LABOUR MIGRATION
IN ENGLAND
1800–1850

by

ARTHUR REDFORD

*formerly Professor of Economic History in
the University of Manchester*

2nd edition

edited and revised by

W. H. CHALONER

*Reader in Modern Economic History in the
University of Manchester*

Augustus M. Kelley · Publishers

New York · 1968

First published
in the United States
1968
by AUGUSTUS M. KELLEY
24 East 22nd Street, New York, N.Y. 10010

Printed in Great Britain by Butler & Tanner Ltd, Frome and London

27643

CONTENTS

PREFACE TO THE SECOND EDITION

IN the preface to the second edition (1932) of his *Economic History of Modern Britain: the Early Railway Age, 1820–1850*, originally published in 1926, the late Sir John Clapham stated: 'Among recent books I am disposed to rank A. Redford's *Labour Migration in England, 1800–1850* (Manchester, 1926) and L. H. Jenks, *The Migration of British Capital to 1875* (New York, 1927) as the most important, perhaps because they would have affected the architecture of the volume most, had I decided to rebuild.' This was high praise indeed, and the passing of nearly forty years, during which time Redford's general conclusions have never been challenged, has further demonstrated the soundness of Sir John Clapham's judgment on the book.

The first of Redford's two main contributions to the study of British population movements was to point out the power of attraction exercised by the rising industrial areas of the period. The rural population was attracted into the towns by the prospect of higher wages and better opportunities for employment, rather than expelled from the countryside by the enclosure movement.[1] The second contribution was to show by analysing census returns, Parliamentary papers, and contemporary literature that internal migration during the Industrial Revolution was for the most part short-distance (or short-wave) migration. The volume of long-distance internal migration was small, although important qualitatively: 'The great majority of the migrants went only a short distance, and migration into any centre of attraction having a wide sphere of influence was not a simple transference of people from the circumference of a circle to its centre, but an exceedingly

---

[1] Redford's conclusions on this point have been strengthened by the evidence assembled in Professor J. D. Chambers's article ('Enclosure and labour supply in the Industrial Revolution', *Economic History Review*, 2nd ser., Vol. V, 1953, pp. 319–43).

complex wave-like motion.'[1] There is now no excuse for what was once a common belief, namely, that the population of the North and Midlands grew during the period 1800–50 largely as the result of an influx of migrants from the over-populated South of England. On the contrary, the only example of substantial long-distance migration from the rural South to the industrial North was exceptional and took place in 1835–7 under the auspices of the Poor Law Commissioners; it affected less than 5,000 persons. In Redford's words: 'London . . . was by far the greatest single centre of attraction, and absorbed the bulk of the migrants from the south and east of England.'[2]

In this connection it should be pointed out that the same conclusions had been reached in the late 1850's by two statisticians who contributed four papers to the *Transactions* of the Historic Society of Lancashire and Cheshire following a study of the census returns for those two counties between 1801 and 1851.[3] After stressing the 'attractive power' of Lancashire in the following words:

> One general conclusion may, however, be very safely adopted, viz.— that the county of Lancaster *has retained among its permanent inhabitants a larger proportion of those born within its bounds than any other county*; and has also drawn very largely from the adjacent counties, and from Ireland and Scotland. It is also apparent that from those parts of England lying at a distance it has received comparatively small contributions to its population.[4]

Danson and Welton went on to state:[5]

> One of the inferences suggested by these figures is that the increase of

---

[1] Infra, p. 186. Irish and Scottish migration was, however, appreciable, the former quantitatively, and the latter both quantitatively and qualitatively.

[2] See also H. A. Shannon, 'Migration and the growth of London, 1841–1891', *Economic History Review*, Vol. V, No. 2, April 1935, pp. 79–86.

[3] J. T. Danson and T. W. Welton, 'On the population of Lancashire and Cheshire and its local distribution during the fifty years 1801–51' (*Trans. Hist. Soc. Lancs & Ches.*, Vol. IX, 1857, pp. 195–212; Vol. X, 1858, pp. 1–36; Vol. XI, 1859, pp. 31–70, and Vol. XII, 1860, pp. 35–74. I am greatly indebted to Mr. T. W. Fletcher of the Department of Agricultural Economics, University of Manchester, for this reference. It is fairly clear that Redford did not know of these articles.

[4] *Trans. Hist. Soc. Lancs & Ches.*, Vol. XI, 1859, p. 41.

[5] *Ibid.*, pp. 48–9.

population, by immigration, here in view, has been principally derived, by each district, from those in its own immediate vicinity, and that this has caused a further but less immigration from other and more distant districts into those immediately surrounding the increasing place. Thus, the districts south of the Ribble increase more rapidly in population than those situate north of that river. A considerable part of their increase is supplied by immigration. A stream of population constantly passes into Preston from the north. This we may reasonable suppose to consist, to a large extent, of persons born in the districts of Fylde, Garstang, and Clitheroe, to whom such a movement is not only obviously profitable, but also comparatively easy. And we conclude that a portion of those who thus leave these districts to proceed southwards are replaced by immigrants into them from the more northern district of Lancaster, which, again, receives from the adjacent parts of Westmoreland and Yorkshire a sufficient number of immigrants to keep its population up to the current demand for labour. If this be the case, each district which is brought into a condition to offer and make known remarkable facilities for the profitable employment of labour, may be held to occasion, as it were, a succession of waves of population pressing after each other from a considerable distance, and gradually increasing in volume up to the point of attraction. Every place of considerable increase no doubt draws a portion from longer distances than those we have thus indicated, but it is conceived that the increase derived from places comparatively near is always much greater than that from a distance.

It should be remembered that Redford's book was published in the same year as Miss M. C. Buer's pioneer *Health, Wealth and Population in the early days of the Industrial Revolution,* when the study of the causes of population increase was still in its infancy. It is not therefore surprising that Redford stuck closely to his last and concentrated on the elucidation of the part played by migration in local population increases. Had he felt able to revise *Labour Migration* thoroughly he might have reviewed his estimate of the relative importance of migration, falling death-rates, and changes in fertility in promoting local population growth. It seems clear that the same forces which caused Lincolnshire villages populated by comfortable small-holder farm labourers to swarm with 'pigs and children',[1] in the 1790's were also at work in the rural coal mining communities and the rising industrial villages of the North and Midlands in the early nineteenth century.

[1] Arthur Young, *General View of the Agriculture of Lincolnshire* (1799), p. 462.

It is not proposed here to detail the work of Talbot Griffith, T. H. Marshall, J. D. Chambers, Habakkuk, Eversley and Krause, which is admirably evaluated and summarized by Phyllis Deane and W. A. Cole in *British Economic Growth, 1688–1959* (1962).[1] These two authors conclude (p. 117):

> Throughout the eighteenth century, not only the north-western catchment area, but the whole of the wider region north and west of the line from the Severn to the Wash—which includes all the major industrial centres of the nineteenth century—had been losing a substantial part of its natural increase by migration; and although this flow from north to south seems to have been checked by the early nineteenth century, the balance of movement in the opposite direction remained negligible. In short, the conclusion drawn by Professor Cairncross that 'the North of England triumphed over the South, mainly by superior fertility (and not, as we used to be taught, by attracting migrants)', appears to be at least as true of the early phases of industrialization as in the period after 1840 to which his evidence relates.[2]

Not a great deal of further work has been published on internal migration since 1926. E. J. Buckatzch's article on 'Places of origin of a group of immigrants into Sheffield, 1624–1799' (*Economic History Review*, 2nd ser., Vol. II, No. 3, 1950, pp. 303–306) confirms that Redford's findings apply to that area in the seventeenth and eighteenth centuries. E. J. Hobsbawm in 'The tramping artisan' (*Economic History Review*, 2nd ser., Vol. III, No. 3, 1951, pp. 299–320) has traced the development of trade union regulations for the purpose of promoting the internal migration of skilled craftsmen in the eighteenth and nineteenth centuries. Some use has been made of the census enumerators' manuscript returns for the censuses of 1841 and 1851 (not available when Redford wrote) by T. C. Barker and J. R. Harris, *A Merseyside Town in the Industrial Revolution: St. Helens, 1750–1900* (1954); W. H. Chaloner, *The Social and Economic Development of Crewe, 1780–1923* (1950); J. F. Ede, *History of Wednesbury*, 1962, pp. 414–15, and R. Lawton, 'The population of Liverpool in the mid-nineteenth century' (*Trans. Historic Society of*

[1] See in particular Chapter III: 'Industrialization and population change in the eighteenth and early nineteenth centuries.'
[2] A. K. Cairncross, *Home and Foreign Investment, 1870–1913* (Cambridge, 1953), p. 79.

Lancashire and Cheshire, Vol. 107, 1955, pp. 89–120). The birth-places of all enumerated persons are given in the 1851 returns, although often with less precision than could be desired, and tabulations made from them confirm Redford's general conclusions. Professor A. K. Cairncross's chapter in *Home and Foreign Investment, 1870–1913* (1953) on 'Internal migration in Victorian England' (pp. 65–83) should also be consulted. His findings are referred to above.

There is now a companion volume to Redford for Scotland: D. F. Macdonald, *Scotland's Shifting Population, 1770–1850* (1937), which may be supplemented by J. F. Handley, *The Irish in Scotland, 1798–1845* (Cork, 1st ed., 1943, 2nd rev. ed., 1945). No systematic study of the migration from North and Central Wales to England has yet been published, although something is known of the reverse movement from England into South Wales (T. M. Hodges, 'The peopling of the hinterland and the port of Cardiff', *Economic History Review,* Vol. XVII, No. 1, 1947, pp. 62–72). On the Irish emigration to England the following should be consulted:

K. H. CONNELL, *The Population of Ireland, 1750–1845* (1950).
T. W. FREEMAN, *Pre-Famine Ireland* (1957).
R. D. EDWARDS and T. D. WILLIAMS, *The Great Famine: Studies in Irish History, 1845–1852* (Dublin, 1956).
C. WOODHAM-SMITH, *The Great Hunger: Ireland, 1845–9* (1962).
R. D. COLLISON BLACK, *Economic Thought and the Irish Question, 1817–1870* (1960).
H. S. IRVINE, 'Some aspects of passenger traffic between Britain and Ireland, 1820–50' (*Journal of Transport History,* Vol. IV, No. 4, Nov. 1960, pp. 224–41).

Much has been written on the subject of emigration from Britain since Redford's book first appeared. Two studies of general interest are: M. A. Jones, *American Immigration* (Chicago, 1960) and W. A. Carrothers, *Emigration from the British Isles, with special reference to the development of the Overseas Dominions* (1929). Particular aspects of the movement are examined in the following works:

R. T. BERTHOFF, *British Immigrants in Industrial America, 1790–1850* (Cambridge, Mass., 1953).

F. Thistlethwaite, 'The Atlantic migration of the pottery industry' (*Economic History Review*, 2nd ser., Vol. XI, No. 2, Dec. 1958, pp. 264–278).

W. S. Shepperson, *British Emigration to North America: projects and opinions in the early Victorian period* (1956).

Helen I. Cowan, *British Emigration to British North America: the first hundred years* (2nd revised and enlarged edition, Toronto, 1961).

W. S. Shepperson, *The Promotion of British Emigration by Agents for American Lands, 1840–60* (Reno, 1954).

F. H. Hitchins, *The Colonial Land and Emigration Commission 1840–78* (Philadelphia, 1931).

O. MacDonagh, *A Pattern of Government Growth, 1800–60: The Passenger Acts and their Enforcement* (1961).

P. Bloomfield, *Edward Gibbon Wakefield: Builder of the British Commonwealth* (1961).

W. H. Chaloner

The University of Manchester

PREFACE TO THE FIRST EDITION

MY interest in problems of migration was first aroused while I was on military service in Macedonia during the late European war. I was struck by the importance of migratory labour in the economy of Balkan life; and later investigation revealed a surprising volume and variety of movement among peasants who, at first sight, might seem as deeply rooted to the soil as the feudal serfs of a medieval manor. A casual study of labour migration in other European countries was sufficient to show that many of the movements which had struck me as peculiar in the Balkans were by no means abnormal, and had their counterparts elsewhere. The regular movement of Vlach shepherds between their winter and summer pastures, the temporary sojourning of Albanian tribesmen as field-labourers in the plains of Thessaly, the annual exodus of Bulgarian harvesters and gardeners to Rumania, Hungary, Serbia, and Russia—all these movements began to appear as particular aspects of a seasonal migration of labour perpetually going on, wherever there are sheep to be folded or crops to be garnered. Alongside this ceaseless periodic movement there are deeper streams of permanent migration and emigration which may persist for centuries, modifying and ultimately transforming the whole structure of human society. Migration, whether seasonal or permanent, is a normal and universal feature of social life. Any far-reaching transition in social conditions is inevitably reflected in the fluctuating currents of human movement; and the study of migration thus becomes a key to the understanding of many problems which remain obscure so long as the factor of human mobility is left out of account.

After the war I returned, from living among the comparatively primitive Balkan peasants, to study the complex changes which underlie the industrial organization of modern society. I wished, for my own peace of mind, to realize the social significance of

xiii

that vast economic transition which is usually called the Industrial Revolution: and on this controversial subject a study of the contemporary movements of population seemed likely to shed a welcome light. My desire to undertake such a study was warmly encouraged by my teachers; the University of Manchester, by electing me to the Langton Fellowship, gave me the means and leisure to pursue my researches; and of such generous encouragement, this book is a tardy and inadequate result. An earlier draft of the book was submitted as a thesis for the Ph.D. degree of the University of Manchester in 1922.

I owe Professor Tout a great debt of gratitude, not merely for his friendly stimulus to the completion of the work, but much more for the patient kindness and tolerance with which he instructed me in the rudiments of historical method during my undergraduate days. My interest in the economic aspect of history arises largely from personal contact with Professor George Unwin during the last few years of his life. I am proud to be considered one of his disciples.

My other obligations are very numerous. Mr. R. H. Tawney and the late Professor Lilian Knowles, my colleagues at the London School of Economics, read the proofs of the book, and made many valuable criticisms. Mr. T. S. Ashton and Miss F. Collier, of the University of Manchester, gave generous help on many points touching their own special studies; and the Secretary of the University Press, Mr. H. M. McKechnie, has allowed me to draw very largely upon his expert knowledge as a publisher. Finally, my wife has rendered indispensable assistance at every stage of the book's progress through the press.

ARTHUR REDFORD

May, 1926

ARTHUR REDFORD (1896-1961)
A MEMOIR

A<small>RTHUR</small> R<small>EDFORD</small>, one of the leading figures in the development of modern economic history, was born at Droylsden near Manchester on May 25th, 1896, the third and youngest child of Arthur Redford (1865–1922), cotton self-actor minder, and his wife Martha (née Street), cotton reeler (1859–1925). Arthur Redford senior later became an overlooker, moving house rather frequently in the years before the first World War, so that young Redford acquired a wide experience of working-class life in Ashton-under-Lyne, Audenshaw, Oldham and Failsworth as well as in Droylsden. He received part of his elementary education at Salem School, Lees Brook, Oldham, and later (c. 1906–8) attended Moorside Council School, Droylsden. From there he entered the Oldham Education Authority's municipal secondary (i.e. grammar) school. He was 'top boy' during the sessions 1910–11 and 1911–12, besides being a promising and versatile athlete. In 1912, having gained an Oldham Education Committee University scholarship of £60 per annum, he entered the Honours School of History in the University of Manchester, where he came under the influence of the great T. F. Tout, graduating with first-class Honours in 1915 after specializing in medieval history. In his third year he was in residence at Dalton Hall. His B.A. thesis on 'The climax of mediaeval Ireland: the administration of Ireland under Edward II', submitted in 1915, has since been much in request by other scholars working in the same field. On the results of his final examination he was awarded a graduate scholarship and took the degree of M.A. in 1916.

During his undergraduate days the family fortunes reached a low ebb (his father in 1914 bought a run-down grocer's shop and general store in Failsworth which did not do well) and at one time Redford seriously considered the possibility of abandoning his university course. Fortunately his father's circumstances seem to have improved somewhat before his death in 1922.

In 1915 Redford joined the Army, and served with the 13th Battalion, the Manchester Regiment, in the Eastern Mediterranean. He was soon commissioned and after a period in the line on the Salonika front, was appointed to serve on the General Staff in Greece and Asia Minor (1917–19), in which capacity he brought to London the official news of the Bulgarian armistice. A by-product of his war experiences is to be found in an unpublished MS on the history of the Balkan peasantry (*c.* 1920).

On demobilization he decided to return to Manchester University to take the honours course in the School of Economics and Political Science and was awarded a first-class degree and the Langton Fellowship in 1920. In his second period at Manchester he came under the spell of Professor George Unwin, holder of the first chair of Economic History to be established in Britain. Unwin's imaginative and creative approach to the subject inspired Redford, although he was critical of the master's difficult lecturing style. During the sessions 1920–1 and 1921–2 he worked under Unwin's supervision on a thesis for the newly-established Ph.D. degree on the subject 'The Migration of Labour in England in 1800–50', for which he was awarded the doctorate in 1922.

In 1922 he accepted a temporary post as lecturer in economic history in the University of Liverpool and two years later was appointed Sir Ernest Cassel lecturer in commerce at the London School of Economics. While in London he married Miss Lucy Ashton, Professor T. S. Ashton's sister, an honours graduate of the English School at Manchester, by whom he had two sons. Mrs. Redford died in 1955. Shortly after Unwin's death in 1925, Redford was made Reader in Economic History in the University of Manchester and twenty years later was given the Chair.

Redford's *Labour Migration in England, 1800–1850,* published in 1926 and based on his Ph.D. thesis, was a pioneering study of this aspect of the Industrial Revolution, and was undoubtedly his most original work. The meticulous scholarship for which he was renowned is here most clearly evident. In 1926–7 he helped to form the Economic History Society and was one of its first council members. In 1931 he published the *Economic History of England, 1760–1860,* and a revised edition was published in 1960. Another of his works was *Manchester Merchants and Foreign Trade,* published in 1934, to which he added a second volume in 1956. He was chosen by the city authorities to write the *History of Local Government in Manchester,* which was completed in three volumes between 1939–40. In 1940 volume I of this work was named by the First Edition Club of London and New York as one of the fifty outstanding books of 1939.

Redford was first and last a Mancunian. The main work of his career was to put Manchester on the map both in its region, in his massive *History of Local Government in Manchester,* and in the sphere of world trade, as evidenced by the activities of its merchants. He was a stimulating teacher, and following Unwin's example, associated many young scholars with himself in his researches. After his promotion to the Chair of Economic History in 1945, he was responsible for the impressive expansion in the teaching of economic history which took place to meet the needs of the post-war generation. In early life he seems to have been extremely and warmly disputatious, and although he later mellowed somewhat in this respect, his general outlook tended to be one of cautious pugnacity.

When he decided in the early part of 1961 to retire, he could justly feel that his life's work, of establishing the subject as one of the main pillars of both historical and economic studies, had been achieved. And this he accomplished under a heavy burden of illness and bereavement. At the same time he always retained a cheerful friendliness and a fund of sage advice.

[This Memoir has been compiled from information kindly supplied by Mr. Timothy Redford, Mr. Maurice Harrison, Director of Education for Oldham, Mr. Herbert Nuttall of Hollinwood, and from obituary notices which appeared in *The Times* and *The Guardian* newspapers.]

B

BIBLIOGRAPHY OF THE MAIN WRITINGS OF ARTHUR REDFORD

1. *Labour Migration in England, 1800–1850* (1926).
2. 'Some problems of the Manchester merchant after the Napoleonic Wars', *Trans. Manchester Statistical Society*, Session 1930–1, pp. 53–87.
3. *The Economic History of England, 1760–1860* (1931, 2nd rev. ed., 1960).
4. 'The emergence of Manchester', *History*, Vol. XXIV, No. 93, June 1939, pp. 32–49.
5. (Assisted by Miss I. S. Russell) *The History of Local Government in Manchester* (3 vols., 1939–40).
6. *Manchester Merchants and Foreign Trade, Vol. I, 1794–1858* (1934), by students in the Honours School of History in the University of Manchester and Arthur Redford.
7. *Manchester Merchants and Foreign Trade, Vol. II, 1850–1939* (1956), (assisted by Brian W. Clapp).
8. 'Portrait of the founder' (a short biography of John Owens (1790–1846), the founder of Owens College), *Manchester Guardian*, August 1st, 1946.
9. 'Historia económica e social (1940–1941)' (*Revista Portuguesa de História*, Vol. III, Coimbra, 1947, pp. 363–70).

LIST OF ABBREVIATIONS

A. & P.—Accounts and Papers.
Adam Smith—A. Smith, *Wealth of Nations*, 1776.
A. H. Johnson—A. H. Johnson, *Disappearance of the Small Landowner*, 1909.
Baines—E. Baines, *History of the Cotton Manufacture in Great Britain*, 1835.
B.B.T.—Bland, Brown, and Tawney, *English Economic History, Select Documents*, 1919.
C.H.O.P.—Calendars of Home Office Papers.
Clapham—J. H. Clapham, *Economic Development of France and Germany, 1815–1914*, 2nd ed., 1923.
Cobbett—W. Cobbett, *Rural Rides*, except where otherwise stated.
Cunningham—W. Cunningham, *Growth of English Industry and Commerce*, Vol. II, 6th ed., 1921.
Daniels—G. W. Daniels, *The Early English Cotton Industry*, 1920.
D.N.B.—Dictionary of National Biography.
Eden—F. M. Eden, *The State of the Poor*, 1797.
E.H.R.—English Historical Review.
E.J.—Economic Journal.
Ernle—Ernle, *English Farming, Past and Present*, 1912.
Fay—C. R. Fay, *Life and Labour in the Nineteenth Century*, 1920.
F.I. Repts.—Factory Inspectors' Reports.
Hansard—Hansard's *Parliamentary Debates.* (*N.S.—New Series.*)
Heaton—H. Heaton (ed.), *Letter Books of J. Holroyd and Sam Hill*, 1914.
J.H.C.—Journals of the House of Commons.
Lancs. Par. Reg. Soc.—Lancashire Parish Register Society.
Le Play—F. Le Play, *Les Ouvriers Européens*, 2nd ed., 1877.
Levasseur—E. Levasseur, *Classes Ouvrières en France, 1789–1870*, 2nd ed., 1903.
Mackay—Nicholls and Mackay, *History of the English Poor Law*, Vol. III, 1899.
Malthus—T. R. Malthus, *Essay on Population*, 7th ed.
Manchester City News, N.Q.—Manchester City News, Notes and Queries.
Mantoux—P. Mantoux, *The Industrial Revolution in the Eighteenth Century*, 2nd rev. ed., 1961.
Muir—Ramsay Muir, *History of Liverpool*, 1907.
Nicholls—Nicholls and Mackay, *History of the English Poor Law*, Vol. II, 1854.
P.L.C.—Poor Law Commissioners.
P.L.C. Rept., 1834—Poor Law Commissioners' Report, 1834.
Rept. D.S. Agric., 1821—Report on the Distressed State of Agriculture, 1821.
Repts. Emig.—Reports on Emigration.
Rept. Employ. Ireland—Report on the Employment of the Poor in Ireland, 1823.

Repts. Hd. Lm. Wvrs.— Reports from Assistant Commissioners on Hand Loom Weavers.

Rept. I. & S. Vag., 1828—Report on the Laws relating to Irish and Scotch Vagrants, 1828.

Rept. I.P., 1835, G.—Report on Irish Poor, 1835, App. G.

Rept. L.W., 1824—Report on Labourers' Wages, 1824.

Rept. M. & B.U., 1841—Report on the Macclesfield and Bolton Unions, 1841.

Rept. Mfs., 1833—Report on Manufactures, Commerce, and Shipping, 1833.

Repts. P.L.—Reports on the Poor Laws.

Repts. P.L.A.A.—Reports on the Operation of the Poor Law Amendment Act.

Rept. P.R., 1854—Report on Poor Removal, 1854.

Rept. S.C.F., 1816—Report on the State of Children in Factories, 1816.

Repts. Set. P.R.—Reports on Settlement and Poor Removal.

Rept. Silk, 1832—Report on the Silk Trade, 1832.

Repts. Soc. B.C.P.—Reports of the Society for Bettering the Condition, etc. of the Poor.

Rept. S.P. Ireland, 1830—Report on the State of the Poor in Ireland, 1830.

Roscher—W. Roscher, *Principles of Political Economy*, trans. 1878.

S. C. Johnson—S. C. Johnson, *History of Emigration from the United Kingdom to North America, 1763–1912*, 1913.

Scot. Hist. R.—Scottish Historical Review.

Sinclair—Sir J. Sinclair, *Statistical Abstract of Scotland*, 1791.

Slater—G. Slater, *The English Peasantry and the Enclosure of Common Fields*, 1907.

Smart—W. Smart, *Economic Annals of the Nineteenth Century*, 1910-17.

S.J.—Statistical Journal: Journal of the Royal Statistical Society.

Toynbee—A. Toynbee, *Lectures on the Industrial Revolution*, 1884.

Unwin—G. Unwin and others, *Samuel Oldknow and the Arkwrights*, 1924.

V.C.H.—Victoria County Histories.

Weber—A. F. Weber, *The Growth of Cities in the Nineteenth Century*, 1899.

Wood—G. H. Wood, *Wages in the Cotton Trade during the past hundred years*, 1910.

CHAPTER I

MIGRATION AND SOCIAL TRANSITION

The European Background

BIRDS of passage, beating northwards in the springtime, awake in man's heart a vague discontent with the routine of settled life and a longing to venture forth in quest of happier surroundings. As the Alpine snows melt and the fresh green spreads again over the high hillside, the sheep and goats drift slowly upwards in search of summer pasture; as the autumn nights draw in and the north wind nips more shrewdly, the grazing flocks edge slowly downwards to the security of their winter fold. The primitive shepherd may be regarded almost as a glorified sheep. He directs, but did not originate, this seasonal migration which has been going on since the days when the man and his dog were alike followers and harriers of the flock.

The annual reaction of birds and beasts and men to seasonal changes in their surroundings typifies, in some degree, the greater waves of human movement by which the population of the earth is always endeavouring to adjust itself more closely to an ever-changing environment. The migration of humankind is a continuous process, working insensibly through countless generations to transform the structure of social life. From this point of view the infiltration of European peoples into the New World, which went on with especial rapidity during the nineteenth century, is seen to be an extension of that westward trend of Asiatic peoples which underlies the history of civilization in Europe. It is, no doubt, a very far cry from the wild incursions of the Goths, Vandals, and Huns to the peaceful movement of poverty-stricken European peasants into the United States, or Canada, or Australia; but there is, after all, some historical connection between the westward pressure of Asiatic races in the Middle Ages and the opening-up of the New World by

I

European emigration in early modern times. The heavily-laden emigrant ship of the nineteenth century followed the sea-trail blazed by the cockboats of Columbus in the fifteenth century; and the European emigrant, wherever he may go, finds himself still confronted with Asiatic or African peoples in the agelong struggle for racial survival.

The modern stream of accelerated emigration from Europe may be said to have begun with the end of the Napoleonic wars in 1815,[1] and during the succeeding years there were many contemporary references to the increased movements of population caused by the misery of the time. There was, apparently, little movement from the westernmost continental countries, the bulk of the emigrants going from Germany and Switzerland. In Central Europe the direction of movement appears to have been determined by the facilities for river communication. From the countries bordering on the Rhine and the Elbe there was a quite vigorous emigration to the United States, which was said to be stimulated by American agents; and by 1819 many thousands were emigrating from Germany to America.[2] From the more easterly parts of Central Europe, which had no direct access to river transport, the main current of movement was eastwards to Russia. Immigration into Russia was deliberately encouraged by the Russian Government. In 1803 the Emperor Alexander promised colonists a full release from taxation for ten years, reduction of taxation for ten years more, freedom from civil and military service, together with grants of land and advances of money. By 1830 the number of such colonists in Russia was estimated at 130,000, mostly Germans. Further regulations (of a less favourable kind) were made in 1833 for immigration into Russia from Poland.[3]

France sent out comparatively few emigrants, owing to the very slow natural increase of her population. Such French emigration as there was, up to the middle of the century, chiefly consisted of Basque peasants. Between 1801 and 1846 there was

---

[1] E. Levasseur, 'Emigration in the Nineteenth Century', translated in *S.J.*, XLVIII, p. 63.
[2] Smart, I, p. 689.   [3] Roscher, II, pp. 350–1.

a considerable increase of population in the Basque Department of Basses-Pyrénées; and it was from that district that 'poor' emigration started in 1832, when an English firm recruited emigrants for a colony in Uruguay. After that the movement grew spontaneously, and was organized by shippers of Bayonne and Bordeaux, the emigrants sometimes contracting to give labour in return for their passage.[1] In the south-east of Europe the partial liberation of Serbia in 1815 led to a migratory movement down the valleys of the Danube and its western tributaries into the valley of the Morava, which was then marshy and thinly populated; from that time there has been a progressive clearing of woodland and scrub in all the surrounding regions, and the population of the valley has increased rapidly. This south-eastern movement into the Balkans gained in strength as the century advanced, and as the European dominions of Turkey became restricted to narrower limits.[2] Emigration from Italy, both to America and to other European countries, constituted one of the most important movements of European population in the later nineteenth century; and from the numerous references to Italians in England and elsewhere it is clear that the movement was already strong in the first half of the century. Little, however, is known of the details of the emigration before 1860. Transatlantic emigration from Italy was throughout the century mainly to South America, where by 1858 there was said to be an Italian colony of 30,000 persons.[3]

World-wide movements of population make a very powerful appeal to the imagination, and it is not easy to overestimate their importance in the history of civilization. Nevertheless, there is some danger lest the spectacular attraction of such mighty currents of racial migration may divert attention from the less striking social changes leading to those short-distance movements which form the great bulk of all human migration. Movement which involves a long sea voyage or overland

[1] Le Play, V, pp. 243 ff.
[2] Jovan Cvijić, *La Péninsule balkanique*, 1918, pp. 301-2.
[3] Foerster, *Italian Emigration*, 1919, p. 5.

trek, the crossing of national boundaries, and entrance into an entirely strange environment, is much more impressive than a mere change of locality within the same social unit. There is, however, a closer kinship between the two kinds of movement than is commonly supposed. The springs of the great streams of international migration may often be discovered in the many trickles of local movement, which are insignificant when studied singly but important in their cumulative effect.

Even a cursory survey of the various currents of short-distance movement reveals a fascinating complexity. Population in Europe has for many generations been slowly shifting from barren to fertile districts, from hilly regions to the plains, from agricultural to manufacturing industry. Beyond these general trends of population, however, are other kinds of movement which seem to go on perpetually without causing any radical redistribution of mankind. There are, for instance, the continual wanderings of pastoral tribes, of pedlars, and of some professional beggars. These may be almost indistinguishable from the seasonal movements of harvesters, mountain shepherds, and masons. Between these seasonal movements and the migrations leading to permanent settlement come the intermediate classes of temporary migration, as of the Mediterranean peasant who returns to his native land as a 'signor' or 'effendi' when he has made his competence overseas. All these different kinds of movement merge into each other very easily. Seasonal migration may crystallize into permanent emigration or degenerate into mere casual vagrancy; while even transatlantic emigration is often seasonal or periodic in character.

The bewildering variety of seasonal migration in continental Europe has hitherto attracted little detailed study in England, and lies beyond the scope of this essay; but even a summary treatment may serve to link up British currents of migration with contemporary movements elsewhere. Particularly interesting are the changes which were taking place during the early nineteenth century in the currents of seasonal migration between France and Spain. From time immemorial migratory labour had been required at certain periods of the year in the great

estates of Andalusia and Castile, and in the principal towns of
Spain. This had been largely furnished by the seasonal movement of French Basques into Spain, the migrants coming from
as far as the mountains of central France, and even from
Limousin. In the early nineteenth century, however, and especially after the collapse of the Spanish colonial empire, the people
from northern Spain ceased to emigrate overseas to Spanish
colonies, and more native labour became available for the work
of the less densely populated regions of central Spain. The
principal Spanish sources of seasonal migration now became
Navarre, the Asturias, and Galicia. Some seasonal migrants
began also to go to France from these regions: for example, as
charcoal-burners to the pine-forests of Gascony.[1]

Other seasonal movements of labour were taking place elsewhere in France, especially to the neighbourhood of Paris. Many
of the masons in Paris were summer migrants from the central
mountainous regions. Other itinerant tradesmen, such as the
water-carriers and porters, came from greater distances and
made longer sojourns in the capital; some came from as far as
Savoy and Piedmont. The general dock-labour round Paris, and
much of the harvesting, was done by seasonal migrants from
Brittany and Normandy; though, as the century advanced, the
Normans were displaced in the harvest work by Belgians.[2]
Similar movements of labour were going on all over Europe.
In Central Europe, there were harvesters going from Württem-
berg and the Odenwald into the valley of the Rhine, and from
Alpine districts into the South German plains; from Galicia
peasants travelled for the season into Poland and Russia, while
on the other hand labourers came from Poland into the Prussian
low country. In Russia, seasonal and periodic migrants jour-
neyed from the central regions to the town labour of St. Peters-
burg and Moscow, and also to the field labour of the southern
steppes. In Italy, the inhabitants of the Abruzzi went to work
in the Roman Campagna, and the Calabrians went to Naples;
while almost all the cultivation of the unhealthy plains of

[1] Le Play, IV, pp. 280 ff.; V, pp. 240 ff., 249.
[2] *Ibid.*, VI, pp. 287 ff., 313 ff., 488 ff.

Tuscany was done by seasonal migrants from the mountainous regions.[1]

The occurrence side by side of so many confused kinds of movement, ranging from transoceanic emigration to merely casual vagrancy, makes any attempt at classification arbitrary and uncertain. It is, nevertheless, important to make a broad distinction between long-distance and short-distance movement, owing to a curious difference in their social effects. Logically, migration might be expected to spread population more evenly over the surface of the earth; and this is, in the main, what long-distance movement has been doing. But while emigration has thus been transferring population from the crowded countries of Europe and Asia to the more recently settled continents, short-distance migration has been mainly from thinly-peopled districts to town areas already comparatively congested.

In the earlier nineteenth century this process of town-growth was more maturely developed in England than anywhere else in the world; and that fact gives a peculiar interest to the study of British townward migration, which forms a central theme of this book. The comparative tardiness of town-growth in continental Europe may, perhaps, be illustrated from the population statistics (imperfect as they are) of France, Germany, and Great Britain. In 1801 less than 7 per cent. of the population of France lived in towns of 20,000 inhabitants or more: in 1851 the corresponding figure was just over 10·5 per cent. In 1816 no less than 73·5 per cent. of the population of Prussia was classed as rural: in 1852 the corresponding figure was 71·5 per cent. In Great Britain, on the other hand, 34 per cent. of the total population was by 1851 living in seventy towns of over 20,000 inhabitants each: in 1801 the seventy towns had contained only 23 per cent. of the total population.[2] Though no exact statistical parallel between the three countries is possible, it will be seen from the figures quoted that the towns in Prussia (which was fairly typical of German conditions) had been growing very little faster than the population of the countryside; town-growth in

---

[1] For a brief survey of seasonal migration see Roscher, II, pp. 375–7.
[2] Clapham, pp. 54, 82; and see p. 16 below.

France had been proceeding at nearly the same *proportionate* rate as in England, but on a much smaller scale. This apparent similarity in the rate of growth of English and French towns hides, however, an important difference in character. In England a great part of the growth of town population during the half-century had been due (as will be seen later) to the mushroom growth of industrial centres. In France, on the other hand, the town-growth had been taking place largely in such old and famous cities as Paris, Marseilles, Lyons, and Toulouse; only two French towns, St. Etienne and Roubaix, grew really rapidly in the period as the direct result of industrial development.

The rapid growth of Paris at the expense of the country districts dates back at least to the sixteenth century, and in the eighteenth century had caused outcries against rural depopulation. During the long Revolutionary and Napoleonic wars the influx of labourers was checked, and the town population apparently diminished; but with the return of peace in 1815 the townward migration revived, especially after 1830. In the first half of the nineteenth century, while the total French population grew by about one-third, that of Paris nearly doubled; that of Lyons more than doubled; Marseilles grew by 75 per cent., and Toulouse by rather more. That the great towns were draining population from the countryside is evident from the contemporary decrease of population in rural districts throughout France. By 1830 about a dozen departments of France had reached their maximum population, and began to show decreases of population at the successive censuses; most of these departments were upland regions. From Normandy the current of migration was towards Paris; in the east, population was decreasing in the Department of the Meuse, and in the southeast there was a drain of population from the Alpine provinces and from Var. The other great region of decreasing population was the upland country stretching from the central mountains of Auvergne to the south-western departments in the Pyrenees.[1]

[1] Levasseur, I, pp. 275-7, 495-6, 613.

Apart from the towns already mentioned, there was no striking growth of town life in France during the first half of the century. Up to the revolution of 1848, industry had changed comparatively little in distribution, and remained mostly in the hands of small artisans and petty tradesmen. By that time, however, the railways were beginning to facilitate the movements of population in France. Between 1846 and 1851 there was evidently a crisis in the rural economy of the country: out of 361 *arrondissements* no fewer than a hundred reached their maximum populations at that time. In the latter half of the century the townward influx from the countryside was as important in France as it had been in England since the beginning of the century, and it displayed the same general characteristics.[1]

This tendency for mankind to congregate in cities is a fundamental feature of all 'civilization'; and in the nineteenth century the acceleration of the process gave rise to the most serious social problems, both in the Old World and in the New. As will be shown later, these problems of town life must be studied primarily as the results of the rapid influx of people from elsewhere. The main force governing this townward influx is undoubtedly the economic motive, the desire to obtain a better livelihood. This implies that the town standard of living is higher than that of the countryside; and therefore the immigration from the country inevitably produces a clash of social standards which may threaten the community with disruption. The difficulty of absorbing the newcomers into the life of the community is frequently aggravated by the scarcity of housing accommodation and by the fluctuating demand for labour in town industries, as well as by differences in language and religion.

Such effects of migration into towns are a matter of common observation; but some other characteristics of the process require further investigation. When an industry leaves one district and becomes established in another, does the industrial population move with it? Is the direction of movement determined mainly

[1] Levasseur, II, pp. 213, 291; G. B. Longstaff, 'Rural Depopulation', in *S.J.*, LVI, p. 398; Toussaint Loua, 'Migrations of the Population in France', in *Journal de la Société de Statistique de Paris*, March 1885, and in *S.J.*, XLVIII, pp. 652–67.

by the previous occupation of the migrant, or by the more general considerations of distance and transport facilities? Is it true to say that 'population follows trade', and in what exact sense is the statement to be understood? How far have the former relations between town and country, and between agricultural and manufacturing industry, been 'revolutionized' by the direction of economic evolution during the last two centuries? On these and many similar questions it seems probable that a patient study of townward migration will throw as much light as is already being gained in other departments of knowledge from studying the migrations of birds, beasts, and fishes.

Evidently the rapid town-growth of the nineteenth century was a reflection of that great economic and social transition which a former generation of scholars named the 'Industrial Revolution'. It is, indeed, not too much to say that 'the best general test of the industrialization of a nation's life under modern conditions is the rate and character of the growth of its towns'.[1] The study of migration thus becomes an avenue of approach to the whole social background of modern industrialism, giving new and sometimes unexpected views of that most controversial field.

Population Changes in England, 1750–1850

The economic transition which ushered in the modern phase of civilization is generally assumed to have reached its most significant rate of development during the later eighteenth and earlier nineteenth centuries; and this assumption is true, so far as England is concerned. A peculiar interest therefore attaches to the movements of population in England during the period: not only because the social effects of modern industrialism first became apparent in this country, but also because it was in England that the process of transition showed most continuity with the past. The student of modern social history may therefore hope to find in the study of labour migration in England

[1] Clapham, p. 53.

the most convenient point of departure for an investigation into the more general questions of social and economic change.

Hitherto the subject has been curiously neglected. With one or two exceptions, English historians of the period have referred to the rapid growth of towns and to the gradual 'depopulation' of the countryside, without giving any detailed consideration to the migration which must have connected the two parallel processes. The reason for this neglect may lie in the difficulty of the subject and the inadequacy of the evidence. Literary references to migration are fairly numerous, but scattered—so scattered as to discourage special investigation. The statistical method, in spite of its subtle pitfalls, is well suited to the subject, and the migration which has taken place since the middle of the nineteenth century has received a great deal of attention from statisticians. Unfortunately, no reliable statistics of migration in England are available earlier than those contained in the census of 1851. The earlier census reports were, no doubt, accurate enough for their main purpose, in giving the approximate numbers of the population and the rates of increase, but the information concerning other matters must be regarded as unreliable. The 1841 census made an experiment in the collection of migration statistics by classifying the persons in each *parish* according to whether they were natives of the county or not; while it also recorded how many of the population of each *hundred* had been born in Scotland, Ireland, the British colonies, and in foreign parts. It was, however, not until the census of 1851 that detailed information was collected concerning the birthplaces of the people; and the statistical study of migration in England has tended to make that date its starting point.

This is particularly unfortunate, because by the middle of the century almost all the great towns of the country had passed their maximum rate of growth; the first great burst of migration to the manufacturing districts was over, and the process was becoming influenced by the increasing use of the railways and by the spread of popular education. It is, therefore, important to study the migration of the earlier formative period as well as the available evidence will allow; and in such a study even the earliest census reports may prove useful as a basis for broad generalizations, though any detailed statistical analysis would probably not be worth doing. For the period after 1811 much information on various aspects of the movement of population is given in the local notes to the successive census returns. As these local census notes form one of the most important sources of information concerning migration, it may be as well to examine their origin and estimate their authority. In 1821, and at the succeeding censuses, the local enumeration officers were asked to account for any remarkable increase or decrease of population in their respective areas during the preceding ten years. In England the local enumeration officers were the Parish Officers (Overseers of the Poor) until the civil registration of births, marriages, and deaths was established in 1837; from 1841 onwards the enumeration was made by officials acting under the District Registrars. In Scotland, which remained without any system of civil registration throughout the period, the enumeration was generally made by the Parochial Schoolmaster, acting under the Sheriff.[1]

The reasons given by the enumeration officers for the local increases or decreases of population were, of course, often inadequate and sometimes ridiculous; nevertheless, they appear to have been given without any conscious or general bias. The returns were made by thousands of persons scattered throughout the country, without any probability of widespread collusion; yet their remarks are in substantial agreement on the main aspects of the movement of population. The Scots schoolmasters were more communicative than the others, the English overseers seem to have been unimaginative but honest, the later registration officials were more cautious and somewhat reticent; but their evidence in most cases hangs together well enough to admit of reasonable interpretation. This general coherence, in the circumstances, greatly strengthens the authority of the statements made. However, even if the local enumeration officers are regarded as incompetent to state the causes of social changes, their remarks still remain valuable as reflecting the popular

[1] See *1851 Census*, Pt. I, Vol. I, Rept., p. xi.

opinion of the place and time. On the whole, it is probably justifiable to accept these local census notes as yielding a valuable body of information dealing with the whole of Great Britain on a fairly uniform basis, and covering a sufficiently wide period of time.

For the study of migration before 1801 the aid of the census returns is absent, and the scattered references in the controversial writings of the time are not very helpful. Even for that period, however, the patient labours of John Rickman and the ingenuity of more modern scholars enable an approximate estimate to be formed of the progress of population. Rickman, who was responsible for the first four censuses, arranged at the first census for the compilation of a Parish Register Abstract, giving the number of baptisms and burials in each district of England and Wales at every tenth year from 1700 to 1780 and in each year afterwards, and the number of marriages in each year since 1753. This Parish Register Abstract was kept up to date by the succeeding censuses until 1841, after which it was superseded by the civil registration returns. From this (incomplete) collection of vital statistics Rickman compiled a tabular estimate of the population of England and Wales, and also of the various counties, for several dates earlier than 1750. This estimate was published posthumously in the 1841 census,[1] and has been used as a basis for historical estimates of population by several later writers. Its accuracy appears to depend on the assumption that population was in the same ratio to the average of baptisms, marriages, and burials at the respective dates as in 1800–1. The validity of this assumption as a guide to the actual numbers of the population may be questioned; but, if the probable error could be assumed to be uniform throughout the area, the figures could be accepted as giving a sufficiently correct idea of the *comparative* rates of increase in different parts of the country.

Reasoning from this and other evidence, Professor Gonner[2]

---

[1] *1841 Census*, Preface, pp. 34–7.
[2] E. C. K. Gonner, 'The Population of England in the Eighteenth Century', in *S.J.*, LXXVI, p. 285.

stated the probable population of England and Wales to be as
follows during the eighteenth century:

1700	5,800,000
1750	6,320,000
1800	8,890,000

This would make the annual increase during the first half of the
century to be more than 10,000, and in the second half of the
century more than 50,000. This great quickening of the rate of
increase may seem improbable; but even this rate of increase
was much below that recorded by the census enumerations in
the early decades of the nineteenth century. The most striking
feature of this general increase of population was the rise in
importance of the counties which were to be the chief centres of
manufacturing and mining industry, and the relatively slight
increase of the agricultural counties. Lancashire, where the textile industries were sustaining a fairly dense population, even
in the seventeenth century, was in 1700 still exceeded in density
of population by the old manufacturing and mining counties
of Worcester, Somerset, and Devon; but after 1750 Lancashire
had a (numerically) denser population than any other county,
excluding Middlesex and Surrey.

In the second half of the eighteenth century the cotton industry was also causing rapid increases of population in Cheshire
and Nottinghamshire. Leicestershire, too, increased in population nearly as rapidly as Nottinghamshire during the century,
but at a much steadier rate. The rising coal and iron districts
of the Midlands (Warwickshire and Staffordshire) grew in
population rapidly throughout the century; but the increase in
the latter half of the century was much less startling than in the
case of Lancashire. In the woollen districts the chief feature of
the half-century was the great increase of population in the
West Riding of Yorkshire, which contrasted sharply with the
slow rates of increase of the older woollen centres in East Anglia
and the West Country. The agricultural counties, which in
1700 were almost as densely peopled as the manufacturing districts, increased only slowly after that date.

c

The movement of population in the early nineteenth century was mainly an accentuation of the tendencies already noticed in the previous half-century. By 1800 most of the modern centres of congested population were unmistakably growing at a quicker rate than the rest of the country. Nevertheless, the differentiation between industrial and agricultural counties was not yet so advanced as is often asserted. London was still the only town of more than 100,000 inhabitants, its importance being reflected also in the relatively crowded population of the neighbouring counties. An area of dense population in Gloucestershire reflected the commercial greatness of Bristol. Of the 'new' manufacturing districts, by far the most thickly peopled was the cotton district of Lancashire and Cheshire. A less remarkable thickening of population in all the other counties encircling Derbyshire reflected the immature growth of the West Riding woollen and worsted industries, the Midland coal and iron districts, and the textile districts of Nottingham and Leicester. In the north, also, the growth of the coal and iron trade of Durham was faintly distinguishable by a slight thickening of the population as compared with the surrounding counties. In the rest of England the distribution of population was fairly uniform. From Cornwall in the south-west to Norfolk in the east there were no remarkable differences of density; the area of scantiest population in England lay in a great arc to the east of the growing manufacturing districts, from Lincolnshire on the south-east through Yorkshire to Westmorland. In Wales the uniformity of distribution according to counties was remarkable; and in Scotland also the only noteworthy clusters of population were at the mouths of the Clyde and the Forth.

Between 1800 and 1850 the population of Great Britain practically doubled itself, increasing from under eleven millions to more than twenty-one millions; and this tremendous increase of more than ten millions occurred in spite of extensive emigration from Scotland and many parts of England. The increase in the ten years between 1840 and 1850 amounted to 2,300,000 persons; this, according to the estimate adopted above, was almost equal to the whole increase in the latter half of the eighteenth century, which was itself a time of unprecedented increase, judged by the standard of previous centuries.[1] The statistics of the distribution of population in 1851[2] show that all parts of the country, except the mountainous counties of Wales and Scotland, had shared in the general increase; but there had been a marked quickening in the differentiation of commercial, manufacturing, and mining areas from the rest of the country. There were now four main areas in which the average population over wide stretches of country exceeded 500 persons to the square mile. London, with 19,375 persons to the square mile, was still by far the densest centre of population; and even the extra-metropolitan districts of Middlesex were more densely peopled than any other part of England except Lancashire. Lancashire maintained an average population of 1,003 persons to the square mile over an area nearly twice the size of Middlesex and Surrey; and the broad stretch of country forming the Lancashire and West Yorkshire textile districts contained more inhabitants than London, Middlesex, Surrey, and Kent all combined.[3] Of the coal and iron districts, the midland counties of Stafford and Warwick had much the densest population, but Durham also had made rapid progress during the half-century. In the South Wales coal and iron field, where the thickening of population was hardly perceptible in 1800, there had since been a continuous and rapid growth; but even in 1850 Glamorganshire had still a sparser population (taking the county as a whole) than such unremarkable counties as Cornwall, Bedford, Somerset, and Flint.[4] In Scotland about one-third of the whole population was clustered into the three shires of Renfrew, Lanark, and Edinburgh, forming an area of dense

---

[1] Cf. *1851 Census*, Pt. I, Vol. I, Rept., p. lxxxii.
[2] See the elaborately shaded maps by Augustus Petermann, *ibid.*, facing p. xlvi.
[3] Lancashire and West Riding = 3,356,731.
London, Middlesex, Surrey, and Kent = 3,185,424.
[4] Glamorgan = 253 to the square mile.
Cornwall = 259 ,, ,, ,, ,,
Bedford = 272 ,, ,, ,, ,, .
Somerset = 289 ,, ,, ,, ,,
Flint = 294 ,, ,, ,, ,,

population stretching across the country from the Clyde to the Forth.

Such broad statements of population density according to counties may be useful as showing the general trend of social changes and the gradual alteration in the relative importance of various parts of the country. In themselves, however, the statements may be misleading, if they are understood to imply a uniform growth of population *within* the counties. Actually, of course, the growth of population within each county was by no means uniform; even the most rapidly progressive counties included large tracts of country in which population was stationary or but slowly increasing, and the extraordinary increase of population was concentrated mainly in a few congested urban areas. It has already been noticed that by 1851 more than one-third of the total population of Great Britain was living in seventy towns of over 20,000 inhabitants each. These large towns had been growing in population much more quickly than the country in general; indeed, the annual rate of increase for the seventy large towns was more than twice that of the rest of the country, including all the towns of less than 20,000 inhabitants in 1851.[1] The bulk of the increased town population was in London and about fifty manufacturing towns; but the smaller towns were in many cases reported to be increasing at a greater *proportionate* rate than the larger.

The study of population changes in England during the earlier nineteenth century thus resolves itself into two main problems, which are closely inter-related. The first question is concerned with the way in which the country (taken as a whole) increased in population; the second concerns the factors making for the growth of great towns. The first of these questions lies outside the scope of this book; but it may be advisable to state the general lines of the problem, as a background for the more limited inquiry into the relation between migration and the growth of towns. The general increase of population in the country does not appear to have been due in any large measure

[1] *1851 Census*, Pt. I, Vol. I, Rept., p. xlviii, Table XXV.

to immigration from abroad. The alien immigration into Great
Britain up to the middle of the nineteenth century was numerically insignificant. There were in 1851 only 56,665 foreign-born
alien subjects living in Great Britain, this number being no more
than 2·7 per 1,000 of the total population.

There was, it is true, a very remarkable influx of labourers
from Ireland into Great Britain, which stands out as the most
noteworthy stream of British migration during the period. This
might be held to account for an appreciable proportion of the
increased population in Great Britain during the half-century;
for in 1851 there were nearly three-quarters of a million of
Irish-born people in Great Britain, to say nothing of the many
persons born in Great Britain of Irish parents. Against this
increase by immigration, however, must be set the loss by emigration overseas. It is, indeed, impossible to balance immigration against emigration with numerical accuracy, owing to the
weakness of contemporary statistics. The Irish influx was not
officially recorded until 1841; and the emigration statistics prior
to that date do not inspire confidence. Moreover, the emigration statistics for the United Kingdom did not distinguish the
emigrations from Great Britain and Ireland respectively until
1853. Nevertheless, it seems clear that the emigrants from Great
Britain were at least as numerous as the immigrants from Ireland and foreign countries,[1] and that the extraordinary increase
of population in this country between 1801 and 1851 was due
not to the effects of migration, but to natural increase, i.e. to the
surplus of births over deaths.

Into the vexed controversy as to whether this natural increase
was due to a rising birth-rate or to a falling death-rate, or to a
coincidence of the two, it is perhaps unwise for the non-statistical
student to venture.[2] Malthus himself, in the course of two extremely difficult chapters on the subject,[3] wrestles desperately
but vainly with the inadequate statistics of the time. No official
figures of the natural increase of population were collected until

[1] But cf. Clapham, *Economic History of Modern Britain*, I, p. 64.
[2] Which blade of the scissors cuts the cloth?
[3] Malthus, Bk. II, Chaps. VIII and IX (2nd and later editions).

1837, and even after that date the returns of births were very defective for the rest of the half-century.

The same problem as to the relation between natural increase and increase by migration presents itself also in discussing the process of town-growth. In this case, however, the gain by migration was apparently greater than the natural increase. Many writers of the eighteenth and earlier nineteenth centuries accepted it as incontrovertible that the main cause of rapid town-growth was migration. Massie, writing in 1758, noticed a general and continual movement of population from the country districts and smaller towns to the large towns, 'more especially in those Towns where considerable Manufacturies are carried on'; and Arthur Young, commenting on the same movement in 1774, exclaimed: 'Let any person go to Glasgow and its neighbourhood, to Birmingham, to Sheffield, or to Manchester. . . . How then have they increased their people? Why, by emigrations from the country!'[1]

There can be no doubt that this was a correct interpretation of the process; nevertheless, many observers of the growth of towns in the early nineteenth century confidently maintained that their extraordinary rates of increase were due, partly at any rate, to special forces stimulating the urban birth-rate. Thus Southey, writing at the beginning of the century, made one of his characters say: 'We are well off for hands in Manchester. . . . Manufactures are favourable to the population; the poor are not afraid of having a family here.'[2] This point of view was more elaborately expressed in many official publications in the following decades, as, for instance, in the Census Report for 1831: 'The Manufacturing Population is invariably on the increase; not only as every short period of prosperity and increased wages produces imprudent marriages, but also because in many Manufactures children are able to maintain themselves at an early age, and so impose little expense on their Parents, to the obvious encouragement of marriage.' The argument was that as the

---

[1] J. Massie, *A Plan for the Establishment of Charity Houses*, p. 99; A. Young, *Political Arithmetic*, p. 63.
[2] *Letters from England*, by 'Don Manuel Alvarez Espriella' (1807), II, p. 143.

introduction of the new machinery increased the demand for child labour relative to adult labour, the possession of children became a valuable asset to a poor man, and the number of children per family increased considerably.[1] It may be noted that a similar argument was pursued to show that in the rural districts the population was being multiplied through the lax administration of the Poor Law and the giving of an extra poor allowance for each child born.

It appeared, then, that the growth of population was being stimulated by special causes, both in the towns and in the country districts. The one argument is as plausible as the other. If both are admitted, they may account partly for the extraordinary increase of population in the country taken as a whole; but the arguments neutralize each other so far as the *relative* increase of the town population is concerned. Indeed, assuming the birth-rate to have been unusually stimulated in both town and country, the towns should (apart from the effect of migration) have been increasing at a slower rate than the country; for the towns were notoriously unhealthy, and the infantile mortality extremely high.

Finally, the fallacy of supposing that the unprecedented growth of the great industrial and commercial towns was due to any abnormal natural increase, as compared with the country districts, is exposed by the records of birth-places, taken at the 1851 census. In almost all the great towns the migrants from elsewhere outnumbered the people born in the town; and, even so, the number of the natives was probably overstated owing to the contemporary position of the settlement question, the effects of which will be discussed later. Here it suffices to notice that any study of the process of town-growth must be based on an investigation of the migration from which the growing towns drew their fresh supplies of labour; and in studying the process of townward migration, we are excavating the foundations of modern society at a point which has not often been laid bare.

[1] *1831 Census*, I, Preface, p. xlvii; cf. Toynbee, p. 110.

CHAPTER II

THE EARLY VILLAGE FACTORIES AND PARISH APPRENTICESHIP[1]

IT is hard for one born in a mature industrial region, inhabited by patient and disciplined factory workers, to realize the difficulties involved in the deliberate formation of a factory community, even where industrial habits and traditions are already well established among the local population. In the course of a generation or two it becomes quite 'natural' for people to work together by hundreds in hot, humid, barrack-like buildings for a fixed number of hours each day, regulating their exertions constantly by the movement of powerful machinery. After a great war, or any other prolonged dislocation of industry, there may be some temporary restlessness among the 'hands'; but the routine soon re-establishes itself as part of the ordinary discipline of life.

The economic value of this factory tradition is, perhaps, only realized when the modern industrial system is breaking new ground: as when a pioneering mill-owner discovers that his factory must close down for a month at a time during the summer, because the workers have all gone home to get in their harvest. Labourers from agricultural or domestic industry do not at first take kindly to the monotony of factory life; and the pioneering employer not infrequently finds great difficulty in building up a stable supply of efficient and willing labour. This same problem presented itself even more strongly to the pioneers of the modern factory system in England during the eighteenth century. When the new water-power factories were

[1] For material concerning the early factory population I am indebted to the late Professor G. Unwin and his collaborators, especially for early access to material later embodied in their book, *Samuel Oldknow and the Arkwrights*; and I owe a special debt of gratitude to Miss F. Collier for information contained in her unpublished M.A. thesis on 'The Family Economy of the Working Classes in the Cotton Industry, 1784–1833'.

established in considerable towns, such as Stockport and Manchester, the nucleus of a labour supply was already available, though its organization called for great administrative skill. Most of the new factories, however, were started on the banks of streams in remote country places, where the population was very sparse. It is true that the labour required was that of much the same class of persons as had hitherto been engaged in domestic spinning; for power-driven machinery and the factory system were, in the first instance, applied to spinning and the other preparatory processes, which had previously been performed largely by the weavers' wives and children. Moreover, the machines of that early period were so small and light that women and children could do most of the work quite efficiently. But the weavers' families were scattered over a wide area, and the immediate effect of the technical inventions in spinning was to increase the prosperity of the weavers;[1] so that there was at first no strong inducement for weavers to migrate for the sake of finding employment for their children.

Even if the early factory masters could have counted on getting the children of the surrounding districts into their mills, they would still have been short of labour. Actually, however, there existed a fairly general prejudice against factory work, which aggravated the difficulty. This peculiar aspect of the labour problem confronting the early factory masters may be clearly illustrated from the history of the Deanston cotton mills, in Perthshire, which were established in 1785 by five brothers named Buchanan. Two of the brothers, John and George, were

intimate acquaintances of Sir Richard Arkwright . . . and were his first agents in Scotland for the sale of cotton-twist at Glasgow. . . . John, being in the habit of attending the great cattle-trysts of Doune was attracted by the beautiful and powerful stream of the Teith, and the prospect of a plentiful supply of operatives from the village of Doune, to think of establishing a cotton-factory in the neighbourhood. He soon acquired part of the small estate of Deanston. A lint dressing mill had been long established on this spot, and there was a good weir or dam-dyke attached to it. . . . At this early period in the process of cotton-spinning it was difficult to find a sufficient number of people with skill and experience for carrying on the work, and it was necessary that most of them should

[1] See Daniels, Chap. V, section III.

be taught personally. . . . A few persons professing knowledge of the art were occasionally got from Glasgow, and some from England; but these were generally of loose and wandering habits, and seldom remained long in the establishment. The more respectable part of the surrounding inhabitants were at first averse to seek employment in the works, as they considered it disreputable to be employed in what they called 'a public work'.[1]

All the scanty evidence available confirms this account of the scarcity of labour for the country mills, the migratory and disreputable character of the early factory population, and the reluctance of the settled population to enter factory life. David Dale, in organizing his factory settlement at New Lanark, in 1783, found that the Scottish peasantry were generally 'disinclined to work in cotton mills';[2] and very few of Samuel Oldknow's weavers, either at Stockport or elsewhere, sent their children into his spinning mills. For most of their adult workers the early factories had to rely on tramp labour. This may account for the markedly casual character of mill-work, as reflected in early factory records. Between 1791 and 1794 over six hundred names appear on the wages lists of Oldknow's mill at Mellor; yet not more than three hundred were ever employed at one time. The same short average period of employment appears also from the wages book of Messrs. Peel, Yates and Peel's Burrs Mill, near Bury. It is reflected, too, in the many advertisements for runaway workers and apprentices which appear in the contemporary newspapers.

About 1785 an enterprising Scotsman named Adam Douglas seems to have made a livelihood by enticing mill-workers from established centres of the cotton trade, like Manchester, to go to the newly-erected mills in scantily populated districts. In that year Messrs. William Douglas and Company, cotton manufacturers, of Pendleton, repeatedly cautioned mill-owners against this man, and advertised for several of their articled servants who had been enticed away,

[1] *F.I. Repts.*, Dec. 1838, App. V, p. 98: James Smith, who provided the history of the firm, was for many years manager of the mills; for his other activities see *D.N.B.*, LIII, 58.
[2] *Rept. S.C.F.*, 1816, p. 22; Robert Owen's *Autobiography*, I, p. 58.

apparently to a mill in the Clitheroe district.[1] Similarly, in 1792 Samuel Oldknow was in correspondence with a firm of Derby manufacturers concerning runaway apprentices from that town, who were thought to be working for him at Mellor. Even so late as the 'thirties of the nineteenth century the younger Samuel Greg was making experiments with a view to eliminating 'that restless and migratory spirit which is one of the peculiar characteristics of the manufacturing population, and perhaps the greatest obstacle to permanent improvement among them'.[2]

This casual, transient character of the early factory population is seen also in the readiness with which workers were transferred from one occupation to another, sometimes within the mill, sometimes outside. Before the coming of the factory system the distinction between agricultural and manufacturing industry had been very loosely drawn. Agricultural workers had found domestic industry a profitable method of employing their spare time in the slack winter months; the industrial workers had, from time immemorial, deserted their looms or frames during the summer to help with the harvest. The interchangeability of agricultural and industrial labour is one aspect of a wider tendency to seasonal migration which will claim attention later; here it is interesting to note that this looseness of differentiation persisted in the country districts for some time after the introduction of the factory system.

Where the new factory was part of a large country estate, as was Samuel Oldknow's factory at Mellor, the employer found outdoor labour a convenient way of keeping his mill-workers occupied during the recurrent periods of slack trade. Thus, in a memorandum book for 1798, Oldknow makes a note of 'Odd jobs for millhands', such as 'a piece of land to be made at the back of the lodge', 'a piece of ground in the orchard to be regularly sloped and planted either with seed or potatoes'. Mellor wage records also reveal instances of persons who at

---

[1] *Manchester Mercury*, Feb. 15th, Feb. 22nd, and March 1st, 1785.
[2] Information from Miss F. Collier, to whom I am indebted for other references to the Greg records.

different times worked at a great variety of occupations, all under the same employer, and at approximately the same rate of wages.[1]

Factory work in that early period might almost be described as a casual employment for unskilled labour; the mill-workers were without any craft tradition or pride in efficient workmanship. The reluctance of the respectable settled population to enter the factories is therefore easy to understand. Disinclination to enter a 'public work' may bear a further interpretation, however, as suggesting that factories were thought of as workhouses. During the eighteenth century most of the numerous schemes for counteracting the increasing burden of pauperism had been 'founded upon an increase in the number of workhouses, and on the employment of the inmates with a view to profit'. The Act of 1723 (9 Geo. I, c. 7), which enabled officials of individual parishes to provide a house for keeping and employing their poor, had led a great many parishes to erect workhouses; more than a hundred such establishments are said to have been built in different parts of the country. 'These workhouses were established, and mainly conducted, with a view to deriving profit from the labour of the inmates. . . . The workhouse was in truth at that time a kind of manufactory . . . employing the worst description of the people.'[2]

Since, then, the workhouse had become a kind of factory, it was perhaps natural that the factory should be regarded as a kind of workhouse. Lest this should be thought too fanciful an explanation of the popular repugnance to factory life, it may be noticed that, throughout the period, assisted emigration or home migration was regarded popularly as a sort of transportation. Thus, when Samuel Oldknow was getting parish apprentices from Clerkenwell his London agent reported that 'some of the Children's Parents, hearing of their intended

---

[1] Cf. Unwin, pp. 168–9.

[2] Nicholls, pp. 18, 58; cf. Eden, I, pp. 269–88. Workshops and works were sometimes called 'workhouses', apart from any connection with the Poor Law: see, e.g., *A View of the Advantages arising to the co-partners or Company of the Mineral Manufacturers at Neath, by making and manufacturing copper, brass, lead, and iron in their workhouses there* [London, 1720, B.M.]

destination, and fearing that it is a kind of transportation, have come crying to beg they may have their Children out again'.[1] When emigration was offered to the Nottinghamshire framework knitters in 1819 'they called it transportation'. Indeed, during the 'twenties and 'thirties of the nineteenth century, 'transportation' became the usual word for government emigration schemes, in the language of such people as Cobbett, Hunt, and the Chartists. While social confidence was so low, it is not very fanciful to suggest that the new factories may have been shunned originally as an insidious sort of workhouse.[2]

This being so, the factory masters turned to the workhouses for a large part of their labour supply. In the early days of the factory system it was apparently the custom for mill-owners to send agents (usually women) round the countryside to get children from their parents. The recruiting agents found that much labour could be got by applying to the overseers of the surrounding parishes, many of whom had poor children on their hands; indeed, the overseers were often only too willing to get rid of the children, either by apprenticeship or otherwise. This practice of scouring the countryside for workhouse labour seems to have been a general method of recruiting workers for the country mills until the 'thirties of the nineteenth century. In 1834 Edmund Ashworth, of Turton, wrote that it was

> often the practice here, if a mill-owner is short of workpeople, to apply to overseers of poor and to workhouses for families supported by the parish: of late this has not always been attended with success. ——[3] who are extensive cotton-spinners and manufacturers, having two establishments in Cheshire and three in Lancashire, have, like ourselves, been in this practice many years; and being this spring short of hands at most of their establishments . . . could not find an overseer in all the county of Chester who was willing to allow a family to leave his parish.[4]

From the mill-owners' point of view the workhouse was a very convenient agency through which to recruit labour, not only in

[1] Oldknow MSS: letter from S. Hall, London, Nov. 24th, 1795.
[2] *Lords' Rept. P.L.*, 1831, pp. 238–9; Cobbett, II, 57, quoted Fay, p. 87; Hansard, *N.S.*, XII, 1360; *ibid.*, 3rd Series, V, 927–8.
[3] The reference is apparently to Samuel Greg and Co., who certainly got much labour in this way.
[4] *P.L.C., 1st Ann. Rept.*, App. C, No. 5, p. 212.

the early days of the factory system, but until comparatively recent times.

The initiative was not always on the side of the mill-owner. In 1787, for instance, the parish of St. Clement Danes, London, offered 'several stout boys' as apprentices, through the medium of a Manchester paper.[1] In 1796, while Samuel Oldknow was asking for parish apprentices from Clerkenwell and the Liberty of the Rolls, he was being offered 'fine healthy boys' from the Ashford Workhouse (Kent).[2] The mill-owners probably preferred to get their apprentices from the large towns, because they could thus get them in bigger batches. Certainly, one main feature of the parish apprenticeship system, in relation to internal migration, was its tendency to cause movement from the great towns to small, unimportant country villages. The great manufacturing towns like Manchester and Glasgow never employed many parish apprentices in their factories; on the other hand, almost all the early owners of cotton mills in country districts seem to have found the system inevitable.

When in 1783 Dale established his mills at New Lanark, he brought his child-labour from the poorhouses of Edinburgh and Glasgow, and the parish authorities insisted that the children should be taken at a very early age. Robert Owen in 1799 found at New Lanark about five hundred such children. In the various mills of the Peels round Bury nearly a thousand parish apprentices were at one time employed, and many of these are known to have been brought from London. Samuel Oldknow got apprentices for his Mellor mill from several London parishes, such as Clerkenwell and Chancery Lane, as well as from other London institutions, such as the Duke of York's Orphanage at Chelsea and the Foundling Hospital. Parish apprentices for the Gregs' mill at Styal were brought from all parts of the country, including London and Liverpool, as well as from many Cheshire parishes.[3] Parish children were being bound not only to the well-known cotton districts, but also to cotton mills in such

---

[1] *Manchester Mercury*, Jan. 2nd, 1787.
[2] Unwin, p. 172.
[3] *Rept. S.C.F.*, 1816, pp. 20, 132–3; H. R. Fox Bourne, *English Merchants*, II, pp. 160, 193; *Palatine Note-book*, II, p. 178; Unwin, pp. 170–2.

outlying places as Holywell and Shrewsbury. Some of the Holywell apprentices came from St. James's, Westminster. The Shrewsbury apprentices were brought from various centres— some from as far as Hull.[1] The practice was being followed also in the other textile industries. The West Riding woollen manufacturers imported much of their child labour from the London workhouses; the Congleton silk mills received apprentices from St. Andrew's, Holborn, in 1800, 1801, and 1805. The children employed in the flax mills at Dundee, and in the neighbouring villages, came from either Edinburgh or Perth.[2]

This exploitation of child pauper labour called forth many weighty denunciations from humanitarian thinkers and radical reformers. Lurid accounts were given of the revolting cruelties practised upon the unfortunate children by their brutal masters, who (it was said) regarded them simply as the 'cheapest raw material in the market'. Even so early as 1784 the Lancashire justices resolved unanimously to refuse their allowance to indentures of parish apprentices bound to owners of cotton and other mills, in which children were obliged to work in the night, or for more than ten hours in the day. This was followed in 1796 by the resolutions of the 'Manchester Board of Health' (Dr. Percival) on the subject of child labour in factories; and in 1800 the West Riding justices passed resolutions even more severe than those of their Lancashire colleagues. Objections to the practice were also made by authorities at Birmingham and Preston.[3] By 1802, when the elder Sir Robert Peel secured his first Factory Act, specially protecting these parish apprentices, the evils of the system were notorious.

So notorious, indeed, did these evils become, that in the popular mind 'factory system' came to mean 'child slavery'; and many persons whose economic principles would have prevented them from agitating for the rights of adult labourers were able

---

[1] *Rept. on Factory Bill*, 1832, pp. 439, 199–203.

[2] Hammond, *The Skilled Labourer*, p. 150, quoting *Annals of Agriculture*, XVI, p. 422; *Rept. S.C.F.*, 1816, p. 76; *Rept. on Factory Bill*, 1832, pp. 339, 388.

[3] *Repts. Soc. B.C.P.*, IV, App. I, Supp. III, p. 19; Supp. IV, p. 20. B.B.T., pp. 495–6; *Rept. S.C.F.*, 1816, pp. 124, 182–3.

to further the same cause by advocating the protection of the defenceless parish apprentices, to whom such phrases as 'freedom of contract' could not possibly be applied. As usually happens when an undoubted social evil becomes the subject of active political controversy, the importance of the parish apprenticeship system was probably exaggerated in the mind of its enemies; nor was the treatment of the apprentices so uniformly cruel (according to the standards of the time) as was often asserted. Moreover, it is not correct to assume that even the country mills were worked *principally* by apprentices, whether pauper children or not.

As already noticed, Dale's mills at New Lanark employed in 1799 about five hundred apprentices; but his colony at that time contained between fifteen hundred and two thousand people, 'of whom all who are capable of work are employed in or about the mills'.[1] On this basis the apprentices might form little more than one-third of the total employed; and this proportion does not seem to have been exceeded in the other factories concerning which it has been possible to get detailed information. In 1793–4 Samuel Oldknow's mill at Mellor employed 285 persons; but of these only twenty were apprentices, and nine of the apprentices were apparently natives of Mellor.[2] Shortly afterwards Oldknow began to take more apprentices; and when, in 1798, he framed an optimistic estimate for a projected extension of the enterprise, he calculated on the basis of 318 mill-hands to 100 apprentices. This number of apprentices (if it was ever realized) seems to have been the maximum ever employed at Mellor.[3] The proportion was substantially higher at the Gregs' Quarry Bank Mill, at Styal, near Wilmslow; in 1790, for instance, the mill employed 183 'free' labourers and about eighty apprentices.[4] But, even so, the percentage did not exceed the proportion employed at Dale's mills. It appears, therefore, that the apprentices, even in

---

[1] *Repts. Soc. B.C.P.*, II, No. LXIX, p. 363; the higher estimate of the inhabitants is given in Bristed's *Pedestrian Tour* (1803), II, p. 670.

[2] Analysis made by Mr. A. Hulme.

[3] Unwin, pp. 172–3.

[4] Analysis made by Miss F. Collier.

country mills, were not usually more than one-third of the total workers employed, and were often not more than one-quarter.

It is to be realized, moreover, that parish apprenticeship as a source of factory labour was already showing signs of decline very early in the nineteenth century. The Factory Act of 1802 restricted the employment of parish apprentices by regulating their hours of work, etc.; and, so far as it was effectual, the tendency of the Act was to encourage the employment of 'free' children at the expense of the apprenticeship system. The Act, however, was never put into full operation in Lancashire and Cheshire, and even in other counties the visitations of magistrates or their nominees soon ceased. By 1816 the Act was recognized as practically a dead letter.[1] By that time, indeed, stronger forces than those of legislation were tending to abolish the system. From the beginning of the century steam-power had been increasingly applied to cotton factories, and the new mills tended to cluster on or near the coalfields, either in existing large towns or in specially favoured villages. As the new mills were thus usually built in more densely populated districts, the demand for child labour from elsewhere was weakened; even in the country mills, the increasing size and weight of machines caused a greater proportion of adult labour to be employed than formerly. Where the country factory communities had been governed humanely from the outset, many of the original parish apprentices had by the beginning of the nineteenth century grown up to be parents of families; and this rendered the country factories still less dependent on imported labour.

A minor reason for the decline of the apprenticeship system lay in the fact that parish apprentices, provided certain conditions had been complied with, might gain a settlement in their new parish. As their master would usually be a considerable ratepayer in the parish in which his mill was situated, this was a danger to be avoided if possible, especially as mill-work might be a blind-alley occupation. There were, it is true, many ways

[1] *Rept. S.C.F.*, 1816, pp. 316–17, 319–22, etc.

D

of taking the apprentices without incurring liability. The indentures were sometimes not properly completed, and might be disowned; a still less scrupulous method was to goad the apprentices into running away before their contract was completed. Some mill-owners, again, managed to build their apprentice house in a different parish from that in which their mill stood. Messrs. Bott and Company, for example, whose cotton mill was at Tutbury, Staffordshire, had their apprentice house across the River Dove in the Derbyshire parish of Hatton, the poor rates of which were correspondingly swollen.[1]

As labour became more plentiful, however, the general practice was to employ 'free' children, under contracts made with their parents, to work at weekly wages for one or more years. It was quite common for such contractual child labour to be employed alongside pauper apprentice labour. Oldknow, for instance, was engaging children on such terms in 1798, and the Peels in 1801. Under such agreements it was much easier to evade the liability of settlement. The work could be made discontinuous, Sundays for example being excluded; or the agreement might be for eleven months only, so as to avoid the settlement which went with a full year's contracted service. The Peels contracted for eleven months' service; Oldknow contracted for service 'for, during, and unto the full end and term of One year', but a large proportion of his workers seem to have been lodged outside the parish of Mellor.

The displacement of parish apprenticeship by this method of contractual child labour is interesting, also, as a further step away from the old conception of apprenticeship. Parish apprenticeship itself had been in form an extension of ordinary industrial apprenticeship; but in practice it easily degenerated into a convenient method by which the parish authorities could dispose of unwanted pauper children, to some person willing to speculate on getting enough work out of them to pay for their keep. The obligation to teach parish apprentices a craft or trade, though retained in form, was abandoned in practice at an early date; and this deterioration of the system,

[1] *J.H.C.*, LXXVII, App. 12, pp. 1342–3.

it may be noted, had taken place before the advent of the factory system.[1] So notorious was this abuse that in some districts parish apprenticeship was apparently not regarded as qualifying for the trade. Thus, in the West Country clothing district, in 1803, it was stated that 'if the apprenticeship regulations were enforced many unapprenticed weavers would be thrown out of employment, *particularly female weavers who may have been parish apprentices*'.[2]

As applied to factories the parish apprenticeship system deviated still further from the original idea of apprenticeship. One of the most important purposes of the apprenticeship system, from the earliest times, had been to restrict entrance to the trade, and so defend the workers' standard of living; but under the factory system the employment of parish apprentices in large numbers was merely a particular method of exploiting unskilled child labour, and almost inevitably tended to overstock the trade with labour. In this, however, parish apprenticeship was only moving in the same direction as ordinary industrial apprenticeship during the same period. The Journals of the House of Commons, during the late eighteenth and early nineteenth centuries, contain frequent petitions against the overstocking of trades with apprentices. Especially was this the case in calico-printing, where the substitution of cylinder printing for hand-block printing, about 1785, made it possible to replace skilled men with semi-skilled boys. In 1804 the journeymen calico-printers complained bitterly against the practice of taking too many outdoor, i.e. 'free', apprentices, and asserted that there were nearly two such apprentices on the average to three journeymen. Subsequent parliamentary investigation established the substantial truth of the journeymen's complaint. The Lancashire firm of Berry and Company was reported to employ fifty-five apprentices and only two journeymen; in the case of Tod and Company, of Dumbarton, there were sixty apprentices and only two journeymen.[3] In this

---

[1] See *P.L.C., 2nd Ann. Rept.*, App. B, No. I, pp. 165–75.
[2] *J.H.C.*, LVIII, App. 32, p. 884.
[3] *J.H.C.*, LIX, p. 100; LXI, App. 99, p. 902.

respect, then, the technical changes affected 'free' apprenticeship and parish apprenticeship similarly; in each case, apprenticeship became little more than a thin disguise for the
contractual hiring of children's labour for the 'minding' or
'tenting' of machinery.

From one cause or another, the system of parish apprenticeship began to decline soon after the beginning of the nineteenth
century. At the time of the discussion on the Factory Act of
1802 the number of children concerned was no doubt considerable; but that was probably the highest point of the system.
The 1807 returns of factory visitations in Derbyshire show that
the method of contractual labour had superseded parish apprenticeship in almost all the local mills. Such mills as still employed
parish apprentices were the smaller and less efficient concerns.[1]
In 1811 the children are said to have been still leaving London
by 'waggon loads at a time';[2] but the total number thus sent
was not very large. The Committee on Parish Apprentices,
which issued its report in 1815, found that many of the London
parishes had never sent children into the provinces, and many
more had not done so since 1802–3. From the returns of the
remaining parishes it appeared that the whole number of
apprentices bound, from the beginning of 1802 to the end of
1811, amounted to 5,815. Of these only 2,026 were bound into
the provinces. About 1,500 children in all were bound apprentices to the cotton trade in the ten years.[3] Assuming that all
these were sent to Lancashire, which is not true, the number
would equal about one per cent. of the increase of population
in the county during the decade.

After the passage of Wilbraham Bootle's Act in 1816 (56 Geo.
III, c. 139) it became illegal to apprentice London children
more than forty miles out; such firms as continued to employ
parish apprentices had henceforth to get them from poorhouses
nearer home. By that time the question had become relatively

---

[1] *Repts. Soc. B.C.P.*, V, App. 24, pp. 171–8.
[2] Romilly's *Diary*, quoted Smart, I, p. 60.
[3] *Rept. on Parish Apprentices*, 1815, printed in *Ann. Reg.*, 1815, App., pp.
557–560. Cf. Smart, I, p. 441.

unimportant so far as factories were concerned, and the system was almost dead in the textile trades by the time of the great Poor Law inquiries in the 'thirties. Even from a remote country mill, which had originally employed a large proportion of apprentices, it was reported in 1824 that 'this mode of working mills is seldom found to answer, and free hands, as they are called, are now generally preferred'.[1] At some few country mills, such as the Gregs' mill at Styal, the apprenticeship system still lingered. The last of the apprentices at Styal did not finish their term of service until 1847; but long before that date the Styal mill was an exception to the general rule. Even in 1833 it was apparently the only mill owned by the Gregs in which the system still survived.[2]

After the Factory Act of 1833 the main home of parish apprenticeship, as of other kinds of child labour, was in coal-mining and the metal trades. It was said that apprenticeship in coal-mines was more common in South Staffordshire than anywhere else; the apprentices there were usually orphans and paupers, sent on trial from the workhouses round Walsall, Wolverhampton, Dudley, and Stourbridge. The practice was common also in the coal-mines of the West Riding. In the Dewsbury Union the miners were allowed to select their own parish apprentices. The overseer of the poor at Oldham said he had recently [1840-2] bound more apprentices to colliers than to any other trade.[3] Along with this persistence of parish apprenticeship in coal-mining went its survival in the allied metal trades. In some of the smaller Midland iron centres the industry was, up to the 'forties, almost entirely carried on by small masters and apprentices, many of the latter being pauper children. A similar survival of the system was noted in the iron trades of Sheffield and among the nail-makers of East Scotland.

---

[1] *P.L.C., 2nd Ann. Rept.*, App. B, No. 20, pp. 414-15; Baines, *History of the County of Lancaster* (1824), II, p. 30, referring to Caton, N. Lancs.

[2] *Repts. from Factory Commssnrs.*, 1833, Rept. I, pp. 24-5, and App. D2, pp. 22-3; Greg MSS; *Rept. Mfs.*, 1833, p. 680; L. Faucher: *Manchester in 1844*, pp. 96-7, *Etudes sur l'Angleterre*, 1845, I, pp. 390-401.

[3] *Rept. Midland Mining Commission*, 1843, p. xli; *1st Rept. Children's Employment Commission (Mines)*, 1842, pp. 40 ff.

In the greater iron towns, such as Birmingham, the practice had declined, and the apprentices were mainly 'free'.[1]

The difficulties attending the initial formation of the early industrial communities did not appear to offer much opportunity for the growth of a healthy social life. Yet the results were in many cases not unhappy. New Lanark, Deanston, Mellor, and Styal are not, perhaps, the worst specimens of industrial civilization; and it was possible for even parish apprentices to grow up into useful men and women. At least two of the apprentices brought by the Gregs to Styal became managers of the mill; several of the original operatives employed at the Deanston mills eventually became managers in different works, and some 'attained to wealth and eminence by engaging in business on their own account'.

The history of the Deanston community may, perhaps, again be utilized to portray the gradual consolidation of a settled industrial population formed from originally unpromising materials. The 'loose and wandering habits' of the first migrants have already been mentioned; this difficulty was aggravated by 'a succession of fevers and other diseases arising from the persons coming in from all quarters, many of them in great poverty, and their bodies consequently susceptible to those diseases'. Yet 'the population thus collected from various quarters, and being of all shades of the lower classes, were gradually moulded into a respectable community. . . . The better part of the surrounding population were ultimately attracted to the work.' A generation later it was possible to report that 'the population connected with the works are much respected by the population of the neighbouring country, and associate freely with those of their own grade; and intermarriages with the agricultural population are not infrequent'.[2]

[1] *2nd Rept. Children's Employment Commission* (*Trades and Manufactures*), 1843, pp. 26–7.
[2] *F.I. Repts.*, Dec. 1838, App. V, p. 98.

[*Editor's note:* for criticisms of some of the views expressed above, see M. D. Morris, 'The recruitment of an industrial labour force in India, with British and American comparisons', *Comparative Studies in Society and History*, Vol. II, 1959–60, pp. 309–15.]

CHAPTER III

INDUSTRIAL CONCENTRATION
AND MIGRATION

THE early importance of water-power and country factories calls attention to the wide dispersion and diffusion of manufacturing industry in the eighteenth century. The specialized industrial districts of the nineteenth century had begun to take definite shape by 1800, and to show a quicker rate of growth than the rest of the country. But the process was still far from being complete, and small-scale domestic industry still showed plenty of vitality. Even after the first quarter of the nineteenth century small-scale industries remained scattered throughout the length and breadth of the country, and still maintained the unequal struggle against factory organization and power-driven machinery.[1] Between 1800 and 1850, however, a considerable change was taking place in the distribution of industry. Some industries were growing rapidly during the period; others were as markedly declining, or were sustaining a parasitic existence on the badly-paid labour of workers displaced from the more progressive industries. Within each industry, also, there was a tendency to concentration in particular areas; and within each area industry tended to become localized round places specially favoured with steam-power, coal and iron, or communications.

From the study of this transition arises the further task of discovering whether, and in what sense, 'population followed trade'. The rapid increase of population round all the rising manufacturing centres seems to justify Arthur Young's conviction that 'wherever there is a demand for hands, there they will abound'. It is not clear, however, to what extent

[1] Summaries of the local manufactures of each county in 1831 will be found at the end of the respective county enumerations in the *1831 Census*. With this cf. the list of local industries about 1800, in Ernle, pp. 308-12.

workers displaced from an industrial occupation by technical advances were reabsorbed into the same industry, either in their own district or in a more rapidly expanding centre. In cases where the displaced worker had to change either his trade or his home, it is important to determine whether considerations of distance or of his previous industrial training influenced more strongly his line of action. Finally, it may be discussed how far industry followed population. Where displaced workers were not reabsorbed into their own industry, some other kindred trade might find it profitable to use the unemployed labour at low wages, thus extending its own field of action and preventing the dispersion of population which would otherwise take place. Industries making an extensive use of such 'reject' labour might often be those lagging behind in the process of transition; and the employment of the displaced workers at low wages would in itself defer the necessity for adopting technical improvements.

THE COTTON INDUSTRY

In the chief textile trades of the country the first half of the nineteenth century was characterized by a general adoption of steam-power, first in spinning and later (more gradually) in weaving. Of this transition the cotton industry was the pioneer, and its lead was followed somewhat tardily by the worsted and woollen trades. The other textile industries (linen, silk, hosiery, etc.) lagged further behind, and were still largely dependent on hand-workers at the end of the period; in none of the textile trades was the transition *complete* by 1850.

At the beginning of the century the British cotton industry was carried on in four main districts, grouped respectively round Manchester, Glasgow, Nottingham, and Belfast. The spinning mills were, as yet, for the most part worked by water-power. It is true that steam mills had been built both in England and in Scotland before the end of the eighteenth century; but water-power was still considered to be the more economical agent, except for its irregularity of working. This predominance of water-power implied a wide dispersion of the industry. The Lancashire and Nottinghamshire cotton areas met in Derbyshire; similarly, the Lancashire area extended northward to Cumberland, while the Scottish area stretched southward into Dumfriesshire. Beyond the main areas, also, isolated mills were to be found scattered in Gloucestershire, Warwickshire, Shropshire, Durham, and in other unlikely parts of the country.

Between 1800 and 1850 the cotton industry as a whole increased very greatly; but the growth was mainly confined to the industrial areas centring round Manchester and Glasgow. As the century advanced, moreover, Glasgow itself was diverted to commerce and shipbuilding, and the cotton trade became more closely identified with Lancashire. This last tendency became apparent in the third and fourth decades of the century. In 1830, the first complete self-actor mule was put on the market by a Manchester firm of machinists, and began to be adopted locally during the 'boom' of 1834–6,[1] though it did not entirely displace the hand mule until after the great cotton panic of the 'sixties. This and other improvements were only adopted very slowly in the Glasgow district,[2] and there the industry began to show signs of decline, though Glasgow itself continued to increase during the later nineteenth century at a quicker rate than the Lancashire towns.

The most striking decline in the cotton trade during the first thirty years of the century was that of the district round Belfast and elsewhere in Ireland. In 1784 and the succeeding years, much money had been spent on promoting a cotton industry in Ireland. Manchester manufacturers of the period fondly hoped that there they would be free from vexatious duties, and would secure cheap labour and water-power.[3] At the beginning of the nineteenth century there was an extensive cotton-spinning

[1] Wood, p. 27.
[2] *Rept. Mfs.*, 1833, pp. 310–11. Cf. G. M. Mitchell, 'The English and Scottish Cotton Industries', in *Scot. Hist. R.*, XXII, pp. 109–14.
[3] Scrap Book, in Chetham's Library, 31366, p. 64: Record of a meeting of Manchester employers (1785) against the imposition of a duty on dyed and bleached cottons; resolved to send delegates to Ireland, to investigate the possibility of conducting an extensive cotton manufacture there.

industry, employing 13,500 persons, in the district round Belfast.[1] With the spinning industry went a flourishing cotton-weaving industry in such widely dispersed counties as Louth, Wicklow, Cork, and Queen's County. By 1830, however, English steam factories had defeated the Irish water-power, and there was severe distress among both cotton spinners and cotton weavers. The decline of cotton-spinning in Ireland was particularly rapid from 1828, after which date the trade tended to be replaced by flax-spinning. In Queen's County the once considerable cotton manufacture was practically extinct by 1830, and the weavers had gone. Up till 1829 there were still between fifteen hundred and two thousand cotton weavers employed round Bandon (Cork); in 1840 there were not more than a hundred and fifty there.[2]

In Great Britain, the gradual concentration of the cotton trade round Lancashire is clearly reflected in the local notes to successive census returns. Between 1811 and 1821 the increases in the number of cotton factories was causing local increases of population, not only throughout southern and central Lancashire, but also in Cheshire, Cumberland, Derbyshire, and the West Riding of Yorkshire. At the same period the establishment of cotton mills was leading to increased population in many towns and villages of Scotland from Dumfriesshire to Aberdeen. On the other hand, the failure of isolated cotton mills was being reported from Cumberland, Derbyshire, Staffordshire, and Warwickshire. The great burst of activity in the Lancashire cotton trade during the third decade of the century was reflected in local increases of population in districts as widely spread as the north of Cumberland and the north of Derbyshire. Many of the country mills in Derbyshire were now failing, however, and the Nottinghamshire village of Papplewick (where the first steam cotton factory is said to have been erected) had decreased in population through the stoppage of a large cotton mill. In Scotland, the increases of population attributed to the expan-

[1] E. Wakefield, *Statistical and Political Account of Ireland*, 1812, I, p. 705.
[2] Sir R. Lloyd Paterson, in *British Industries*, ed. Ashley, pp. 124–6; cf. *Rept. Employ. Ireland*, 1823, pp. 21, 187; *Rept. S.P. Ireland*, 1830, p. 419; *Repts. Hd. Lm. Wvrs., Ireland*, 1840, p. 657.

sion of the cotton trade were now mainly in Renfrew; and mills in the less accessible parts of the country were being abandoned. It is thus possible to trace, in the changes of population between 1810 and 1830, that gradual concentration of cotton-spinning round the Lancashire textile district which became so pronounced in the succeeding generations. The movements of individual workers from one cotton district to another are necessarily harder to trace. Nevertheless, the drift towards Lancashire may be illustrated from the cases of two very well-known immigrants, who came respectively from the Irish and Nottinghamshire cotton districts. John Doherty, the leader of the Lancashire spinners in the late 'twenties and early 'thirties, was born at Buncrana, Inishowen, Donegal, in the closing years of the eighteenth century. About 1809 he migrated to the east of Ireland, and found work in a cotton mill at Larne, in Antrim. At the end of the French wars he made the further journey to Manchester, where he soon acquired great influence among the operative spinners.[1]

Robert Blincoe, the celebrated parish apprentice,[2] was originally bound apprentice to a firm of cotton spinners near Nottingham in 1799. The mill stopped about 1803–4, and the children working there were turned over to a mill-owner at Litton, in Derbyshire, where Blincoe finished his term of apprenticeship towards the end of the French wars. After staying on at Litton for a short time as a paid worker, Blincoe made his way northwards through Derbyshire and Cheshire to Manchester, stopping at each cotton mill on the way to work for a week or two. From Litton he came first to New Mills, but could get no work there; he therefore pushed on to Mellor, where for a time he earned eleven shillings a week at Old-know's mill. Then, after an interval at Bollington, he again struck north, and worked at two Stalybridge factories before finally settling in Manchester.

[1] Austin Doherty, in *Manchester City News*, N.Q., VII, p. 228; *1st Rept. on Combinations*, 1838, p. 259; cf. Webbs' *Trade Unionism*, 1919, p. 117n.

[2] See John Brown's *Memoir of Robert Blincoe*, 1828; reprinted by J. Doherty, 1832, pp. 55–62; A. E. Musson, 'Robert Blincoe and the early factory system', *Derbyshire Miscellany*, I, Feb. 1958, 111–17.

It is not to be inferred, from the cases mentioned, that any great proportion of the cotton spinners displaced in the Scottish, Irish, or Nottinghamshire centres migrated to Lancashire; of that there is little evidence, and it seems probable that such special industrial migration was almost insignificant compared with the volume of general migration into Lancashire which was taking place.

The transition in the cotton industry so far described has concerned mainly the spinning mills. In cotton-weaving a contemporary transition was going on from handloom weaving in the home or in small 'loom shops' to power-loom weaving in factories. This caused severe distress among the displaced handloom weavers, although the transition was by no means sudden. The position of the handloom weavers became especially precarious after 1825. The first great burst of power-loom weaving seems to have occurred during the period of improved trade which culminated in the 'boom' of 1825. In Oldham and district, for instance, the weaving of fustians by power began about 1823, and the change was practically complete in that district ten years later. Moreover, when the profits of cotton-spinning fell off after 1825, many employers began to combine spinning and power-loom weaving in the same establishment; so that from the middle 'thirties onwards cotton handloom weaving decreased rapidly in importance.[1]

The consequent distress among the handloom weavers was one of the most serious social problems of the time, and the absorption of the displaced workers into other occupations seemed to contemporary observers to be protracted by a prejudice against mill life. It was said that the weavers were willing to starve rather than submit to factory discipline. This general repugnance to mill life has already been noticed, and was an important factor in the situation. It did not, however, prevent considerable numbers of handloom weavers from flocking to the growing factory towns, to seek employment either for themselves or their children. The growth of such new cotton towns as Staly-

[1] *Rept. Mfs.*, 1833, pp. 565, 659; Wheeler's *Manchester*, p. 233; Cunningham, p. 638.

bridge and Ashton-under-Lyne was based largely on labour drawn from the handloom districts in other parts of the county. Villages such as Leigh and Chadderton, which later grew considerably as factory centres, were in the early decades of the nineteenth century *losing* population through this migration of handloom weavers. Flixton, a small village seven miles from Manchester, was decreasing in population through the exodus of weavers to the town. Some handloom weaving villages became practically deserted, the houses being left empty as their tenants departed. Loom shops were abandoned, looms sold or broken up, and whole families went to the mill-towns.[1]

The distress among handloom weavers was most severe in the country districts (where the opportunities for factory employment were less plentiful), and especially in parts of north-central Lancashire. There were few spinning mills in that region, and the weavers were mainly employed on the plainer kinds of work at very low wages. The migration of weavers from these districts was not so active as from the districts near the great towns. Nevertheless, considerable numbers of weavers from out-districts like Colne and Burnley found employment in the mills of southern Lancashire. From other out-districts, such as Clitheroe, many weavers went into calico-printing works as dyers, washers, and labourers.[2] The unwillingness of the handloom weavers to submit to factory discipline is therefore not to be over-emphasized.

A partial explanation of the long persistence of handloom weaving, in face of the power-loom and the factory system, lies in the continually increasing immigration of Irish weavers throughout the period. This was swelled between 1826 and 1833 because of the decline of many Irish manufacturing centres. The newcomers were accustomed to a lower standard of living than the native English. Moreover, many Irish who described themselves as weavers were peasants who had previously woven

[1] *P.L.C.*, *1st Ann. Rept.*, App. C, No. 5, p. 216; *1831 Census*, I, pp. 297, 300; *1841 Census*, p. 146; John Ward: *Moston Characters at Play*, 1905, p. 2; *P.L.C. Rept.*, 1834, App. A, Pt. I, No. 22, pp. 909–10; Wheeler's *Manchester*, p. 233.
[2] *Repts. Hd. Lm. Wvrs., Lancs.*, 1839, pp. 602–7; cf. *Ann. Reg.* 1818, p. 128; *P.L.C.*, *1st Ann. Rept.*, App. B, No. 11, p. 188; *Rept. Mfs.*, 1833, p. 245.

only for domestic purposes, and who therefore took any wages offered, in order to learn the trade. In Lancashire there was said to be a regular progression of skill: the Irish migrants, in moving up from Liverpool to the cotton towns, first began by learning to weave calicoes at Wigan, and then moved on to learn the weaving of muslins at Bolton.[1] The invasion was, of course, encouraged by the extreme ease with which the plainer branches of weaving could be learned; it is said that three weeks was the time allowed at the New Bailey, Manchester, to teach a prisoner how to weave calico.[2] The evidence suggests, therefore, that as the English and Scots handloom weavers left the trade, or died, their places were taken by low-grade Irish labour at starvation rates of wages. The handloom weaving industry was thus able to drag out a parasitic existence for another generation.

THE WOOLLEN AND WORSTED INDUSTRIES

In the woollen and worsted manufactures the characteristic feature of the earlier nineteenth century was the concentration of the industries in the West Riding of Yorkshire, and the decline of the ancient clothing centres of East Anglia and the West Country. This migration of industry may easily be ante-dated. So early as 1737 Sam Hill, of Halifax, was dealing in 'Bocking Long Broad Bays', and also in 'white Serges call'd Exeter Long Ells', and thought it was 'now very evident these Manufactories will come in Spite of fate into these northern Countys'.[3] The process of transition was, however, not to be completed for another century.

Up to the industrial developments of the later eighteenth century Norwich ranked as the third town in England, coming only after London and Bristol in numbers. By 1801 it had fallen to the tenth place but still remained one of the chief towns of the kingdom. Its decline is said to have begun soon

[1] *Rept. Mfs.*, 1833, p. 704.   [2] *Ann. Reg., loc. cit.*
[3] Heaton, p. 41, No. 133. Ironically enough, Hill started the manufacture of these southern specialities to retain some of his workmen who threatened to desert to the southern centres.

after the middle of the eighteenth century, but this does not imply that its population was not increasing. In 1771 Arthur Young believed that the trade of the town had increased four-fold since the beginning of the century; and there were no very convincing signs of industrial decline until after the end of the Napoleonic wars in 1815.[1]

In the fifteen years after the return of peace Norwich showed every sign of trade prosperity. Its population was increasing fairly rapidly, though on a smaller scale than that of the northern textile towns; dwellings in the centre of the city were being converted into warehouses, and building was increasing in the suburbs. In the 'thirties experiments were being made with Jacquard looms for the weaving of figured silks, and power-driven mills were built, both for spinning alone and for spinning and weaving combined.[2] In short, up to the serious trade depression after 1836 Norwich seems to have maintained itself in second-rate prosperity as a textile centre, though out-lying parts of the East Anglian clothing district had long been in decay, and 'the migrations which have introduced so much Norfolk blood into the population of Bradford had begun'. The trade depression after 1836 may be regarded as the end of the greatness of Norwich as a textile town. In 1838 only about four thousand looms were at work in the town and its suburbs, while in 1841 there were only about 4,600 men and women in the whole of Norfolk who described themselves as weavers. The population of the town had been almost stationary in number for the previous ten years, and there were other signs of industrial stagnation.[3]

The West Country clothing industry suffered more severely

[1] *1831 Census*, I, Preface, p. xxiii; Mantoux, p. 361; N. Kent: *Norfolk* (1794), p. 6; cf. Hammond: *The Skilled Labourer*, pp. 141–2. On the whole question, see J. H. Clapham: 'Transition of the Worsted Industry from Norfolk to the West Riding', in *E.J.*, XX, p. 196; D. C. Coleman, 'Growth and decay during the Industrial Revolution: the case of East Anglia', *Scandinavian Economic History Review*, X, No. 2, 1962, pp. 115–27.

[2] *1831 Census*, I, pp. 422, 426; C. B. Hawkins: *Norwich*, 1910, pp. 6–8; cf. *Rept. on Poor Rate Returns*, 1822, App. E, p. 30.

[3] See *1851 Census*, Pt. I, Vol. I, App. to Rept., p. cxxvi, Table 42; M. F. Lloyd Prichard, 'The decline of Norwich', *Economic History Review*, III, No. 3, 1951, pp. 371–7.

from the introduction of power-driven machinery than did the East Anglian, and was not so fortunately situated for the adoption of 'replacement' industries. During the later eighteenth century the population of the West Country, like that of East Anglia, had increased relatively slowly. Some of the clothing towns, like Tiverton, actually declined in population, and others began to assume a decayed appearance. Yet at Chippenham, Wiltshire, it was said in 1803 that the manufacture of superfine broadcloth had doubled within living memory; weavers had been scarce, and had been drawn from a distance of nine or ten miles round. Moreover, in 1811, which was a time of general trade depression, it was reported that the clothiers of Wiltshire, Gloucestershire, and Somerset were in fairly good employment on the finest Spanish wools, 'and there can be no doubt that this branch of the manufacture will resume its former prosperity'.[1]

In the years after the war the West Country, like Norwich, showed signs of returning prosperity. Clothing towns in all the counties round Bristol were increasing in population through the flourishing state of the woollen manufacture, and were still attracting migrants from the surrounding countryside.[2] The ancient woollen manufacture did not seem to be in any immediate danger when one Somerset village could ascribe its increase of population to the cultivation of teasels! The years immediately after the war were, in fact, a high-water mark in the prosperity of the district;[3] after that time the decline was continuous, and fairly rapid. Even by 1821, the woollen manufacture was visibly decaying at Wilton, and many of the workers were returning to agriculture.[4]

Cobbett, riding through the West Country in 1826, found signs of great distress throughout the clothing district, and was convinced 'not that the cloth making is at an end, but that it

---

[1] Mantoux, *loc. cit.*; *J.H.C.*, LVIII, App. 32, p. 885; Lord Sheffield's report on the trade in wool and woollens for 1811, in *The Pamphleteer*, III, No. VI, p. 294.

[2] *1821 Census*, pp. 105, 279–80, 282, 357, 361.

[3] Hammond, *op. cit.*, p. 138; cf. Cunningham, p. 799n.

[4] *1821 Census*, p. 356.

never will be again what it has been'. Frome, that 'very small Manchester', was in a state of 'irretrievable decay', and the other clothing towns in the area were in the same condition. By 1831 some of the towns (especially in Wiltshire) were showing actual decreases of population, which were locally ascribed to the declining state of the woollen trade, the closing down of manufactories, and similar causes. In the outlying counties some new manufactories were springing up; but such increases of population as occurred in the principal towns were mostly due to the 'replacement' manufactures of linen, lace, and silk.[1] The Poor Law Commission in 1832–3 found ample confirmation for Cobbett's pessimistic description. Frome, which had been one of the principal clothing centres, was especially badly hit. The town had formerly contained about fifty small firms of clothiers; these, however, had failed one by one, being unable to compete with the businesses with larger capital in the West Riding. Smaller places like Boughton Gifford and North Bradley were said to be 'broken down by weavers and shearers thrown out of employment, and by an accumulated population for which there is no work'.[2]

Against this evidence of distress in the West Country districts in the early 'thirties it must be remembered that trade in general was then seriously depressed, and that when trade began to revive in 1833, hopes were as high there as in the northern districts. In certain specialities Gloucestershire was beginning to win back its trade from Yorkshire. By 1833 many of the mills in Gloucestershire were driven by steam, and the transition had been greatly quickened during the previous dozen years.[3] It was in vain, however, that the West Country clothiers tried to keep pace with the Yorkshire industry. By the middle of the century migration and emigration were general from all the south-western counties, and at many places the cloth manufacture was extinct. Uley, a typical small clothing town in

[1] Cobbett, Sept. 1st, Sept. 2nd, and Sept. 30th, 1826; *1831 Census*, I, pp. 127, 152, 201, 535, 537–8, 541–2, 550; II, pp. 692, 702.
[2] *P.L.C. Rept.*, 1834, App. A, Pt. I, No. 15, pp. 444, 497, 505.
[3] *Rept. Mfs.*, 1833, pp. 30, 67–8; *P.L.C. Rept.*, 1834, App. A, Pt. I, No. 21, p. 883.

E

Gloucestershire, lost exactly half of its population between 1821 and 1851. Four extensive manufactories there were abandoned between 1831 and 1841, and by 1851 the trade had been 'discontinued'.[1] Almost all the clothing towns in Gloucester, Somerset, Wiltshire, and Devon decreased in population between 1841 and 1851, and in most cases the decay of the woollen manufacture was mentioned as a specific cause. The towns in which new factories for the production of silk, etc., had been established were by that time in as grievous decay as the rest of the district.

Meanwhile, the woollen and worsted towns of the West Riding were growing rapidly in much the same way as the cotton towns of South Lancashire, though on a smaller scale. Up to the beginning of the nineteenth century the West Riding woollen trade was 'conducted by a multitude of master manufacturers, generally possessing a very small and scarcely ever any great extent of capital'. Nevertheless, the new factory system which transformed the Lancashire cotton industry was also beginning to invade the Yorkshire industry. The first water-power mills for the manufacture of worsted were built in 1784 and 1787, at Dolphinholme and Addingham; the first steam mill at Bradford was built in 1800.[2] In 1794, when many of the woollen centres were petitioning against the use of wool-combing machinery, the special grievance of the Yorkshire workers was the attempt on the part of Halifax and Leeds clothiers to establish large factories, and so monopolize the industry.[3] From that time onwards the numerous petitions of the Yorkshire hand-workers could not stop the advance of the new technique, and Yorkshire thus drew ahead of both the West Country and the East Anglian clothing districts in the adoption of power-driven machinery and the factory system. This competitive advantage, reinforced by superior access to coal, and by the comparative weakness of corporate restrictions in the West Riding, may partly explain the concentration of the

[1] *1841 Census*, p. 99; *1851 Census*, Pt. I, Vol. I, Divn. VI, pp. 18–19; K. G. Ponting, *The West of England Cloth Industry*, 1957.

[2] James, *History of the Worsted Manufacture*, 1857, pp. 327, 592.

[3] *J.H.C.*, XLIX, pp. 275, 431, 501; cf. pp. 491, 552, 564–5, 599.

worsted and woollen industries in Yorkshire during the ensuing half-century, and the decline of the older districts.

During the first years of the nineteenth century the West Riding suffered much less from war conditions than did the other clothing districts, and increased steadily in both trade and population.[1] It is easily understood that the war-time demand favoured rough stuffs, suitable for army clothing, to the neglect of the finer fabrics; so that the 'bread and butter' stuffs of the West Riding found a readier market than either the 'superfine broadcloths' of the West Country or the bombazines, shawls, crapes, and camlets of East Anglia. Throughout the first half of the century such towns as Bradford, Leeds, Halifax, and Huddersfield continued to grow rapidly. Bradford, the chief town of the worsted industry, almost doubled its population between 1801 and 1821, and increased about eightfold between 1801 and 1851.[2] Leeds, the centre of the woollen trade, had a slower rate of increase at the beginning of the century than either Manchester or Liverpool; but by 1831 it was growing as rapidly as any of the Lancashire towns, in proportion to its size. In the early 'thirties an 'enormous' number of new mills were being built in Yorkshire. To the eyes of an American-born observer the northern textile districts seemed to be a second America, so rapidly were they growing in population. 'In Yorkshire there seemed to me to be occasionally entire villages just out of the hands of the masons, consisting of beautiful little cottages.'[3]

It is possible, then, to trace a process of concentration going on in the woollen as well as in the cotton industry during the earlier nineteenth century; and, as in the cotton, so also in the woollen industry, the question arises whether the migration of industry was accompanied by the migration of the industrial population. The question is of particular interest in the woollen industry, because craft tradition was much stronger there than

[1] Lord Sheffield's report on the trade in wool and woollens for 1809, in *The Pamphleteer*, III, No. VI, pp. 282–3. For the history of the trade up to 1806 see *Rept. on the State of the Woollen Manufacture*, 1806.
[2] *1851 Census*, Pt. I, Vol. I, App. to Rept., p. cxxvii, Table 42.
[3] *Rept. Mfs.*, 1833, p. 48.

in the cotton industry, and because the decaying clothing districts were widely separated from the West Riding and from each other. This makes it easier to see whether the decaying clothing districts sent a *disproportionate* number of migrants to the West Riding, and helps to decide whether distance or previous industrial experience was predominant in determining the direction of movement.

There were, of course, many migrants to the West Riding from the other woollen districts during the period. The poor persons passed back from the West Riding towns in the 'slump' years 1841–3 included woollen workers from all the decaying clothing districts. From the Bradford district woolcombers were sent back to Dean Prior and Hemyock (Devon), to Wellington (Somerset), to Bury St. Edmunds, and to Kidderminster. Halifax removed persons to Woolpit (Suffolk), Plymstock and Ashreigney (Devon), and to Timberscombe (Somerset). The Huddersfield removals included a weaver sent to Chippenham (Wilts.) and a wool sorter sent to Bermondsey. Leeds removed a wool dresser to Frome, hecklers to Alcester and Bridport, and a wool comber to East Dereham (Norfolk).[1] If, however, these migrants from other woollen centres are considered in relation to the many thousands of migrants who were sent back to other counties, the disturbance due to special industrial migration is seen to be extremely slight (see Map C in Appendix). Similarly, if the total migration to the chief towns of West Yorkshire from the other woollen districts is placed in relation to the total migration from elsewhere, no disturbance of the main trend of townward migration is discernible.

It is evident, then, that the industrial migration from East Anglia and the West Country did not set strongly in the direction of the northern woollen districts. What was its direction and character? In the first place, many of the displaced workers emigrated overseas. Internal migration from the East Anglian counties set very strongly in the direction of London (see Map D in Appendix). The attraction of London was strong also in all the south-western counties; but from these counties there was

[1] *A. & P.*, 1846, XII, No. 209.

also an important stream of movement to the iron and coal districts of South Wales. The majority of applicants for casual relief in Cardiff were said to be single young men from Somerset or Wiltshire. It is known, moreover, that many whole families were migrating into Wales from the West Country clothing towns in search of employment at the ironworks.[1]

THE MINOR TEXTILE INDUSTRIES

In none of the other textile industries were technical improvements so quickly adopted, or the processes of industrial transition so marked, as in the cotton and woollen industries. If the textile industries were grouped according to the rapidity with which they improved in technique, cotton would in the earlier nineteenth century be the typical progressive industry; while the typical parasitic industry would be silk, which seems to have maintained its position during the period largely through its use of the labour displaced from the more progressive trades. In such a grouping of industries linen would occupy a midway place.

In the eighteenth century the chief seat of the British linen manufacture was the north of Ireland. In England there was an important manufacture of linen in the west of Lancashire and the north of Yorkshire; in Scotland the industry was carried on in most of the southern shires, and had attained a considerable development by 1770. Beyond these defined areas the manufacture of sailcloth and coarse linens was carried on at many ports throughout the country, for the satisfaction of local demand. During the earlier nineteenth century it is possible to trace a process of concentration in the linen industry similar to that going on in the cotton and woollen trades, though on a much smaller scale. The decline of the domestic manufacture of linen was an important cause of the emigration from North Ireland in the later eighteenth century. This decline continued in the following half-century, and by 1840 only the elderly linen weavers were left in the district round Londonderry. 'The fine,

[1] *A. & P.*, 1847–8, XV, No. 987, p. 30; *1851 Census*, Pt. I, Vol. I, Divn. V, p. 23.

sturdy young men who once came to market have now gone out of the trade.'[1] Meanwhile, the Irish linen industry was being reborn through the introduction of flax-spinning by machinery, about 1828. The new factory industry grew up round Belfast, and at first drew most of its labour from the surrounding cotton and linen districts.[2]

One great cause for the general decline of the linen manufacture was the increasing cheapness of cotton goods. The growth of the Lancashire cotton industry hit the Irish linen trade particularly, because the extension of the cotton manufacture tended to drive out of Lancashire the manufacture of both linen and fustian (cotton and linen mixed), which had previously been made in Lancashire from Irish yarn.[3] A gradual transition from linen to cotton can be traced in the parish records of some villages in West Lancashire, during the eighteenth century. In Walton-le-Dale, for instance, most of the families were those of linen weavers at the beginning of the century, apart from the ordinary village craftsmen. By 1720, however, fustian men and chapmen in fustians begin to be mentioned. In 1775 a 'cotton and linen printer' was married there, and from about 1786 there are frequent references to calico-printers, one of whom came from Hampshire. By 1798 a cotton-spinning factory had been built in the parish, and in the following years there are references to manufacturers of calico and muslin. Mule spinners begin to be mentioned about 1808.[4] This transition appears to have been general in the west of Lancashire. Between 1770 and 1780 the linen manufacture in Lancashire decreased considerably, while the cotton manufacture is said to have doubled itself within the same period,[5] and by the beginning of the nineteenth century the linen industry of Lancashire had shrunk to very small dimensions.

---

[1] Arthur Young, *Tour in Ireland*, 1780, Pt. II, p. 30; *Political Arithmetic*, pp. 319–20; *Repts. Hd. Lm. Wvrs., Ireland*, 1840, p. 725.

[2] See E. R. R. Green, *The Lagan Valley, 1800–1850*, 1949, Chap. V, 'The Industrial Revolution in the Linen Industry'.

[3] Daniels, pp. 9, 58.

[4] *Lancashire Parish Register Society*, XXXVII, *passim*.

[5] *J.H.C.*, XXXVIII, p. 926.

The same transference from linen to cotton took place all over the west of Scotland, between 1778 and 1790;[1] and in the succeeding generation the manufacture of cotton spread with surprising rapidity through almost all the southern shires. As the cotton manufacture gradually became concentrated round Lancashire, however, the group of shires round Dundee returned to the linen trade.[2] Here the main source of labour was the Highlands; but there was also a strong influx of linen weavers from Ireland. Abbotshall, in Fifeshire, may serve as an illustration of the process of transition. At the end of the eighteenth century Abbotshall was increasing in population through the manufacture of checks and bed-ticks. The parish contained five cotton manufactories, with spinning 'Jeanies' (worked with a horse engine); these employed about two hundred persons, including many children. By 1831, however, the parish was concentrating on flax-spinning; this had been considerably extended, 'thereby furnishing employment to poor families from other quarters, particularly from Ireland'.[3]

Meanwhile the Yorkshire linen trade was tending to become concentrated in the West Riding, round Barnsley, and in neighbouring places like Silkstone and Dodworth. This coincided with a rapid decline in the domestic linen trade of the North Riding for which Knaresborough was the centre. Between 1821 and 1831 the population of Knaresborough showed a marked falling-off in the rate of increase, and by 1840 it was said that only family ties could keep any weavers there at all. There were 130 cottages empty, and many others for which no rent or rates could be paid. In the neighbouring country villages, such as Darley, Hampsthwaite, and Dacre, wages were even lower than at Knaresborough. The weavers, who were migrating in large numbers, went mainly to Barnsley.[4]

The lace and hosiery trades of the framework-knitting districts

[1] G. M. Mitchell, *loc. cit.*, pp. 101–4, quoting J. Cleland: *Annals of Glasgow*, II, p. 372.
[2] *1821 Census*, pp. 508–9, 511–12; *1831 Census*, II, pp. 977–9, 982–5, 1014.
[3] Sinclair, IV, pp. 186, 189; *1831 Census*, II, p. 978.
[4] *1821 Census*, pp. 418, 420; *1831 Census*, II, p. 817; *Rept. Mfs.*, 1833, p. 597; *Repts. Hd. Lm. Wvrs., Yorkshire*, 1840, pp. 485, 488.

round Nottingham and Leicester were not, in the earlier nineteenth century, transformed by the adoption of steam-power, as were the textile trades already mentioned.[1] Yet the framework knitters throughout the period were as miserable a class as the handloom weavers in the other textile districts, and were as prominent in the social disturbances of the half-century. Like the London framework knitters at an earlier date, the Midland knitters complained that the undue number of apprentices trained to the trade had driven wages below the subsistence level. In the closing years of the eighteenth century a great many parish apprentices are said to have been brought from Northamptonshire and Warwickshire. 'They came from Northamptonshire and all about, with ten pounds to put an apprentice out—some would have eleven, or twelve, or thirteen apprentices.' In the next generation cheap labour was being introduced from Ireland and Scotland, with a deteriorating effect on the standard of work. 'If they get into a frame for twelve months or so they think they are masters of it.'[2]

Both Nottingham and Leicester were growing at a respectable rate during the period, and were capturing the local specialities in hosiery and lace-making which had hitherto employed the population of small villages in various parts of the country. A factor contributing to the growth of Nottingham was the extension of the 'Nottingham' lace manufacture into the neighbouring counties of Northampton, Lincoln, and Derby, wherever cheap labour could be found. These extensions led to a local influx of labour into Nottingham and its surrounding villages, which manufactured the necessary lace machines.[3] Taking the counties as units, both Nottinghamshire and Leicestershire were losing on balance by migration, Leicestershire showing the heavier loss. From Nottinghamshire the predominant trend was to the Yorkshire textile districts. From Leicestershire the strongest streams of labour flowed towards the Midland coal and iron towns, and towards London.

[1] *Rept. on Framework Knitters*, 1845, Pt. I, App., pp. 56, 394; cf. p. 405.
[2] *Ibid.*, Pt. I, pp. 10, 108; Pt. II, p. 52.
[3] *1821 Census*, pp. 222–3; *1831 Census*, I, pp. 335, 480–1, 487; *1841 Census*, p. 51.

During the eighteenth century the British silk industry had made notable progress, especially in provincial centres such as Derby, Macclesfield, and Coventry. 'In 1700 Spitalfields was the only centre of a considerable silk trade. . . . By the year 1800 the industry had been entirely transformed, and ranked among England's greatest undertakings.'[1] During the nineteenth century, however, the silk manufacture did not fulfil its earlier promise. The change from handloom to power-loom did not take place in the silk trade until the later nineteenth century, except for a limited class of goods; consequently the trade became an asylum for handloom weavers from the cotton and woollen trades. This involved a further migration of the silk trade from the old centres like Spitalfields to the northern districts, especially those round Manchester and Macclesfield. Manchester is said to have possessed ten thousand silk weavers in 1815, and the next decade saw a great expansion of the industry there. The great majority of the Lancashire silk weavers at that time had formerly been cotton weavers, the transition being especially active between 1816 and 1826.[2] The change from cotton to silk affected mainly the more highly skilled workers, such as the weavers of nankeens, ginghams, and muslins; it did not necessarily involve any migration of population, though there seems to have been some transference of weavers to Manchester from Macclesfield.[3]

Meanwhile, the wages of the Spitalfields silk workers remained depressed, in spite of the regulatory Act of 1773, and there were many complaints that, even so, the Act tended to drive the trade to the provinces. In the post-war generation the problem of pauperism among the silk weavers increased greatly,

[1] G. B. Hertz, 'The English Silk Industry in the Eighteenth Century', in *E.H.R.*, XXIV, p. 721.
[2] *Rept. Silk*, 1832, pp. 740, 792, 819, 822, 826.
[3] *Rept. Mfs.*, 1833, pp. 296, 305–6. 'In 1825, the population of Macclesfield amounted to about 20,000; and in the newspapers of February of that year may be seen advertisements to "overseers, guardians of the poor, and families desirous of settling in Macclesfield. Wanted immediately, from four to five thousand persons, from seven to twenty years of age, to be employed in the throwing and manufacturing of silk". Again: "Wanted to be built immediately, one thousand houses" ' (H. Martineau, *History of the Thirty Years' Peace*, 1877 ed., II, p. 19).

and observers were already of the opinion that the silk trade
would eventually leave Spitalfields.[1] This became still more
likely after the reduction of the protective duties in 1824–6, and
the decline was reflected in a contemporary movement of
weavers out of London.[2] In the early 'thirties there remained in
Spitalfields about five thousand male weavers. The manufacture of narrow goods had been almost entirely discontinued,
and the local firms were employing looms in the country, as
far afield as Devonshire. Some of the London weavers weathered
the recurrent periods of unemployment by turning to the
miscellaneous odd jobs on the docks (which were then extending) and in the warehouses. Silk weavers, however, had a
special prejudice against doing any other kind of work. 'If we
went to labouring work we should never be able to return to
weaving, for our hands would be in that state that we should
not be able to handle the silk.' Most of the weavers who
migrated seem to have gone to other silk-manufacturing centres,
such as Macclesfield, Coventry, Bocking, and Braintree.[3]

This decline of the London silk industry affected also the
domestic workers in the old clothing counties round about
(especially Essex and Surrey), where the woollen trade had
been almost entirely superseded by silk.[4] In the counties to the
north of London the situation was relieved by the erection of
silk-throwing factories, which gave employment to the younger
people and caused local increases of population.[5] The Essex
section of the industry was particularly vigorous, and has already been noticed as attracting weavers from Spitalfields.
Attempts were also made to import silk-workers from Coventry,
but without much success:

> . . . I have gone to Coventry, and found a good many out of work; I give
> them two guineas to go to Coggeshall, they have gone and staid a week,

---

[1] *Rept. P.L.*, 1817, pp. 40–2.

[2] *Rept. Mfs.*, 1833, p. 113.

[3] *1831 Census*, I, pp. 368, 382; *Rept. Silk*, 1832, pp. 608, 734–5; *Rept.
M. & B.U.*, 1841, p. 7.

[4] *P.L.C. Rept.*, 1834, App. A, Pt. I, No. 8, p. 229 (Hinckford); *1831
Census*, II, p. 633 (Haslemere).

[5] *1821 Census*, pp. 96, 216; *1831 Census*, I, pp. 187, 197; II, pp. 606, 626,

and they would stay no longer. . . . During the worst of distress, I had many men from Coventry come to me, and the moment they had got enough to travel back they have gone.

There was actually a scarcity of workers in some silk-throwing centres of Essex, which caused the trade to spread still further afield into Suffolk.[1]

THE COAL AND IRON INDUSTRIES

The transition to the use of steam-driven machinery in the textile industries during the nineteenth century involved an expansion of the coal and iron trades of the country. These two trades had a very close relationship to each other, not only because the increased demand for iron and steel was largely caused by the transition to steam-power, but also through the modern use of coal in iron-smelting, and through the juxtaposition of the ores which is usual in England. Almost all the chief coalfields of the country increased rapidly in population throughout the first half of the nineteenth century; but the greatest increases naturally occurred in districts which combined coal-mining with metal or textile manufactures. The coal districts of the West Midlands (especially South Staffordshire) were growing more rapidly than the others, but the Black Country coal trade was closely bound up with its iron and steel manufactures. Of the areas depending more narrowly on coal-mining, Durham was the most important throughout the period; though the most notable increase of population through the extension of the coal trade was probably in the South Wales area.

South Wales had long possessed a considerable iron industry. Its modern importance as a coalfield did not, however, begin to emerge until the later eighteenth century.[2] Up to that time coal had been shipped to Cardiff from Pembrokeshire. In the closing years of the century canals were opened between Merthyr and

[1] *Rept. Silk*, 1832, p. 383; *Repts. Hd. Lm. Wvrs., East of England*, 1840, p. 291.
[2] On population changes in the South Wales coalfield see Dr. A. E. Trueman, in *Geographical Journal*, June 1919, pp. 410 ff.

Cardiff (1798) and between Pontypool and Newport. These canals stimulated the export trade in both coal and iron, and caused the rapid growth of the two ports. During the earlier decades of the nineteenth century Newport grew more rapidly than Cardiff, because the eastern valleys were opened up first. The exportation of the smokeless coals from the north-west districts began about 1830; from that time may be said to date the modern growth of Cardiff, the Merthyr and Aberdare valleys becoming increasingly important.

The main trends of coal-mining migration during the half-century were obscured by the fact that much local movement of no great significance was always going on within the various districts. This was due largely to the primitive mining methods of the time. Pits were small, pumping and ventilation were not well understood, and it was often considered safer to open up a new shaft than to proceed further with an existing one. The resultant ebb and flow of population was especially prominent in the Northumbrian coalfield, where the coals presented peculiar difficulties owing to 'their great depth beneath the surface, their comparative softness, and the profusion of inflammable air'. The same tendency occurred, however, in many of the other coal-mining districts, such as Lancashire, Yorkshire, Gloucester, Ayr, and Fife; this may in part explain why coal-mining acquired the reputation of being a migratory trade.[1]

In general, the evidence for any strong influx of labour into coal-mining is not plentiful. A large part of the supply of new labour required by the expansion of the industry probably came from the natural increase of a notoriously prolific section of the population. To contemporary observers the coal-mining population afforded

an example of the principle of population operating in full vigour, in the

___

[1] See *Ann. Reg.*, 1815, App., pp. 507–8; cf. *ibid.*, Chronicle, pp. 38, 50, etc.; *1821 Census*, pp. 87–8, 235; *1831 Census*, I, pp. 170, 175, 454; *1841 Census*, pp. 81–8, 212–22; *1851 Census*, Pt. I, Vol. II, Divn. X, pp. 11–39; Dr. A. Ure's *Dictionary of Arts, Manufactures, and Mines*, 4th ed., 1853, II, p. 409; on the technique of coal-mining during the period see *ibid.*, articles on 'Pit-coal' and 'Mines'; T. S. Ashton and J. Sykes, *The Coal Industry of the Eighteenth Century*, 1929, pp. 152–5.

absence of external influence, and (hitherto) of internal checks. Pitmen must be bred to their work from childhood ... their numbers cannot be recruited from any other class. .... The increase of the pit-population solely from internal sources has in consequence been such that ... one hundred and twenty-five families attached to a single colliery were capable of annually supplying twenty to twenty-five youths fit for hewers.[1]

The most notable outside source of labour for the coal-mines was found in the lead-mining industry, which declined considerably during the period. The Derbyshire lead-mines were already declining before the end of the eighteenth century, and people were leaving such mining villages as Eyam, Winster, Bradwell, Castleton, and Wirksworth. This local exodus went on throughout the earlier nineteenth century, in spite of efforts to revive lead-mining by the introduction of improved pumping machinery and the importation of lead-miners from Cornwall. Some of the Derbyshire lead-miners went to the textile districts of Lancashire and Cheshire; many others, especially from the more southerly mines, found employment in the Staffordshire collieries, while some went to the iron-stone mines of South Yorkshire.[2]

Most of the other lead-mining districts felt the effects of depression as keenly as Derbyshire. In the villages of Durham and Northumberland the lead-miners were receiving only one-half the rate of wages earned in the neighbouring coal-pits,[3] and many lead-miners' families were emigrating to the United States. The mine-owners were, therefore, under strong temptation to introduce lead-miners into the coal-pits in any dispute with the colliers. In the great Durham coal strike of 1832 lead-miners were imported into the coal-pits at Callerton, Coxlodge, and Waldridge, in spite of forcible opposition from the desperate colliers. In that strike, indeed, miners were brought not only from the neighbouring lead-mines, but from Yorkshire,

---

[1] *P.L.C. Rept.*, 1834, App. A, Pt. I, No. 5, p. 130.
[2] Aikin's *Manchester*, 1795, pp. 81, 484, 494, 497–8; Eden, II, p. 130; *1821 Census*, p. 54; *1831 Census*, I, p. 105; *1851 Census*, Pt. I, Vol. II, Divn. VII, pp. 77–9; *1841 Census*, p. 51; *P.L.C. Rept.*, 1834, App. A, Pt. I, No. 13, p. 390; M. H. Habershon: *Chapeltown Researches*, 1893, pp. 139–40.
[3] Hammond, *op. cit.*, pp. 37–8, quoting *Newcastle Chronicle* and *Tyne Mercury*.

Staffordshire, and even Wales.[1] About that time, almost all the British lead-mining centres were petitioning against the importation of foreign ore, which had halved the price of lead in seven years. Petitions came from places so far apart as Ireland, Scotland, Cumberland, Northumberland, Yorkshire, Flintshire, and Derbyshire. Most of the lead-mining districts were declining in population through the migration of miners in search of employment. At Alston Moor, Cumberland, where lead-mining had been carried on since the Middle Ages, the population declined by over one-quarter between 1831 and 1833, and 400–500 houses were left empty. Some of the families emigrated to Canada, others moved to the neighbouring coal-mines in West Cumberland.[2]

Apart from this transference of labour from lead-mining to coal-mining, there is some evidence that the coal-mines were attracting labour from the distressed workers of other industries. As early as 1777 the West Country coal-pits were finding employment for felt-makers from Bristol in times of depressed trade. When, in 1837, the Lanarkshire miners struck work, starving handloom weavers were brought in from the surrounding districts, and are said to have earned as much in a day as colliers as they could earn in a week as weavers. About the same time the Durham coal-mines were attracting distressed linen weavers from the North Riding of Yorkshire; and, as the Factory Act of 1833 prevented the handloom weavers from sending their young children into the factories, many sent them into the mines.[3] It is probable, however, that the attraction of labour to coal-mining from manufacturing industry was not very important. The work was too arduous and dangerous, the social status of the miners too low, for the occupation to prove very attractive. It was said that respectable people never

[1] Hansard, *3rd Series*, XIII, pp. 1152–4; Webb: *Story of the Durham Miners*, 1921, pp. 35–6.

[2] *J.H.C.*, LXXXV, pp. 211, 284, 474, 479, 593; LXXXIII, p. 385; *1831 Census*, I, p. 105; II, pp. 769, 770, 965; *P.L.C. Rept.*, 1834, App. A, Pt. I, No. 11, p. 320.

[3] *J.H.C.*, XXXVI, p. 307; *1st Rept. on Combinations*, 1838, pp. 151–2; *Repts. Hd. Lm. Wvrs., Yorkshire Linen Weavers*, 1840, p. 489; *Ibid., Gen. Rept.* 1840, pp. 49–50.

apprenticed their children to mining except as a last resource. This dislike of the native workers for coal-mining partly accounts for the large number of Irish immigrants who adopted that occupation.

Population changes in the iron trade had necessarily a close similarity to those in the coal-mining industry; there are, however, clearer indications of a process of concentration in the former than in the latter. In the earlier decades of the century increases of population through the extension of iron-works were being reported, not only from the main centres, but from various places in Essex, Hereford, Somerset, and Gloucester; and iron-founding was also being carried on in such counties as Wiltshire, Devonshire, and Denbigh.[1] Gradually, however, the industry was becoming more closely concentrated round Birmingham, South Wales, and Sheffield. The Cleveland iron district was not yet in the first rank.

In the iron districts of the Midlands the balance of importance was shifting from Shropshire to the group of iron and coal towns round Birmingham. During the eighteenth century the growth of ironworks about Coalbrookdale and Broseley had made this corner of Shropshire the chief centre of iron production in the country, and from the local records of population it is clear that an influx of single men from elsewhere had taken place.[2] Before the end of the eighteenth century, however, the smelting of iron with pit-coal was driving the industry eastwards, and Shropshire was becoming a centre of dispersion. In the early nineteenth century, while the iron towns of Staffordshire and Worcestershire were increasing continuously, Shropshire reported both increases and decreases of population, in fairly equal proportions, through fluctuations of the iron trade. In 1821, for instance, Eardington reported an increase through the extension of ironworks, but Bridgnorth was decreasing for the opposite reason. In 1831 Dawley and Stirchley were said to be increasing through the establishment

[1] *1821 Census*, pp. 96, 122, 279; *1831 Census*, I, p. 203; *1851 Census*, Pt. I, Vol. I, Divn. V, pp. 27, 47; Vol. II, Divn. XI, p. 55.
[2] T. S. Ashton, *Iron and Steel in the Industrial Revolution*, 1924, p. 199.

of blast furnaces, forges, and mills for the manufacture of bar-
iron; Broseley, on the other hand, had decreased through the
stoppage of five blast furnaces, and Upton Magna was similarly
declining.[1]

Many of the Shropshire ironmasters migrated to the Black
Country coalfield. Among those coming from Broseley were
the Thorneycrofts, of Tipton and Wolverhampton, and the
Bagnalls, of Tipton, Wednesbury, and West Bromwich. The
Williamses, of Wednesbury, came from Ludlow, and the
Parkers, of Tipton, were among the families coming from Coalbrookdale. Other families of ironmasters migrating from
Shropshire were the Joneses, of Shakerley, and the Baldwins.
Bilston, which increased its population fourfold between 1780
and 1820, is known to have been drawing miners and iron-
workers from both Shropshire and Wales.[2] It would be interesting to know whether this special industrial migration in the
iron trade was important enough to modify the general trend
of movement into the main centres of the industry. Where
records of individual firms are available, they suggest that the
workers for new ironworks were collected largely from among
the experienced workers at old-established centres, and that
when an ironmaster migrated he took his skilled workers with
him. The histories of the trade record the attraction of iron-
workers to Furness from Cheshire, Ireland, South Wales, and
Yorkshire, and from Shropshire to Scotland and South Wales.
In the last quarter of the eighteenth century there was apparently a considerable influx into South Wales from the Midlands,
especially from the Stourbridge district.[3]

It is not possible, however, to determine whether these
special industrial migrants formed any large proportion of the
volume of labour flowing into all the rising iron centres during
the earlier nineteenth century. The migration of iron-workers
from Shropshire to the Black Country was certainly strong
enough to have left its mark on the census statistics of migra-

[1] *1821 Census*, p. 272; *1831 Census*, I, pp. 514, 526.
[2] Ashton, *op. cit.*, p. 53; S. Griffiths: *Iron Trade of Great Britain*, 1873,
p. 110; Lawley, *History of Bilston*, 1893, pp. 171–2.
[3] Ashton, *op. cit.*, p. 199.

tion.[1] Migration into the Midland iron towns was appreciably stronger from Shropshire than from the counties to the east of the Black Country. On the other hand, the special migrations into South Wales from the great iron and coal districts did not produce any marked disturbance of the general trend of movement. Almost all the new labour required for South Wales seems to have been drawn from the surrounding Welsh counties and the south-western counties of England.

[1] See *1851 Census*, Pt. II, Vol. I, Divn. VI, p. 526.

F

CHAPTER IV

MUSHROOM TOWN-GROWTH AND AGRARIAN MIGRATION

THE TOWNWARD DRIFT

THE movements of population in England during the generation following the Napoleonic wars have been shown to
reflect a steady process of industrial concentration and localization. Many of the old-fashioned industrial districts were
declining, and their place was being taken by those rising
manufacturing districts which reached maturity during the
later nineteenth century. From the standpoint of social organization, the transition taking place was from rural and village
industry to town industry and the peculiar problems of town
life. The unprecedented increases of population in the 'new'
industrial areas were mainly confined to a comparatively small
number of great towns, most of which reached their maximum
decennial rate of growth during the period 1821–31.[1] It is
important to know whence the new town population came, and
to understand the forces which lay behind the movement.

The problem is not so simple as might be presumed from
the casual attention it has generally received. Since the manufacturing towns in question were mostly situated in the west-
midland and north-western counties, it is tempting to assume
that the transition was, in the main, brought about by a
movement of population from the southern and eastern counties
to the midlands and the north. This conception of the change
as a migration from south to north may, indeed, be regarded
as the established view. Ernle, for instance, states that

> in the latter half of the following [eighteenth] century not only wealth
> but population migrated northwards, and the inhabitants of rural districts

---

[1] R. Price-Williams, 'On the Increase of Population in England and
Wales', in *S.J.*, XLIII, pp. 464–9.

began to flow into the centres of trade and manufacture. . . . Population was shifting from the south to the north, and advancing by leaps and bounds in crowded manufacturing towns. . . . It was now [about 1800] that the industrial population was shifting from the south to the north.[1]

In discussing the rapid increase of population in the early nineteenth century, the Rev. A. H. Johnson said it was then that 'population began to shift from the south and east, which had hitherto been the industrial parts of England, to the north and west, the homes of the new industries'.[2] Mantoux confessed himself baffled as to the way in which the transition of population took place. 'In 1750 the trend of population towards the north and west had begun to show itself. It seemed to be moving towards the Atlantic . . . What is the meaning of this migration towards the north and west?'[3]

It is, perhaps, reasonable to suppose from such statements that there was during the period a noticeable rush of population from the south of the country to the rising manufacturing districts, as to a newly-discovered El Dorado. Curiously enough, however, the most careful contemporary observers knew nothing of any such 'Klondyke rush'; on the contrary, they asserted that no appreciable movement at all had taken place from the southern counties into the manufacturing districts. This may be illustrated from the results of inquiries made in the Lancashire cotton districts in 1834–5. Dr. J. P. Kay declared that up to that time few or no migrants had come from the counties south of Derbyshire or Staffordshire; and Henry Ashworth, of Turton, had only heard of one family from further south than Derbyshire, 'that of a bricklayer from Northants'.[4]

A great proportion of the migrants into Lancashire had come from the surrounding counties:

An extensive migration of miners proceeded from the valleys and

[1] Ernle, pp. 147, 205, 308.
[2] A. H. Johnson, pp. 112–13.
[3] Mantoux, p. 354; cf. pp. 182–3, 359.
[4] *P.L.C., 1st Ann. Rpt.*, App. B, No. 11, p. 185; App. C, No. V, p. 217; cf. *A. & P.*, 1843, XVI, No. 254, pp. 2–4. The fact is also mentioned in *P.L.C., 2nd Ann. Rpt.*, App. B, No. 20, p. 430, and App. C, No. 15, p. 490.

moorlands of the Peak. . . . The north-west of Yorkshire had likewise, at
former periods, supplied the flannel district of Rochdale and the cotton
districts of Todmorden, Bacup, and Burnley, etc., with many workmen.
Cheshire and Wales have also both been the sources of a more partial
migration, as well as the more distant northern counties and Scotland.
. . . One source of a vast supply of workmen to this district yet remains
to be mentioned, viz. Ireland.[1]

The scattered and scanty references to migration into particular towns confirm this account. The parish registers of
Manchester, for instance, show that even from the seventeenth
century there had been a gradual influx of population from all
the surrounding counties, and it had been quite common for
the yeomen of North Lancashire, Yorkshire, and Cumberland to establish their sons in Manchester as clothworkers,
haberdashers, glovers, linen-drapers, woollen-drapers, and felt
makers. Before 1815 both Manchester and Liverpool were also
drawing population from the eastern counties of North Wales,
and Liverpool was receiving migrants from as far west as Anglesey. From the fact that a 'Salopian Amicable Society' was
projected in Manchester so early as 1785 it may be inferred
that there was a considerable number of migrants from
Shropshire: while the migrants from Staffordshire included such
successful commercial families as the Philipses, in the early
eighteenth century, and the Coopers, a century later.[2] Most of
the long-distance migrants to Manchester came either from
Ireland or from Scotland. The histories of such smaller Lancashire towns as Oldham, Ashton-under-Lyne, and Stalybridge
show that practically all the migrants came either from the
north and west of Lancashire, from the surrounding counties,
or from Ireland.[3] It is important to realize that although
Lancashire was increasing in population very rapidly during
the early nineteenth century, many rural districts in the north

[1] Cf. *17th Rept. P.L.A.A.*, 1838, p. 1.
[2] John Owen, *Extracts from the Parish Registers of Manchester*, 1879—see
especially pp. 15–20; *E.J.*, XV, pp. 216–17; *Manchester City News, N.Q.*,
II, p. 124; *1821 Census*, pp. 432, 455; *Harrop's Manchester Mercury*, Feb. 1st,
1785.
[3] See E. Butterworth's *Historical Account of Ashton-under-Lyne, etc.*, p. 94;
Mantoux, p. 372, quoting Butterworth's *History of Oldham*.

and west of the county were decreasing in population through the migration of families to the growing towns.[1]

Migration into the other great centres of manufacturing and mining industry showed the same short-distance movement from all neighbouring counties. The woollen towns of the West Riding received much labour from the north and east of Yorkshire, as well as from Lincolnshire.[2] Birmingham and the neighbouring group of towns drew labourers from the rural parts of Staffordshire and Warwickshire, together with considerable numbers from Shropshire on the west and Northamptonshire on the east.[3]

In Scotland the situation was affected by the general efflux from the Highlands, which increased the population of towns in all parts of the country. Glasgow, like most of the other towns, received many highland migrants; but the town also drew largely on the rural districts of the Lowlands, and in particular on the upland farming districts of the Lothians. During the earlier decades of the nineteenth century Glasgow experienced a greater aggregate increase of population than any other manufacturing town; a contemporary analysis of its population is therefore important:

> Taking Glasgow as the centre, there are persons who have come to it from all sides, within a circuit of sixty miles. My father originally came from the Lothians, and had been a country farmer; he was driven out by the improvements in farming, became a mechanic, and settled in Glasgow. Most of my acquaintances either were born in the country or their parents came directly from the country. When the extinction of small farms took place, and the cottiers were driven in from their agricultural and pastoral employments, they first collected in villages, and then gradually inclined to the large towns, especially to Glasgow, from the Lothians. In my opinion, the population of Glasgow may be divided into five parts, of which the native inhabitants would be one-fifth, the Lowlanders two-fifths, the Highlanders one-fifth, and the Irish one-fifth.[4]

Apart from its general interest, this account of the migration

[1] E.g. *1831 Census*, I, pp. 291, 294; *1841 Census*, p. 142.
[2] Cf. Toynbee, pp. 69–70.
[3] Wedge, *Warwick*, 1794, p. 21; A. W. Ashby, *One Hundred Years of Poor Law Administration in a Warwickshire Village*, pp. 24–5; *P.L.C., 2nd Ann. Rpt.*, App. B, No. XV, p. 381.
[4] Report by Tait, quoted in *17th Rept. P.L.A.A.*, 1838, p. 3.

into Glasgow raises the question whether the small towns and country villages were acting as concentration centres for the subsequent movement to the greater towns. Statistically, if comparison is made between rural and urban communities at equal distances from a great town, the urban district will be found to contribute a greater proportion of its population.[1] There are other examples of this migration by stages in Scotland. Loudoun (Ayrshire) had been growing quite steadily during the later eighteenth century, though many weavers had migrated to Glasgow and Paisley; their places had been filled by an immigration of farmers' widows and daughters, who came to assist the local weavers and so learn the trade. The same process of local concentration was reported from many other lowland villages which were supplying Glasgow with labour.[2]

In England the process was not so evident; but it appears to have been taking place in the West Country clothing district. Frome, for instance, decreased markedly between 1821 and 1841; yet in 1833 it was said that one-sixth of the population of the town (two thousand out of twelve thousand) were migrants from neighbouring villages, and it was known that a thousand persons had come from Shepton Mallet alone. Similarly, Calne, in Wiltshire, decreased slightly between 1841 and 1851; yet such neighbouring villages as Blackland, Cherhill, Compton Bassett, and Highway were attributing their local decreases to the removal of families to Calne.[3]

So far, then, as can be discovered from the scanty evidence available, the extraordinary burst of town-growth in this country between 1821 and 1831 was not due to any cataclysmic transference of population from the southern to the northern counties. The movement was a drift, rather than a migration in the ordinary sense of the word. Most of the people flocking into the rising towns came from the rural districts of the surrounding counties. They were a mixed company, in which

[1] See Weber, pp. 267–72.
[2] Sinclair, I, pp. 82–3, 319, 321; II, pp. 195–6, 226, 325; III, pp. 103–4; etc.
[3] *P.L.C. Rept.*, 1834, App. A, Pt. I, No. 15, pp. 496–7, 498; *1851 Census*, Pt. I, Vol. I, Divn. V, pp. 18–19.

cobblers and tailors rubbed shoulders with starving handloom weavers and gawky husbandmen; but the workers coming from agriculture far outnumbered the rest.[1] Agriculture was, indeed, the most promising recruiting ground for the manufacturing towns during the post-war generation; the difficulty is not to explain why migration from agriculture took place, but to determine its character and social significance.

AGRARIAN TRANSITION AND RURAL 'DEPOPULATION'

A curious confusion of opinion on the subject of agrarian migration shows itself among the writers of the period. Cobbett and his school asserted that the English countryside was being turned into a desert by the monstrous growth of towns, and the depopulating effects of agrarian transition:

> The farmhouses have long been growing fewer and fewer; the labourers' houses fewer and fewer; and it is manifest to every man who has eyes to see with that the villages are regularly wasting away. . . . In all the real agricultural villages and parts of the kingdom there is a *shocking decay*. . . . I am quite convinced that the population, upon the whole, has not increased, in England, one single soul since I was born. . . . The country has never varied much in the gross amount of its population, but formerly the people were pretty evenly spread over the country, instead of being . . . collected together in great masses. . . . No doubt Lancashire, part of Yorkshire, and some other parts, are more populous than they formerly were. . . . One part of the nation has been depopulated to increase the population of another part.[2]

This view of Cobbett's, it will be noticed, agrees tolerably well with the opinions of the more modern writers already quoted, in assuming that a general migration of agricultural labourers was taking place from the southern to the northern counties. The tendency is to regard the agrarian revolution as exactly parallel and supplementary to the industrial revolution; so that while industrial forces (the 'factory system') were attracting people into the towns, agricultural forces (the 'enclosure movement') were compelling people to leave the countryside.

[1] *Rept. of Factory Commssnrs.*, 1834, D. 1, p. 169.
[2] Cobbett, *Rural Rides*, Oct. 31st and Nov. 24th, 1822; Sept. 4th, 1826; *Political Register*, April 10th, 1823; *Political Works*, VI, pp. 337–8; and many other similar references.

On the other hand, there were, during the period under discussion, innumerable complaints from the agricultural counties that agricultural labour was super-abundant, that the migration of labour was being prevented by the action of the Poor Laws, and that the rural population was increasing in an unhealthy fashion. In effect, to Cobbett's plaint that the nation's life-blood was ebbing away from the countryside, the agriculturalists retorted: 'We only wish it were; a little blood-letting of that sort would do no harm!'

This latter point of view tends to corroborate the statements of those observers in the northern manufacturing towns who asserted that there had been remarkably little migration from the southern agricultural counties, and that the agricultural migrants to the towns had come in the main from the immediately surrounding counties. Throughout the period it was remarked that agricultural wages were highest in the neighbourhood of the growing towns, and many instances were quoted to show that this arose from the local scarcity of agricultural labour due to the attraction of higher wages in industry.[1]

Agricultural labourers were most highly paid round the textile districts of Lancashire and the West Riding;[2] the next

---

[1] Adam Smith, Bk. I, Chaps. VIII and X; cf. Mantoux, pp. 359, n. 3, 421–3; Steffen, *Geschichte der englischen Lohnarbeiter*, Pt. II, Chap. XIII, pp. 11–27.

[2] This statement has been criticized by E. W. Gilboy (*Wages in Eighteenth-Century England*, 1934, pp. 189–90), who wrote: 'Some exception must be taken, however, to Redford's statement that "agricultural labourers were most highly paid round the textile districts of Lancashire and the West Riding", if by that he means to exclude entirely districts further afield. As far as the general labourer, who worked on the county bridges and roads, was concerned, his wage was as high in the North Riding, and the more purely agricultural districts of Lancashire as in the immediate neighbourhood of the manufacturing towns. It became even more true as the century went on and applied particularly to the period after 1750. Whether this may be explained by the diffusion of the industrial demand for labour over areas somewhat larger than Redford appears to have in mind, or by other reasons, we can only surmise. It is plausible to suppose, especially in Lancashire, that as industry became organized and factories increased, the demand for labour reached out even to the most rural districts with a consequent effect on the rate of wages. This explanation is not as convincing in the case of the North Riding, however. In the first place, the West Riding woollen industry did not develop as fast as the cotton industry in Lancashire and the need for labourers in factories would not therefore be as great. More

highest group was composed of the districts immediately bordering on London. In Lancashire it had been observed, so early as 1794, that the rate of agricultural wages was in inverse proportion to the distance from the manufacturing centres. At Chorley a common labourer got 3s. a day, with ale; at Euxton 2s. or 2s. 6d.; at Eccleston 1s. 6d. or 2s.; whilst at Mawdsley and Bispham labourers could be got, even in harvest time, for 1s. 2d. or 1s. 4d. In Cheshire, in 1808, the competition for children's labour was so keen round Macclesfield, Stockport, and the other manufacturing towns that few boys were being brought up to farming, and it was there 'as difficult to get a boy to drive the plough as a man to hold it'.[1] A similar drain of agricultural labour was observable in the neighbourhood of the other manufacturing and mining centres. In the 'thirties, for instance, agricultural wages were rising in South Wales through the increasing demand for labour in the iron and coal centres of Glamorganshire; and in Herefordshire wages were higher in the south of the county than in the north, for the same reason.[2] It goes without saying that wages in the manufacturing towns were everywhere higher than agricultural wages, throughout the period.

Such gradations in wages may reasonably be taken to imply that the higher wages in manufacturing towns were attracting agricultural labourers from the surrounding districts, and that

---

than that, the West Riding had a much larger area to draw upon in itself than Lancashire, and it would not appear necessary to induce labour from the North Riding at that period.' See also J. D. Marshall, 'The Lancashire rural labourer in the early nineteenth century', *Trans. Lancs. & Ches. Antiq. Soc.*, LXXI, 1963, pp. 90–9.

[1] J. Holt, *Lancashire*, 1795, p. 179; H. Holland, *Cheshire*, 1808, p. 296. Compare T. Wedge, *Cheshire*, 1794, p. 26: 'The effect of manufactories upon agriculture has been an increased demand for the produce of the land, and more especially for the luxuries of life: they have at the same time seriously increased the price of labour, and occasioned a scarcity of useful hands for husbandry. This was severely felt by the farmers, in the harvest of 1792, many of whom were obliged to pay for labourers at the rate of three shillings, three shillings and sixpence, and upwards per day, besides victuals and drink.'

[2] *Rept. L.W.*, 1824, printed in *Ann. Reg.*, 1824, App., p. 50; see also *Ann. Reg.*, 1825, App., p. 284; *1st Rept. Agric. Distress*, 1836, q. 4379, p. 206; *P.L.C., 2nd Ann. Rept.*, App. B, No. XIII, p. 364, and No. XIV, p. 371.

the attraction diminished as the distance from the manufacturing town increased. Agrarian migration, according to this interpretation of the evidence, was a short-distance, centripetal movement; and the motive force controlling the migration was the positive attraction of industry rather than the negative repulsion of agriculture. Before this conclusion can be accepted, however, it is necessary to investigate more closely the effect of the contemporary agrarian changes upon the rural population —a vexed question, upon which it is, perhaps, futile to hope for any final judgment. The difficulty of the subject was aptly illustrated by Sir James Steuart, writing in the middle of the eighteenth century:

> I know of cornfields, where villages formerly stood, the inhabitants of which fed themselves with the pure produce of absolute agriculture; that is, with a bit of garden ground and the milk of a cow; this surely is a proof of depopulation: but at a small distance from the place where those villages stood I see cornfields, where nothing but heath was to be met with; this proves an increase of population.[1]

As a result of the long-continued controversy concerning the relation between enclosures and population, general agreement has been reached on a few of the many contentious questions involved. It is agreed that where the land after enclosure was used for corn-growing, depopulation was less likely to occur than where it was used for pasturage (especially for sheep pasturage). It is further agreed that enclosure of the common waste was less likely to lead to depopulation than the enclosure of common field arable; and that the enclosure of extensive wastes, such as the marshes, forests, moorlands, and heaths which formerly covered a great part of England, led almost inevitably to local increases of population.[2]

Down to the later decades of the eighteenth century the most profitable form of enclosure was to use the enclosed land for arable or pasture, following the capacity of the soil; but by the end of the century wartime scarcity made corn-growing more

---

[1] Sir James Steuart, *Works*, 1805 ed., I, pp. 178–9.
[2] Slater, pp. 1–7, 104; Ernle, p. 299; A. H. Johnson, p. 97; Gonner, in *E.H.R.*, XXIII, p. 501n.

profitable than pasture-farming, and a higher proportion of land was enclosed for arable purposes. In December, 1800, a Parliamentary Committee was appointed to consider the high prices of foodstuffs. It inquired into the increase or decrease of land under the different crops in the districts which had been enclosed by private Acts of Parliament during the previous forty-five years (i.e. since 1755). The result showed a net gain in the area under wheat of 10,265 acres, out of 1,767,651 acres enclosed; the area under wheat had been 155,572 acres before enclosure, and was 165,837 acres after enclosure. The increased acreage under wheat had apparently been due mainly to the enclosure of waste; for if the cases where the enclosure was of waste only had been left out of the calculation, the result would have shown a decrease in the acreage under wheat, especially in such midland counties as Northants, Leicester, Buckingham, Warwick, and Bedford. In the other divisions of the country, however, the acreage under wheat would have been shown as increased even on this basis, especially in such eastern counties as Norfolk, Suffolk, Cambridge, and Hertford.[1]

Reasoning from the points of general agreement already mentioned, it might be presumed, then, that the enclosures between 1760 and 1800 had not been an active force in lessening agricultural employment, or depleting the rural population. Local decreases in some parts of the country had been more than offset by increases in other districts. On this basis, however, it would appear that the enclosures of the next generation must have been even more favourable to the growth of population; 'nor is there any period of the nineteenth century in which any serious rural depopulation as a result of enclosure . . . could be asserted'.[2] Not only did the home growth of wheat increase considerably between 1800 and 1840, but the enclosures of that period included a far greater proportion of waste land than had been the case in the enclosure movement of the eighteenth century. While the enclosure of the common field by

[1] Slater, pp. 108–9, quoting Board of Agriculture's *Gen. Rept. on Enclosures*, 1808, pp. 39, 232.
[2] Slater, p. 93.

private Acts took place most rapidly between 1760 and 1800, the great period for the enclosing of waste came in the succeeding generation.[1]

It has never been strongly held that the enclosure of waste caused depopulation. In the eighteenth and earlier nineteenth centuries, indeed, as in previous periods, it was often advocated as an antidote to the injurious social effects arising from the enclosure of the common field.

> The enclosure of waste lands should accompany that of common fields. . . . The only way [to avoid depopulation] is to counteract the effect of lessening the growth of corn on good land by bringing the bad and unimproved land into cultivation by a universal enclosure and improvement of waste lands, at present almost wholly unproductive; this is a matter of much greater public importance than common field enclosures. . . .[2] By the enclosure and conversion of waste lands population must in some degree be encouraged; and this should operate as one among the motives and ends of enclosing.[3]

This point of view found much support during the early decades of the nineteenth century; and in 1831 legislation was passed allowing the parish authorities to enclose a limited area of waste in or near the parish for the use and benefit of the poor persons of the parish. In the same year the legislation was extended to permit enclosure from forest or waste lands belonging to the Crown.[4]

During the periods of wartime scarcity in the later eighteenth and earlier nineteenth century large stretches of waste were enclosed, which had never supported any population, and on which no considerable common rights had been exercised. The Board of Agriculture's Report for Nottinghamshire records that 14,666 acres had recently been enclosed from Sherwood Forest alone. In 1801 three enclosures of Lincolnshire fens amounted to 53,500 acres; and the same year saw the enclosure of nearly 10,000 acres from Needwood Forest (Staffordshire), and 3,500 acres from Enfield Chase (Middlesex). In

---

[1] A. H. Johnson, pp. 90, 94. On the increase in the home production of wheat see Lord Welby, in *S.J.*, LXXVIII, p. 4.

[2] W. Pitt, *Leicester*, 1809, pp. 70, 79.

[3] T. Rudge, *Gloucester*, 1807, p. 91.

[4] *Rept. P.L.*, 1817, pp. 19, 128; 1 and 2 Wm. IV, c. 42; and 1 and 2 Wm. IV, c. 59.

1803 two enclosures in Cumberland, at Alston Moor and Penrith, totalled between them 48,000 acres. Two years later 9,000 acres of Canford Heath (Dorset) were enclosed; in 1808, 10,000 acres were enclosed at Hathersage (Derbyshire), and 18,000 acres from Charnwood Forest (Leicestershire). Nearly 3,000 acres of Quernmoor Forest (near Lancaster) were ordered to be enclosed in 1811; in Cheshire the enclosure of part of Delamere Forest gave rise to an entirely new parish. Many local increases of population were reported as following the enclosure of Inglewood Forest, in Cumberland. In the counties near London the same trend is shown in the enclosure of Bere Forest (Hampshire), Bexley Heath (Kent), and Hampton Common (Middlesex).[1]

The drainage, enclosure, and allotment to smallholders of large tracts of land in Lincolnshire was an especially prominent cause of local increases of population, and was coupled with an extension of cultivation on parts of the Lincoln Wolds. The population of the Soke of Bolingbroke increased considerably through the creation of small allotments of ten acres each, leased on condition that houses were built thereon. An Act of 1812 stated the public utility of dividing 14,000 acres into seven townships. The townships of Carrington, East-Ville, Mid-Ville, West-Ville, Langrick-Ville, and Thornton-le-Fen were thus created, and other villages increased. With this Lincolnshire reclamation of fenland is to be compared the parallel movement in Norfolk, and smaller drainages of marshes elsewhere.[2] Such extensive enclosures of hitherto uncultivated and uninhabited country must have tended to cause local increases of population; and, indeed, this is specifically reported in most of the cases mentioned.

While the French wars continued there can be no doubt that the progress of the enclosure movement tended to increase the rural population. Wartime scarcity favoured the agricultural interest, agricultural wages rose, and agricultural employment

[1] R. Lowe, *Nottingham* (1798), Apps. III and IV, pp. 149–50; Sir R. Hunter, in *S.J.*, LX, p. 383; *1821 Census*, pp. 28, 45, 47, 49, 50, 155, 165–6, 292, 299, 305; *1831 Census*, I, pp. 276, 369.
[2] *1821 Census*, pp. 171–84, 212, 431–3, 500; *1831 Census*, I, pp. 337–58.

increased through the extension of tillage; consequently a check was placed on the rural migration which had been in progress before the war. After 1814, however, agricultural prospects became unsettled; and in the post-war years petitions and speeches complaining of the distressed state of agriculture were very plentiful. The prices of agricultural produce fluctuated alarmingly, and it was said that landed property had fallen to one-half of its wartime value. Much arable land was said to be going out of cultivation. 'In some places the lands are actually deserted, and growing no other crop than weeds. In Huntingdonshire it is said that a circuit of three thousand acres is abandoned.' Allowing for rhetorical exaggeration, it is clear that the agricultural depression was acute, and that agricultural labourers were suffering through unemployment and reduced wages.

This, in its turn, tended to revive the townward migration from agriculture, and to raise again the question as to the relation between agrarian changes and rural depopulation.

> It has been observable . . . in some of the manufacturing districts that persons who had been supported on farms, by employment there during the war, for want of regular employ in manufactures, were, on the revival of the manufactures in which they had been educated, drawn from the farms by the temptation of higher wages. . . . Whole parishes had been deserted, and the crowd of paupers, increasing in numbers as they went from parish to parish, spread wider and wider this awful desolation.[1]

In these circumstances the enclosure of waste lands inevitably fell off sharply after the war; of the 939,043 acres of unmixed waste enclosed between 1802 and 1845 no less than 739,743 acres had been enclosed before 1815.[2] Nevertheless, local increases of population ascribed to the enclosure and allotment of waste continued to be reported from many parts of the

---

[1] See speeches by R. Preston, M.P., and C. C. Western, M.P., in *The Pamphleteer*, VII, No. XIII, pp. 81–124, and No. XIV, pp. 503–29; also in Hansard, XXXIII, pp. 31, 667. On the extension of tillage during the war see *Commons' Rept. on Corn Laws*, 1814, *Lords' Rept. on Grain Trade*, 1814, and *Commons' Rept. on Corn Trade*, 1813; W. F. Galpin, *The Grain Supply of England during the Napoleonic Period*, New York, 1925; on the deterioration of cultivation between 1814 and 1821 see *Rept. D.S. Agric.*, 1821; L. P. Adams, *Agricultural Depression and Farm Relief in England, 1813–1852*, 1932.

[2] Slater, App. A, p. 267.

country for the remainder of the half-century. The strength of the movement in the north of England, even after the end of the wars, may be seen from the enclosure of 18,300 acres at Holme (West Riding) in 1828, and of 1,360 acres of Haltwhistle Common (Northumberland) in 1844.[1]

The widespread distress among agricultural labourers was not merely an aspect of the post-war panic; it persisted in varying degree for the rest of the half-century, and was mentioned as the cause of decreased population in many small villages scattered throughout the country. Such rural decreases of population imply that migration was taking place; and the movement, in the circumstances, must have been mainly to the towns. In the country districts round rapidly-growing towns this can be clearly seen: in the town of Cardiff, for instance, the increase of population previous to 1831 was ascribed to the 'number of families who have deserted the neighbouring villages, through the depressed state of agriculture, and now reside in houses of the lowest description, built by speculators for their accommodation'.[2] In this respect, then, agricultural conditions were certainly tending to stimulate migration from the country to the towns, though as yet the movement was not causing depopulation over any large areas.

'Agricultural distress' is, however, a vague phrase, which may have had no necessary connection with the complex changes in agricultural methods and tenure commonly known as the agrarian revolution. Fortunately, the main aspects of agrarian transition are distinguished in the local census notes for the post-war period; and a brief analysis of the notes may throw some light on this controversial subject. The changes in agricultural methods and tenure reported to be causing local increases or decreases of population during the period may be grouped under the five heads of (i) enclosures, (ii) allotments, (iii) 'agricultural improvement' (a vague phrase), (iv) the enlargement or consolidation of farms, and (v) the conversion of

---

[1] *1851 Census*, Pt. I, Vol. II, Divn. X, p. 31; for Holme, see Sir R. Hunter, *loc. cit.*; for Haltwhistle, see Slater, App. B, p. 294.
[2] *1831 Census*, II, p. 895.

land from tillage to pasture. It may be remarked that the last two heads were closely related. When farms were 'thrown together' the change was usually for pasture-farming, and especially for sheep-rearing. The local reports concerning the effects of these five movements are practically unanimous. With very few exceptions, wherever enclosures, allotments, or agricultural improvements are mentioned, it is as a cause of increased population; with still fewer exceptions, the enlargement of farms and the laying down of land to pasture are reported to have caused decreases of population. It is therefore important to discover whether the various movements affected distinct areas or occurred in scattered fashion throughout the country.

In 1821 the influence of the wartime enclosures of waste was still strong; the local increases reported from this cause were most numerous in the eastern counties, but occurred also over a great part of England. There were, however, none in the southern Midlands, west of Cambridgeshire and north of Berkshire; the only reports of decreased population following enclosure were in Leicestershire (Drayton) and Lincolnshire (North Thoresby). In a great many counties enclosure was associated with allotments or agricultural improvements as a cause of increase; and in some parts of Scotland increases were attributed to the cultivation of hitherto untouched mountain land, or to the practice of 'feuing' small parcels of land. This was especially the case in the shires of Aberdeen, Kincardine, and Dumfries, where the policy was being adopted partly as a remedial measure for the settlement of Highlanders driven into the Lowlands by the extension of large-scale sheep-farming.

The enlargement of farms was frequently reported in Scotland, especially in the highland districts of Perthshire and Sutherland, where much land was being converted to sheep-farming; nevertheless, the population of the shires was increasing. In Berwickshire improved agriculture was said in two instances to have thrown small farms together and caused depopulation; in Glamorganshire, on the other hand, an *increase* of population was in one case reported to be due to the union of the whole parish in the occupation of one person, and to the introduction of improved agriculture. In England the solitary reference to the incorporation of small farms was in Suffolk (Walsham-le-Willows), and was said to have caused increased population through the improvident marriages of farm labourers who had 'formerly lived in'.

There were many other references in the southern and eastern counties to this peculiar cause of increased population. In some districts the practice of giving board wages to agricultural servants was being discontinued; the farm labourers were thus in many cases impelled to marry and set up house earlier than they would have done under the old system. Evidently the matter had no necessary connection with the consolidation of farms. Cobbett found the change symptomatic of social rottenness, due to the 'infernal stock-jobbing system'.

> Everything about this farmhouse was formerly the scene of plain manners and plentiful living. . . . But all appeared to be in a state of decay and nearly of disuse. There appeared to have been hardly any family in that house, where formerly there were, in all probability, from ten to fifteen men, boys, and maids. . . . Why do not farmers now feed and lodge their workpeople, as they did formerly? Because they cannot keep them upon so little as they give them in wages. This is the real cause of the change.

Other contemporary writers thought that the decay of the living-in system was due to the higher social standards of the farmers' families. ' . . . In the present day the wives and daughters of great farmers are of a different description. . . . They have been educated at boarding schools . . . and the false pride they have acquired makes them esteem it a drudgery to provide food for a number of workmen. . . . The latter are consequently obliged to get food and lodging where they can.'

A contributory cause preventing the keeping of indoor servants may have been the fear that they would thereby acquire a settlement.[1]

In 1831 the reports of increased population through enclosure continued without much abatement; there were many special references to the enclosure of waste, mainly in the south-eastern

[1] Cobbett, Oct. 20th, 1825; *Rept. D.S. Agric.*, 1821, p. 40; Davies, *Hints to Philanthropists*, 1820, p. 97 (reference kindly indicated by Prof. L. C. A. Knowles).

counties, but also in such nothern parts as Derbyshire and the West Riding. The increases through allotments and smallholdings continued to be most numerous in Lincolnshire, as in the previous decade. In Scotland, Aberdeenshire showed by far the greatest number of increases through enclosure and kindred causes; next came the neighbouring shires of Banff and Kincardine; but similar increases were reported (less frequently) as occurring in many other shires, from Caithness in the north-east to Wigtown in the south-west. Throughout Scotland, however, the decreases attributed to the enlargement of farms were very numerous in 1831, and affected about two-thirds of the more considerable shires, especially Argyll, Dumfries, Forfar, and Perth. In England, there were only two reports of local decreases from this cause, one in Suffolk, and the other in Cumberland, on the Scottish border; scattered instances also occurred in Wales.

By 1841 the enclosure movement had fallen off considerably; the three increases of population reported from this cause occurred in counties so widely separated as Cambridge, Devon, and Derby.[1] The only instance of increase through allotments was in Gloucestershire, where the system had been recently introduced. In Scotland the enlargement of farms continued with increasing strength between 1831 and 1851, and was the main cause of the general emigration of that period. The tendency was quite general throughout the Highlands, and was in most places for the purpose of sheep-farming; in the south of Scotland, Dumfriesshire seems to have suffered most heavily from this cause, but the tendency was present throughout the Lowlands, except along the south-west coast. The period was one of intense distress in many parts of Scotland, and one local decrease (in the shire of Inverness) was reported to be due to 'the insufficiency of food'. South of the Scots border, decreases through the enlargement of farms became more numerous towards the middle of the century. This was reported from both Cumberland and Northumberland, from Wales, and from the

---

[1] Bratton-Fleming, in Devon, reported the enclosure of 1,800 acres of waste, apparently from Exmoor.

Lincoln Wolds, as well as from Devonshire, Wiltshire, and Ox-
fordshire. The movement seems to have been especially strong
in Devonshire.

If these scattered references to the effects of agricultural
changes are considered in relation to their geographical distribution, the significance of the movement becomes clearer. The
increases attributed to enclosure, etc., were most numerous in
the eastern counties of England, especially in the fen counties of
Lincoln and Norfolk. The decreases through the enlargement of
farms and conversions to pasture were most numerous in the
Highlands of Scotland, especially in Sutherland, Inverness,
Argyll, and Perth. Between these two extremes there were many
districts in which the significance of agrarian change is not at
first sight apparent. If, however, the geographical distribution
of population changes consequent on agrarian transition is compared with maps showing the main agricultural areas of Great
Britain,[1] it appears probable that the agrarian changes of the
early nineteenth century were part of an evolutionary process
by which the rural population of each district was specializing
in the kind of agriculture to which the district was physically
and climatically suited.

This is clearly the case in the corn-growing districts of south-
east England, and in the Highlands of north-west Scotland. In
north-east Scotland the area reporting increases of population
through agrarian changes corresponded to the districts which
were physically suitable to mixed agriculture, and this was also
the case in the south-east of Scotland. The districts showing
most decreases in the Scottish Lowlands were the shires containing a high proportion of upland pasture. The regions of upland
pasture suitable for sheep were declining in population in eastern
Wales and in Devon; while many other English counties record-
ing occasional decreases contained considerable areas of upland
pasture, such as the Lincoln Wolds, the Marlborough Downs,
and the Chiltern Hills. On the other hand, the districts of mixed

[1] For the distribution of crops in England during the *third* quarter of the
nineteenth century see *S.J.*, XXXI, pp. 222–7, where six coloured maps
are given.

agriculture, and those where dairy-farming and cattle-rearing are most important, were reporting increases of population.[1]

Whether this interpretation of the agrarian transition be accepted or not, Cobbett's fear of widespread rural depopulation was not justified by the facts of his time—if by rural depopulation is meant the actual decrease of population in the country districts. It is true that large numbers of agricultural labourers were migrating from the countryside to the towns; and in some cases this was causing local decreases of population. But the local decreases recorded were quite insignificant compared with the general and continuous growth of population in all the English counties, as shown by the census returns. During Cobbett's lifetime no single county in England, Wales, Scotland, or Ireland reported a decreased population at *any* of the successive census returns. Cobbett countered this argument by flatly refusing to believe the census returns; but in this he was narrowly anticipating Dame Partington's opposition to the Atlantic Ocean.

[1] For a summary of recent research and opinions on the enclosure movement, see R. A. C. Parker, *Enclosures in the Eighteenth Century*, Historical Association, 1960.

CHAPTER V

'SURPLUS LABOUR' AND THE SETTLEMENT QUESTION

U NLIKE Cobbett, the landowners and other ratepayers in country parishes had no doubt that the rural population was increasing, and in a most unhealthy fashion; for, while the supply of agricultural labour was increasing, the demand for it was falling off, during the post-war depression. The apparent result was the growth of an ominous surplus of agricultural labour in most of the southern and eastern counties. This in turn led to a tremendous increase in the burden of the poor rates, already swollen by the lax administration and financial inefficiency of the war period.

Since the labour surplus depended on the coincidence of an increasing supply of labour with a diminishing demand for it, the underlying causes were presumably complex; and it is hard to decide how much weight should be attached to each factor in the situation. It seems probable that the wartime stimulus to agricultural production, followed by the inevitable and disastrous reaction on the return of peace, was as important a cause of agricultural unemployment as any of the changes in agricultural methods and tenure which were going on during the earlier nineteenth century.

> This surplus has been growing for years; but it commenced with the peace. . . . The first cause, when the peace was declared, was that the old soldiers and sailors were paid off and came home; and . . . we could not get vent for our young men in the army or navy. . . . And another cause was that soon after the peace the price of corn fell, and that was the ruin of a great many small farmers, and from that the great farmers have driven the small farmers out of the market. . . . The consequence was the increase of poor-rate; we have now to keep persons, who were originally farmers, as paupers. . . . Another cause is that we farmers make labourers do more work now than they used to do formerly.[1]

[1] *18th Rept. P.L.A.A.*, 1837, p. 16; evidence of John Stapley, a Sussex farmer.

In spite of the protective corn laws, less land was being kept under the plough, the intensive methods of wartime cultivation were being abandoned, and farmers were being forced to economize labour wherever possible. This was so not only on the inferior land taken into cultivation during the war, but also in many of the ancient corn-growing districts. To economize labour, however, was not so simple a matter as might have been thought, since in many cases the choice was between employing the labourer in agriculture or supporting him as a pauper. The poor rates in some agricultural districts rose at an almost incredible pace from this and other causes. One Buckinghamshire village reported in 1822 that its expenditure on poor relief was fully eight times the amount it had been in 1795, and more than the rental of the whole parish had been at the former date.[1] In the Weald of Sussex rent and poor rate had changed places exactly between 1792 and 1833: rent at the earlier date was eight shillings an acre and poor rate four shillings, whereas at the latter date rent was four shillings an acre and poor rate eight shillings.[2]

While the post-war agrarian depression was causing a reduction in the demand for agricultural labour, and necessarily increasing the problem of pauperism, it was freely asserted that a considerable part of the trouble was caused either by the poor-law system itself or by the laxity of its administration. In particular it was said (and with much justice) that the 'Speenhamland' system of subsidizing wages from the poor rates tended to reduce the demand for independent wage-labour, by allowing landowners and farmers to pay their labourers less than a living wage, thus shifting part of their labour cost on to the other ratepayers. Apart from its demoralizing effect in reducing the demand for free labour the Speenhamland system was declared to act as a direct incentive to the unhealthy increase of population, through the giving of an extra poor allowance for each child born.

[1] *Rept. on Poor Rate Returns*, 1822, printed in *J.H.C.*, LXXVII, App. 12, pp. 1342–3.
[2] *Rept. on Agriculture*, 1833, printed in *Ann. Reg.*, 1833, App., pp. 342–3.

Men who receive but a small pittance know that they have only to marry, and that pittance will be augmented in proportion to the number of their children. . . . An intelligent witness, who is much in the habit of employing labourers, states that when complaining of their allowance they frequently say to him: 'We will marry, and you must maintain us.' . . . But there was one thing better than to marry and have a family, and that was to marry a mother of bastards. . . . As one young woman of twenty-four with four bastard children put it: 'If she had one more, she should be very comfortable.'[1]

It is impossible to decide how far (if at all) the undoubted natural increase of population during the period was stimulated by this endowment of parenthood. 'Look at Ireland! There were no poor laws in that country; and would any man say that there was not a vast increase of population there!'[2] Assuming, however, that the Speenhamland policy was stimulating the supply of labour, while at the same time it was reducing the effective demand for it in the agricultural counties, it was still necessary to explain why the surplus labour persisted in staying at home on a starvation pittance when much higher wages were to be had in the rising manufacturing districts or in the overseas colonies.

One result of thinking constantly in terms of capital and labour as co-ordinate factors in production was the assumption that there was a 'circulation of labour' in the same sense as there was a 'circulation of capital'; and this sometimes led to the further assumption that labour was, in itself, as mobile as capital, and that to transfer either capital or labour from one industry to another was not very difficult. It is true that the most acute economic thinkers did not fall into this crude fallacy. Adam Smith, while he assumed that the 'free circulation of labour' was natural in the absence of special impediments, also realized 'from experience that a man is of all sorts of luggage the most difficult to be transported'. Ricardo's earlier position was that the application of labour-saving machinery 'was a general good,

[1] *Rept. L.W.*, 1824, printed in *Ann. Reg.*, 1824, App., pp. 49–50; *P.L.C. Rept.*, 1834, pp. 92–6, and App. A, Pt. I, p. 136; Hammond, *The Village Labourer*, p. 228.
[2] Hansard, *3rd Series*, XXV, p. 254; Lord Wynford on the second reading of the Poor Law Amendment Bill.

accompanied only with that portion of inconvenience which in most cases attends the removal of capital and labour from one employment to another'; but he later came to realize that considerations applying to capital in such cases did not necessarily apply to labour.[1] Such refinements of analysis, however, were wasted on the average employer of labour, to whom labour was a commodity 'the supplies of which are regulated on the same principles which regulate the supplies of articles of consumption and commerce'.

Why, then, should there be a recurrent scarcity of labour in the manufacturing districts, where wages were comparatively high, while in the agricultural counties of the south there was a vast, inert mass of redundant labour subsisting on starvation wages or on the pauper's dole? There must (it was thought) be some artificial hindrance to the free circulation of labour; otherwise labour would move from place to place until supply was equated to demand and wage rates for the same classes of labour were at approximately the same level throughout the country. The most obvious impediment to the adjustment of the labour supply was considered to be the restrictive effect of the poor laws in binding a man to his parish of settlement.

Adam Smith's condemnation of the system is well known.

> To remove a man who has committed no misdemeanour from the parish where he chooses to reside is an evident violation of natural liberty and justice. . . . There is scarce a poor man in England, I will venture to say, who has not in some part of his life felt himself most cruelly oppressed by this ill-contrived law of settlements.

That the settlement regulations restricted the migration of labourers was maintained before all the parliamentary committees which considered the matter, among them being the Committees on the Poor Laws in 1817 and 1818, the Committee on Emigration in 1826, the Committee on the State of the Poor in Ireland in 1830, and the Lords' Committee on the Poor Laws in 1831. In 1833 the restrictive effect of the law of settlement was noticed by the Factory Commissioners, the Poor Law Commissioners, and by the Committee on the State of Agriculture.

[1] Ricardo, *Political Economy and Taxation*, Chap. XXXI, 'On Machinery'.

It is evident, therefore, that there was a strong body of contemporary opinion which held that the settlement laws and regulations were mistaken in principle and pernicious (or at least vexatious) in practice.[1]

There was, however, another side to the question. Even in the eighteenth century, Sir Francis M. Eden, whose opinion on such a matter was as weighty as that of Adam Smith, considered that the evil effects of the settlement regulations had been greatly exaggerated. He did not defend the principle of the regulations, but thought that they were too often evaded or disregarded to be a serious hindrance to migration.[2] He agreed with Howlett that, as to servants in industry, 'they range from parish to parish, and from county to county, unthinking of and unrestrained by the laws of settlement'.[3] Half a century later almost identical language was being used; the industrial districts were 'drawing the labour from the different parishes, and drawing men from their parochial settlements, merely by an increase of wages . . . as if there were no settlement at all . . . increasing the wages has always got the men, and always will; parochial settlement will make no difference'.[4]

To decide where truth lies between these extremes is rendered more difficult by the extreme complexity of the settlement laws themselves. The determination of settlement in disputed cases was one of the most prominent questions in the legal history of the period, and many of the technical issues are quite beyond the comprehension of a layman. So intricate did the network of regulations and precedents become that a prominent lawyer with much experience in such cases advocated the total repeal of all settlement legislation and its removal 'from the region of Legislation into that of History, there to serve with other now abrogated absurdities . . . as memorable examples of the slow

[1] *Rept. P.L.*, 1817, pp. 24–8; *Rept. P.L.*, 1818, *passim*; *Rept. Emig.* 1826, q. 2357, p. 216; *Repts. S.P. Ireland*, 1830, qq. 6455–6665 (evidence of J. R. M'Culloch); *Repts. from Factory Commssnrs.*, I, 1833, pp. 62–3; *P.L.C. Rept.*, 1834, App. A, Pt. I, No. 7, p. 158.
[2] Eden, I, pp. 296–9.
[3] Howlett, *Examination of Mr. Pitt's Speech*, 1796, p. 14.
[4] *6th Rept. Set. P.R.*, 1847, pp. 204–5.

progress of reason and justice'.[1] Nevertheless, settlement laws survived into the twentieth century to puzzle the brains of magistrates and guardians.

The broad lines of the question, so far as it directly affected migration, may be stated fairly simply. The relief of the poor in England had, since the sixteenth century, been on a parochial basis: each parish was held responsible for the relief of its own poor. Hence there arose the difficult problem of deciding to which parish any particular pauper belonged. The problem might have been simple if no movement had occurred from one parish to another; but the very fact that one parish was richer than another would, in itself, tend to cause some movement of population from the poorer to the richer parish. In such a case, one of the two parishes concerned was bound to feel aggrieved when the migrant became destitute and applied for relief. It was obviously unjust that one parish should have to support poor persons coming from another; on the other hand, a parish would be unjustly treated if its poor, after spending the best years of their working life in another parish, should be forced to come home for poor relief in old age or infirmity.

The Settlement Law of 1662 had attempted to determine the question by enacting that new-comers into a parish could, within forty days of their arrival, be removed to their last parish of settlement if they were thought *likely* to become chargeable. This statute was clearly unjust to the migrant, and many attempts were made to modify its restrictive action, but without much success. In the law of 1662 the seasonal movement of harvesters had been specially allowed, if they had a certificate of settlement in their original parish. This was extended by an important law of 1697, which facilitated the migration of poor persons, provided that their parish of settlement gave them a certificate accepting responsibility for their poor relief in case of necessity. If such 'certificated' migrants became destitute, their parish of settlement was responsible not only for their maintenance, but also for their removal. The parishes of settlement could not be

---

[1] Robert Pashley, Q.C., *Pauperism and Poor Laws*, 1852; see also his expert evidence in *Rept. P.R.*, 1854, especially App. 17.

compelled to grant such certificates, and there was no strong inducement for them to do so in the majority of cases. Some parishes never gave certificates; others allowed migrants to go only a limited distance from their settlement.[1] The power to refuse certificates became, therefore, a serious check upon the circulation of labour, and the law failed in its purpose. This was the position of the settlement question in Adam Smith's day, and goes far to justify his assertion that in England 'it is often more difficult for a poor man to pass the artificial boundary of a parish than an arm of the sea or a ridge of high mountains'.

In 1795, however, an important relaxation of the law of settlement was effected by a statute forbidding the removal of poor persons to their place of settlement until they actually became chargeable. This apparently philanthropic Act, together with the misguided Speenhamland policy initiated in the same year, may have been occasioned by the increased burden of pauperism due to the war against France. But when every allowance has been made for the effect of war and economic change in stimulating alterations in the poor-law system, the Poor Removal Act of 1795 still seems curiously mild, in the contemporary circumstances. The country was at war with a revolutionary Government, and there was some reason to fear the spread of revolutionary ideas at home. Trade clubs were being prohibited, and corresponding societies suppressed. Yet the Government relaxed the settlement laws for the express purpose of increasing freedom of movement! The reaction of war upon migration policy was certainly quite different in France and Germany.

In France the old restrictions on movement were strengthened under the Napoleonic régime by the law of 1803, by which employers were forbidden to take on any journeyman unless he was furnished with a certificate from his former employer showing that he had fulfilled all previous engagements. In the same way employers were forbidden to take as workman any apprentice who was not furnished with a quittance from his master, to show that he had finished his apprenticeship. The workman's leaving certificate was similar to a passport, but was not valid

[1] Hammond, *The Village Labourer*, pp. 116-19.

as such. Any journeyman working without either certificate or passport was to be treated as a vagrant, and was liable to six months' imprisonment. This regimentation was at best vexatious, and at worst might be little removed from serfdom. Its repressive effect in the Napoleonic period was increased by its association with the police, who had inherited the tradition of the pre-revolutionary régime.[1]

In Prussia a similar system had been established in 1731, by which the migrating workman had to possess an 'information card', which acted as a sort of good-conduct certificate. This system was confirmed by the Prussian law of 1794, which also ordered workers in large workshops to carry a leaving certificate. The passport law of 1807 held that such certificates were not valid as passports, and manual workers had to obtain a separate pass, even for journeys within the country. In the next year (1808) Bavaria introduced a system for the registration of migration, the various journeyings of the workman being all recorded in his 'Wanderbuch'.[2] The English system of settlement and poor removal, as amended in 1795, can hardly have tended to restrict migration so severely as did these contemporary regulations of the continental countries.

Apart from its primary effect in increasing freedom of migration, the English Poor Removal Act of 1795 had the important feature of reversing the responsibility for the expenses of removal. Whereas under the certificate system the parish settlement was responsible for the expense incurred in bringing the pauper home, after 1795 the responsibility for such expenses lay upon the parish ordering the removal. Under the former system it was to the interest of the parish settlement that its poor people (if they did migrate) should not go far from home—since, the further they went, the more expensive it was to bring them home. After 1795, however, parishes were anxious, not lest their poor persons should wander too far, but lest they should not migrate far enough. The further a man migrated the less chance

---

[1] Levasseur, I, pp. 377–87, 548, 558; II, pp. 67, 504–7.
[2] See W. Stieda, article 'Arbeitsbuch', in Conrad's *Handwörterbuch der Staatswissenschaften*, I, 1890, pp. 598–602.

there was of his being sent back under a poor removal order, and the less likelihood of his returning independently. It is thus possible to argue that during the early nineteenth century the power of poor removal discriminated against short-distance migration as compared with long-distance migration.

Whether this had any serious influence upon the character (as distinct from the volume) of migration may be questioned, since the expense of removal was presumably insignificant compared with the cost of maintenance. The contemporary records of Parliament and parliamentary committees resound, however, with complaints against the heavy expense of poor removal; and when, in 1800, William Baker introduced a Bill to suspend removal of the casual poor, one of his opponents argued that the Bill was unnecessary, as poor removal was so expensive that paupers would seldom be removed![1] However this may be, it seems clear that poor removal cannot have been responsible for the predominantly short-distance character of migration in the nineteenth century. It is, at the same time, evident that the system was not unduly restricting the *volume* of migration; the towns, not only in the manufacturing districts but throughout the country, were growing at an unprecedented rate by migration from the country.

The landowners and ratepayers of the southern agricultural counties complained that their surplus labourers refused to make a long and hazardous journey to the manufacturing districts in the north of England; this, they maintained, was due to the fear of poor removal, which made the labourers unwilling to leave a secure settlement for the prospect of high but uncertain wages in industry. The opposing points of view may be illustrated by the comments made concerning poor removal at the time of James Scarlett's abortive Bill for the amendment of the Poor Laws in 1821 and 1822. Scarlett's proposal for dealing with the settlement question was to prohibit poor removal, which would have been equivalent to abolishing the law of settlement. The effect of the settlement laws, he said, was to restrict the free circulation of labour.

[1] Cobbett, *Parliamentary History*, XXXV, pp. 198-9.

One of the most striking effects upon the poor themselves was that they were driven from where they could find labour and accumulated where no labour was to be found. . . . From the returns it appeared that Sussex, with an inferior population and a taxable income of £915,348, paid £275,000 of poor-rates; while Lancashire, with a superior population and a taxable income of £3,087,777, paid £261,730. . . . In populous districts where there were large manufacturing towns the poor-rates were always lower than in thinly-inhabited agricultural districts. The cause of all this . . . was obviously the removal of the poor.[1]

On the other side, it was pointed out that if the towns were deprived of this power of self-defence they would become simply the dumping ground for all the pauperism of the agricultural counties. The landlords were making every possible effort to stimulate migration artificially; in particular, they were pulling down cottages wherever possible, and thereby aggravating an already serious housing problem.

The effect of the Bill would be to send every idler from the country parishes into the towns . . . under the present system every device was practised to throw paupers in the country parishes on the towns for maintenance.

J. B. Monck instanced the county of Berkshire, where the farmers kept only sufficient labourers on the land for the ordinary routine operations.

The farmers draw labourers for the harvest from the workhouses of Reading, Abingdon, and Newbury. For six weeks they are well fed by the farmers; get beer and large wages; but afterwards they are cast out, and for the rest of the year are to be maintained by the towns.[2]

Cobbett supported Scarlett's Bill because of its attack on poor removal from the large manufacturing towns.

Under the present system, when there was any cessation of employment in a manufacturing town the labourers were scattered all over England. From Manchester, for instance, he had seen loads sent to London by coach, and some even to the west of England. . . . The effect on that town was that in Manchester the rates were less than in any agricultural parish in England. . . . The poor, who had enriched the town of Manchester by their labour, were sent away . . . to burden agricultural parishes that had derived no benefit from them.[3]

---

[1] Hansard, N.S., VII, pp. 767–8.
[2] Ibid., p. 773.
[3] Cobbett, Political Register, May 14th, 1821; reprinted in Political Works, VI, p. 112.

The opposite point of view was stated equally clearly by Prentice, the Manchester historian:

> Mr. Scarlett . . . calculated on the support of the landowners who after having been released of the burden of supporting a portion of their poor, who had migrated to the manufacturing districts, might be supposed very willing to have a guarantee against their return to their native parishes.[1]

Cobbett's account of wholesale removals from Manchester was probably correct. The period 1819–21 saw much distress and social disturbance in the manufacturing towns; and the 1821 census gives several instances of recent increases of population in country parishes ascribed to the return of paupers from the towns, either voluntarily or under removal orders. Poor removal was not, however, the only method of providing for non-settled paupers at Manchester: many of the country parishes preferred to give temporary relief to their absent poor in the town[2] (in the hope that the revival of trade would once more make them independent) rather than have them sent home under removal orders.

A single instance may illustrate the custom. Wray, a remote little village in North Lancashire, was decreasing in population during the post-war period through 'dullness of trade'.[3] Some of its surplus labourers had migrated to Manchester, and had there fallen on evil times; but they were not sent back to their place of settlement. At the very time to which Cobbett was referring (1819–20) the township of Wray was giving relief through its own private agent (a Manchester shopkeeper) to several persons living in Manchester but 'settled' in Wray. One of the cases, that of Hannah Withers, was of some complexity. She was about sixty years old, and had lived in Manchester more than twenty-six years. Her husband, through whose settlement she claimed relief, was during his life a servant of Mr. Barlow, a drysalter of Manchester, but formerly of Hornby. The woman's husband had been dead nearly fifteen years; but she declared that his last whole year's (contracted) service was with John Hodgson, of Wray. Several other circumstances of

---

[1] Prentice, *Manchester, 1792–1832*, pp. 233–4.
[2] *Lords' Rept. P.L.*, 1818, p. 156.　　　[3] *1831 Census*, I, p. 294.

the case were doubtful, and might have made a long law-suit; but the overseer of Wray sent relief money to the woman without much demur.[1]

Even when there was no such private arrangement to obviate the necessity for poor removal, it is not clear that removal was the normal method of dealing with non-settled pauperism. It has been generally assumed that the receiving parishes were always anxious to pass back migrants as soon as they became paupers. In the case of the growing manufacturing towns, however, there was no strong reason why the town authorities should be anxious to check immigration by a harsh use of their power of poor removal. At most times the manufacturers were only too eager to get workmen, and welcomed a surplus of labour, both for its utility as an industrial reserve in times of trade expansion and for its effect in keeping wages down. Where the manufacturers were not in a predominant position the municipal authorities might inconvenience them by a strict enforcement of the settlement laws;[2] but in most of the large towns the manufacturers were the ruling party, and were willing to spend the public funds (to which others as well as themselves contributed) in order to keep a plentiful supply of labour in the parish.

There is some evidence that even in prolonged trade depressions the towns aimed at retaining labour by giving poor relief to non-settled persons. In 1841, for instance, Mr. William Tattersall, the relief officer for Manchester, attributed the great burden of pauperism in the town partly to the laxity of the local authorities concerning settlement. The influential manufacturers, he said, had encouraged the payment of liberal relief on the ground that they must have some surplus labour. Again, in 1854 it was remarked that the stipendiary magistrate of Manchester was very cautious in granting orders of poor removal. 'He takes a very great deal of trouble before he ever submits to pass or to sign these orders.'[3]

[1] Letters of Robert Howson, Overseer of the Poor for Wray, shown to me by Mr. W. G. Howson.
[2] *J.H.C.*, quoted in Hammond, *The Village Labourer*, p. 116, n. 1.
[3] *Rept. M. & B.U.*, 1841, pp. 50-2; *Rept. P.R.*, 1854, p. 20.

There can be no doubt that the settlement regulations and the practice of poor removal were extremely vexatious during the period. The very complexity of the law made it uncertain where the responsibility for maintenance would lie in many cases. It thus happened that the unfortunate pauper might be bandied about from one parish to another, until at length the question of settlement was finally decided. The notoriety of such cases may have had an indirect effect in *deterring* agricultural labourers in the southern counties from migrating. On the whole, however, it seems probable that the action of the Old Poor Law in restricting migration was not so much due to the effects of the settlement system as to the mistaken and lax administration of poor relief in the southern counties previous to the Poor Law Amendment Act of 1834.

Any parochial system of poor relief must have some effect in deterring poor persons from migrating, in so far as it protects them from absolute starvation. It was said that, whereas the English labourer was bound to his parish by the law of settlement, the Irish labourer was unhindered by such considerations, and so migrated much more freely; but the Irishman had this freedom simply because there was no Poor Law system in Ireland, and because the destitute there had either to migrate or to starve. So long as the English system of poor relief was to be maintained on a local basis the settlement system and the power of poor removal could not be abolished entirely; and so long as settlement and poor removal survived cases of hardship were bound to arise after any period of active migration.

The general effect of poor relief as a deterrent from migration is naturally greater when the administration of relief is more generous; and it is well known that the English poor-law administration was much more liberal in the early decades of the nineteenth century than had been intended by the legislation on which it was based. The giving of outdoor relief to able-bodied labourers, the encouragement of early marriages and large families, the giving of relief in money instead of in kind, all tended to pauperize the rural population and to restrict migration, quite apart from any question of settlement or poor removal.

H

The census returns for the period between 1811 and 1831 contain frequent references to the demoralization caused by lax administration of the Poor Laws; but complaints of this kind were confined mainly to the southern, and especially the southeastern counties. It was in those districts, and particularly in the counties of Norfolk, Suffolk, Huntingdon, Bedford, Buckingham, Surrey, Dorset, Wilts., and Devon that the practice of making up labourers' wages out of the poor rates was most prevalent; it was, moreover, from those same counties that the most persistent reports of surplus agricultural labour were received.[1]

The immobility of the southern agricultural labourer was not, however, entirely due to the action of the Old Poor Law. The difficulties of transport were, up to the middle of the nineteenth century, a much more serious check on migration. It was, for instance, much easier and cheaper to get to the northern manufacturing districts from Ireland than from the southern counties of England. In the 'twenties there was already a regular service of steamships between Ireland and England, making the voyage in fourteen hours on an average, at a charge of half-a-crown per head; in the recurring 'rate wars' between the different steamship companies the fare was often reduced to as little as a shilling. In 1827 the steam packets between Ireland and Liverpool were bringing many immigrants at fourpence or fivepence each.[2] The English labourer from the southern counties would have had to pay much more in making his way to the northern counties, whether he went by coach, canal boat, waggon, or on foot.

Ironically enough, the cheapest way of migrating from the south to the north of England was by taking advantage of the free travelling facilities offered by the vagrancy laws and the poor removal system! It was only necessary to wander off from one's parish in any direction until apprehended as a vagrant and ordered to be 'passed back'. The appropriate method was

---

[1] *Rept. L.W.*, 1824, printed in *Ann. Reg.*, 1824, App., pp. 49–50.
[2] J. B. Bryan, *A Practical View of Ireland*, 1831, p. 126; Smart, II, p. 435; Hansard, *N.S.*, XVI, p. 499.

then to swear to a settlement in (say) Cumberland, and to receive free conveyance with maintenance during the northward journey. It was quite easy to slip off the waggon at Manchester, or wherever prospects seemed promising; such things could be arranged, for the constables were only human. The constables, indeed, seem to have made a good profit out of the system. The constable of one Staffordshire parish near Birmingham received thirty shillings for the expense of passing each pauper to Manchester (presumably by coach); he found it possible, however, to contract with the Manchester waggoner to take them for five shillings each, pocketing the difference.[1]

The regular vagrants made good use of the opportunities for free conveyance afforded them by the vagrancy acts and bragged of being able to ride about at the public expense, while many Irish vagrants were said to make a living by being removed backwards and forwards. Many hundreds of Irish paupers declared that they were Scots when they wished to travel in that direction, and others exercised a nice discretion in swearing to settlements in the north or south of England according to the season of the year. Meanwhile the number of Irish poor in England was increasing very rapidly, and the burden of 'passing' lay heavily on such places as Bristol, Liverpool, and Cumberland.[2]

While the 'old hands' and the Irish thus found travelling cheap in England, the English agricultural labourers were apparently not acute enough to make much use of the facilities offered. This mental obtuseness of the English peasantry suggests that, even in the absence of special impediments, the ideal of a free circulation of labour could not have been realized. Peasants, especially uneducated peasants, are immobile except under the spur of extreme necessity. They do not migrate whenever it is to their economic interest, but only when they must. To Adam Smith's assumption that there is naturally a 'free circulation of labour' may be opposed the assumption of Malthus that 'a state of sloth, and not of restlessness and activity

---

[1] Hansard, *N.S.*, IV, pp. 1216–19.
[2] *Rept. on Vagrants*, 1821, *passim*; *Rept. D.S. Agric.*, 1821, p. 62.

seems evidently to be the natural state of man; and this latter
disposition could not have been generated but by the strong
goad of necessity'.[1]

Education, it is true, may add the spur of mental necessity
to the whip of physical want; but there was an almost total lack
of education among the English peasantry of the early nineteenth century. Such education as there was did not include
the dangerous subject of geography; even in the National and
British schools of the period (to say nothing of the workhouse
schools) there was such a prejudice against the teaching of
geography that in many cases the schoolmaster was forbidden
to hang any map on the walls of the schoolroom.[2] Where rural
life was broken into by such an event as the cutting of a canal
the young people were said to learn much from mixing with the
'navigators'; but in general the account of country life given by
a Dorset witness in 1847 is probably typical of agricultural
England up to that time: 'In Dorset we very much vegetate
where we are born, and live very close indeed.'[3] If this was true
in 1847, when the railway was becoming a considerable factor
in migration, it must have been still truer in the period before
1834, irrespective of the influence of the Poor Laws. Even after
1834, and despite the utmost efforts of the Poor Law Commissioners, the 'rooted antipathy to locomotion which nature
seems to have implanted in the breast of the Sussex labourers'[4]
proved a strong obstacle to movement, not only from Sussex,
but from most of the southern agricultural counties.

[1] Bk. I, Chap. VI.   [2] *40th Rept. P.L.A.A.*, 1838, p. 1.
[3] *6th Rept. Sel. P.R.*, 1847, pp. 157, 173.
[4] *P.L.C., 2nd Ann. Rept.*, App. B, No. 3, p. 211.

[*Editor's note:* Miss Dorothy Marshall has shown that the Settlement Act
of 1662 did not present any serious obstacle, particularly after 1697, to
the industrial mobility of artisans and labourers in the prime of life if they
were really determined to seek work in a parish not of their settlement
('The Old Poor Law, 1662–1795', *Economic History Review*, Nov. 1937,
pp. 38–47). This vindicates the judgment of Sir Francis M. Eden, as
against that of Adam Smith.]

CHAPTER VI

MIGRATION UNDER THE NEW POOR LAW
(1834–1837)

WHATEVER may have been the fundamental causes of the disease, there is abundant evidence that the cancer of pauperism had spread ominously over a great part of England during the generation following the French wars. Throughout the southern and eastern counties of England the hardy peasantry of bygone times seemed to have degenerated into a stagnant mass of demoralized paupers; nor did the 'labouring and bending of great minds in the Upper House, in order to find employment for the overplus labourers in the corn-growing districts',[1] offer any immediate remedy. In the autumn of 1830 riots, machine-breaking, and rick-burning had convulsed southern England from Kent to Wiltshire; so that, among the many problems confronting the Ministry which came into power at this time, the most urgent as well as the most difficult was the radical amendment of the Poor Laws and the finding of employment for the mutinous labourers in the agricultural counties.

It was to this end that the famous Royal Commission on the Administration and Practical Operation of the Poor Laws was appointed, early in 1832; the report of this Commission, and the Poor Law Amendment Act of 1834 which was founded upon it, aimed at making a clean sweep of the existing abuses, and remained the foundation of the English Poor Law system for the rest of the nineteenth century. The Commissioners recognized that the stagnation of labour in the agricultural counties was not to be traced to the machinery of the settlement laws so much as to the lax administration of outdoor relief to able-bodied persons, which was a legacy of wartime conditions. Many of the evils ascribed to the machinery of settlement and poor

---

[1] *Rept. Silk*, 1832, p. 826, referring to *Lords' Committee on Poor Laws*, 1831.

97

removal, they pointed out, were necessarily implied in the 'mere existence of a law of settlement, whatever that law may be', and could be removed only by its entire abolition; this, however, was impossible while poor relief remained on a local basis. In their specific recommendations on the settlement question the Commissioners therefore confined themselves to the abolition of such special qualifications as settlement by hiring, apprenticeship, and renting, leaving almost untouched the main questions concerning settlement by parentage, birth, and marriage. In this the Commissioners may fairly be said to have progressed backwards; since the types of settlement they recommended for abolition had originally been introduced to aid mobility.[1]

On the question of outdoor relief and the various forms of the allowance system in aid of wages their opinion was much more decided and their remedies more drastic. Their main specific recommendation on the subject was that with two unimportant exceptions 'all relief whatever to able-bodied persons or to their families, otherwise than in well-regulated workhouses . . . shall be declared unlawful and shall cease'. It was realized that to bring into full operation such a drastic reversal of existing practice would require time and caution; but the principle expressed was the ideal aimed at during the first ten years after the passing of the Poor Law Amendment Act, and was then embodied in a definite prohibitory order.[2]

If outdoor relief was to be abolished, what was to become of the surplus labourers who were unable to find sufficient work to maintain their families, and who had hitherto been dependent on the parish? In many counties this class was reported to be too large a proportion of the population to be accommodated in the new workhouses, however large. The Commissioners believed that a great part of this 'surplus' was imaginary, and would automatically vanish with the stoppage of outdoor relief in aid of wages. The workhouse test, it was considered, would 'dissipate at once nearly the whole of this false and unreal appearance of surplus labour'.

This, however, was a theoretical judgment, and it was thought

[1] Cf. Fay, p. 99.   [2] B.B.T., pp. 662, 664–5.

necessary to form some particular scheme for the absorption of the surplus of labour, if such was really proved to exist during the transition from the old to the new system. The official remedy for redundant population, then, as now, was emigration to the colonies. Many parishes in the southern counties were already promoting emigration from the local parish funds, as a means of relieving the poor rates. The Poor Law Commissioners were therefore not breaking new ground in recommending emigration as an outlet for surplus labour in 1834. The most active Commissioner, Nassau W. Senior, who was mainly responsible for the drafting of the Commission's report, had long been an ardent advocate of Government assistance to emigration. In 1830 he had maintained that emigration was a necessary prelude to any depauperization of the southern counties.

> The only immediate remedy for an actual excess in any one class of the population is the ancient and proved one, *coloniam deducere*. . . . Who, in the present state of these districts, will venture to carry into execution a real and effectual alteration of the poor laws? Remove by emigration the pauperism that now oppresses these districts, and such an alteration, though it may remain difficult, will cease to be impracticable.[1]

It was inevitable, therefore, that the Poor Law Commissioners should include emigration, 'which has been one of the most innocent palliatives of the evils of the present system', as a remedial measure for the disposal of surplus pauperized population. They recommended 'that the vestry of each parish be empowered to order the payment, out of the rates raised for the relief of the poor, of the expenses of the emigration of any persons having settlements within such parish, who may be willing to emigrate'. Sections in accordance with this recommendation were included in the Poor Law Amendment Act of 1834, and £1,457 was voted for the payment of seven emigration agents stationed at Liverpool, Bristol, Dublin, Belfast, Cork, Limerick, and Greenock. The Poor Law Commissioners appointed under the Amendment Act issued to the parishes a circular letter giving instructions facilitating emigration, but

---

[1] *Three Lectures on the Rate of Wages*, 1830, quoted Mackay, p. 32.

very few parishes took any action. In the first year only 320
persons were sent out under parochial arrangements, nearly
half the number coming from Sussex; of the remainder, all
except nine came from the southern counties.[1]

From emigration it was an easy mental transition to suggest a scheme of home migration from the agricultural to the
manufacturing districts. Cobbett, in 1826, had poked much fun
at the 'Scotch feelosofers', and especially 'Dr.' Black, for insist-
ing that the only remedy for distress in the farming districts
was the transfer of labourers to manufacturing industry;[2] nevertheless, in the distressed years which followed, the possibili-
ties of 'home colonization' were often discussed alongside the
schemes for assisting emigration overseas. One difficulty of the
preceding period was that manufactures, as well as agriculture,
were severely depressed; so that in some industrial districts it
was a question whether 'the new conditions of society' would
not best be suited 'by giving facility to the unemployed manufacturers to acquire settlements in rural districts, and to
make it more difficult for agriculturists to gain settlements in
towns'.[3]

For the encouragement of home migration the New Poor Law
was well timed, for in 1833 a revival of manufacturing prosperity had begun to show itself. By the summer of 1834, industry
in general, and the Lancashire cotton industry in particular,
was recovering from its long and severe depression. Wages were
rising, especially those of unskilled operatives; trades unionism
had assumed a formidable aspect, and there was undeniably a
real scarcity of labour in the manufacturing districts. Even in
1833 Messrs. Greg had found some difficulty in getting hands
for their spinning mills.

> At Bollington we have had considerable difficulty in procuring piecers;
> and at Bury I have made great exertions to procure water spinners, and I
> have only been enabled to do it to a limited extent. . . . I have sent to
> Bolton and Oldham and other places to procure them, and I have found

---

[1] *P.L.C., 1st Ann. Rept.*, pp. 23-4, and App. A, No. 8.
[2] *Rural Rides*, Sept. 4th, 1826. For John Black (1783-1855), see *D.N.B.*
[3] *P.L.C. Rept.*, 1834, App. A, Pt. I, No. 15, p. 498.

it impossible. . . . There was a great demand for all hands except mule spinners.[1]

At Stockport it was reckoned that a thousand families would be required from outside for the mills then building. The cotton trade of Lancashire and the woollen trades of the West Riding were at that time expanding more rapidly than any other industries; and a most unusual activity in building was noticeable throughout the textile districts. The employers' desire to tap new sources of labour was, no doubt, partly due to the curtailment of child labour in mills under the Factory Act of 1833; nevertheless, the demand for hands cannot be wholly ascribed to that cause. A very significant feature of the situation was that labour scarcity was apparently much keener in the country districts than in the towns. The trade depression after 1825 had almost ruined many old-established spinning mills of the country type. This had led manufacturers to combine spinning with power-weaving in the same establishment; and this, in turn, was causing a considerable extension of steam-power in the country mills and smaller centres. Altogether, Dr. J. P. Kay estimated in 1835 that about ninety thousand people would be required from outside the cotton area; and on the basis he adopted for his calculation this must be regarded as a conservative estimate. He estimated that in the years immediately following 1835 the steam-power employed in the north-western cotton area would be increased by 7,507 horse-power. As a matter of fact, between 1835 and 1838 the increase in steam-power in Lancashire and Cheshire equalled 17,413 horse-power, of which 15,377 horse-power was in the cotton manufacture alone.[2]

On June 9th, 1834, Edmund Ashworth wrote to his 'Respected Friend, E. Chadwick', the secretary of the Poor Law Commissioners, pointing out the exceptional demand for labour in the northern textile districts, and suggesting the encouragement of migration from the pauperized areas.[3] This letter was

[1] *Rept. Mfs.*, 1833, pp. 621, 632, 677.
[2] *P.L.C., 1st Ann. Rept.*, App. B, No. 11, p. 187; *S.J.*, I, pp. 315–16.
[3] *P.L.C., 1st Ann. Rept.*, App. C, No. 5, pp. 312–13.

printed in the London newspapers, and was brought to the notice of the Government. In the debate on the Poor Law Amendment Bill, a week later, Mr. Secretary Rice gave a very cautious promise to consider the matter.

> If there were to be an excess of labour in Sussex, for instance, while labour was in demand in Lancashire, it could be taken from the one county and provided for in the other. . . . There undoubtedly might be cases in which the application of this particular remedy would become a point well deserving the consideration of the legislature.[1]

Later in the summer further accounts of the labour scarcity in Lancashire were sent to the Commissioners: R. H. Greg reported that 'our machinery in one mill has been standing for twelve months for hands. In another mill we cannot start our new machinery for the same want.' Nothing was done, however, until the following December, when the question was reopened by a pathetic letter received by the Commissioners and published in *The Times*, from thirty-two paupers of Great Bledlow (Bucks.), asking for work or relief. This led the Commissioners to make an experiment in the encouragement of home migration. They acted as intermediaries between the Bledlow authorities and the mill-owners; as a first trial it was arranged to send a few families to the Gregs' mill near Wilmslow and the Ashworths' mills near Bolton.

The difficulty was to persuade the labourers to leave home. The Assistant Commissioner who went down for that purpose found the whole parish in a state of disorder—the men lying about on the roads or poaching in the woods. 'Robberies had taken place. The overseer's ploughs and agricultural instruments had been frequently damaged in the night, and a bullet had been fired into his house. . . . The parish was in the control of the able-bodied paupers.' Work had been provided at a place fifteen miles away, but the labourers would not move; they were willing to work inside, but not outside, their parish. 'At first there was not a single pauper that would consent. . . . After many visits, I at last succeeded in persuading one family to go. Their next neighbour then consented to accompany them. The

[1] Hansard, *3rd Series*, XXIV, p. 467.

parish provided conveyance by the canal for them and their families and furniture; and one of the five officers went with them.'[1] By March 1835, four or five families had been 'forwarded' to Messrs. Greg at Styal, near Wilmslow, and one family to Messrs. Ashworth, at Egerton, near Bolton;[2] both employers and migrants expressed themselves as highly satisfied with the results of the experiment, and the example was soon followed by several neighbouring villages where the problem of unemployment was equally severe.

In particular, the publicity given to the first experiment by the *Manchester Guardian* attracted the attention of the Rev. James Beard, rector of Cranfield (Bedfordshire), who knew the Manchester district personally.[3] Mr. Beard asked to be put in touch with persons requiring labourers, and in June 1835, several families were sent from his parish to Samuel Oldknow's old mill at Mellor, which was now being run by Oldknow's half-brother, John Clayton, on behalf of the Arkwright family. Beard himself came north in July to visit the migrants, and to make further arrangements with several leading cotton spinners of Stalybridge and Hyde.[4]

A little later in the summer of 1835 two parishes near Cranfield (Woburn and Ampthill) discussed the advisability of sending an agent to the manufacturing districts to report on the demand for labour and to make terms with any mill-owner willing to receive migrants. John Langston, of Cranfield, volunteered for the task, and was appointed joint agent for the two parishes, apparently in September 1835.[5] He reported in October, to the effect that there were good openings for children in such towns as Manchester and Stockport, though his inquiries in the smaller centres in Staffordshire, Derbyshire, and Cheshire were not particularly encouraging. Another deputation (from

---

[1] *P.L.C., 1st Ann. Rept.*, p. 22; App. B, No. 6, p. 150; Mackay, pp. 213–14.

[2] *Manchester Guardian*, March 21st, 1835.

[3] In 1833 we find him speaking at a political dinner in Stockport (*Manchester Guardian*, Feb. 2nd, 1833); and in 1835 he was apparently staying at Hope Hall, Manchester, as a guest.

[4] *P.L.C., 1st Ann. Rept.*, App. B, No. 11, pp. 197–9; App. C, No. 5, pp. 220–21.

[5] *37th–39th Repts. P.L.A.A.*, 1838, pp. 41–3.

an Essex union), which visited the cotton districts shortly afterwards, found a good demand for young persons in Stalybridge,
Hyde, Oldham, and Rochdale; offers of employment were also
forthcoming from the West Riding.[1]

By this time it was becoming clear that some centralized
organization and official supervision of the movement was necessary. Ugly rumours were spreading about the country. 'System-
mongers' (as the *Manchester Guardian* politely called them) were
placarding the agricultural districts with bills representing the
migrants as having been 'transported into slavery'[2]—an ingenious combination of Oastler's 'industrial slavery' cry with a
reference to the transportation of the Dorchester labourers in
1834? In particular, it was said that some of the Buckinghamshire migrants had found themselves 'turned adrift on the streets
of Manchester';[3] and even the friends of the movement were
constrained to admit that 'on one or two occasions families have
arrived in Manchester without any suitable arrangements having been made for their reception, and without funds to enable
them to reach their ultimate destination'.[4]

A pathetic case came to light on October 12th, 1835, when a
party of eighteen migrants (men, women, and children) appeared before the magistrates at the New Bailey, Manchester.
Their spokesman stated that they came from Towersey, in
Buckinghamshire. The farmers, he said, called a meeting to
know if any of the parishioners would go down to Manchester.
'Several of us said we would go; they told us they thought our
families would do well to go down . . . they said there would
be houses for us to go into when we got there, and everything
provided for our use.' The farmers engaged a man named
Clarke, who took the families to Glossop. 'We were brought
from our own county to Glossop in a boat, and from Glossop
Mr. Waterhouse sent us forward in a cart.' They were lodged
for three weeks in a warehouse, lying on straw; 'but yesterday

[1] *P.L.C., 2nd Ann. Rept.,* App. B, No. 20, pp. 428–30.
[2] *Manchester Guardian,* July 11th, 1835.
[3] *37th–39th Repts. P.L.A.A.,* 1838, p. 42.
[4] *Manchester Guardian,* July 18th, 1835.

he hired a cart, and sent us in a cart to Manchester; the carter put us down in the street, and left us'.[1]

The Poor Law Commissioners had already taken steps to organize and control the movement, to prevent the recurrence of such cases of hardship. The manufacturers who wrote the first letters asking for labour from the south had not seen the necessity for any elaborate official scheme of migration. They were, in general, not willing to take the responsibility for the maintenance of migrants, and at least one of them was definitely opposed to any system of contracts or official supervision. After all, the Irish immigrants into the cotton towns shifted for themselves, and made their own bargains with the employers; why should not the English families do the same?[2] All that the mill-owners wanted was assistance from the parishes to the migrants to cover travelling expenses. Even in 1834, however, R. H. Greg had suggested the opening of migration offices in several Lancashire towns. This hint had been followed up by John Langston, who, during his visit of inspection, had tried to secure permanent local agents. Dr. J. P. Kay thought the situation would be best met by the appointment of one part-time agent in Manchester, to whom manufacturers could apply when they came to town on 'Change days. In this he was supported by the opinion of Thomas Ashton, sen., of Hyde.[3]

Ultimately the Commissioners decided to appoint two full-time agents, one in Manchester for the Lancashire cotton trade, the other in Leeds for the woollen towns of the West Riding. In the summer of 1835 these two agents set up their offices, R. M. Muggeridge in Lever Street, Manchester, and Robert Baker in Leeds. It was not until October 1835, that the migrants under the official scheme actually began to arrive in the factory districts. The official method of procedure was somewhat lengthy. The agent first received offers of employment from the mill-owners; he inquired what wages the employers would give, usually (but not always) with reference to a three

---

[1] *Ann. Reg.*, 1835, Chronicle, pp. 144–5.
[2] *P.L.C., 1st Ann. Rept.*, App. C, No. 5, pp. 215–16; letter of Henry Ashworth.
[3] *Ibid.*, App. B, No. 11, pp. 188–9; App. C, No. 5, p. 221.

years' contract. Then he forwarded the information, through the Poor Law Commissioners, to the parishes. If the parish authorities accepted the terms, particulars were sent of the families ready for migration. Both parties being agreeable to the transfer, the three years' contract was signed, in which the wages of the migrants were expressly stated for each year of the contract. After all formalities had been completed the migrants were sent from the parishes by waggon or coach to London; there they were met by Mr. Marshall, an agent of the Commissioners, who conducted them to the Paddington basin of the Grand Junction Canal. At that point they were put aboard a Pickford's boat, and travelled without further change to Manchester. The voyage took four or five days, and the fare was fourteen shillings for adults, children being taken at half-price.[1]

Migration under this scheme went on from October 1835, to May 1837, when the deepening depression of trade made the efforts of the migration agents futile. The falling-off of trade was already apparent before the end of 1836, and the ensuing 'slump' proved to be as severe as any the country had experienced since the end of the French wars. Many firms in Lancashire went bankrupt. 'The entire trade of the district was all at once paralysed. . . . Large numbers of the native workpeople were temporarily thrown out of employment.' The official migration scheme dragged on for another five months, Muggeridge trying, without much success, to turn the stream of migrants into other occupations. The migration agents were finally relieved of their responsibilities, and the scheme came to a rather obscure end.[2]

By a lucky chance, an almost complete list of the migrants is available in printed form, from which the broad features of the movement can be easily studied. On February 21st, 1843, after an extraordinary spate of poor removals from the manufacturing towns of Lancashire, Cheshire, and Yorkshire, the House of Commons ordered a return to be made of the contracts for the hire of labourers made under the supervision of Muggeridge,

[1] *P.L.C., 2nd Ann. Rept.*, App. B, No. 20, p. 426.
[2] *P.L.C., 3rd Ann. Rept.*, App. B, No. 4, p. 90; cf. *4th Ann. Rept.*, pp. 35–6.

with the terms of such contracts, and the names and ages of the persons on whose behalf the contracts had been made.[1] It was then found that few of the documents relating to the transference of labourers had been preserved, except some registers produced by Muggeridge and some reports made by Baker. These, however, gave the substance of the information required.[2]

The return accounted for 4,684 Poor Law migrants between 1835 and 1837, of whom 1,233 had apparently been placed through the agency of Baker. As will be seen from the accompanying tables and map, about half of the migrants came from Suffolk. For the rest, the migrants were drawn mainly from the band of counties stretching south-west from Norfolk to Wilts. The counties to the south and east of London sent relatively few migrants, as emigration overseas was more favoured there. Middlesex sent only three migrants; the counties immediately north and south (Hertford and Surrey) sent none at all, because the attraction of London was strong enough there to prevent appreciable movement to the north-west. To the north the migration faded out in Northampton, Huntingdon, and Lincoln, and to the south-west in Dorset.

More than four-fifths of the migrants went to the textile districts of Lancashire, Cheshire, and the West Riding; the movement into Lancashire was naturally strongest. Derbyshire attracted an undue number of migrants, considering that on balance it was an area of dispersion rather than of absorption. Evidently the small country factories, which were still numerous in Derbyshire, took advantage readily of the cheap labour offered by the migration scheme. The midland metal towns absorbed very few of the Poor Law migrants; they were, indeed, too near the sources of the migration for any official intervention to be necessary.[3]

---

[1] *J.H.C.*, XCVIII, p. 39; Hansard, *3rd Series*, LXVI, p. 1026.
[2] See *A. & P.*, 1843, XVI, No. 254: 'Return relative to the Removal of Labourers from Agricultural Districts to Manufacturing Districts, 1835-7'; in some cases the origin or destination of the migrant is not easily traced to its proper county.
[3] See Tables I and II, and Map B in Appendix.

TABLE I

SOURCES OF POOR LAW MIGRATION, 1835–7: COUNTIES FROM WHICH
APPROXIMATELY 4,320 MIGRANTS WERE TAKEN

County	No.	County	No.
Bedford	298	Lincoln	9
Berks	93	Middlesex	3
Bucks	389	Norfolk	583
Cambs	154	Northants	8
Dorset	10	Oxford	117
Essex	134	Suffolk	2,128
Hants	48	Sussex	78
Hunts	10	Wilts	86
Kent	175		
		Total	4,323

TABLE II

DESTINATION OF POOR LAW MIGRATION, 1835–7: COUNTIES TO WHICH
APPROXIMATELY 4,615 MIGRANTS WERE TAKEN

County	No.	County	No.
Cheshire	860	Warwick	75
Derby	471	Westmorland	48
Lancs	1,785	Worcester	8
Somerset	18	Yorks W.R.	125,6
Stafford	94		
		Total	4,615

With this attempt to stimulate long-distance migration from
the south to the north of England by means of official organization it is instructive to compare the Poor Law emigration overseas which was going on at the same time. If the statistics of the
two movements are considered together, it will be seen that they
are really complementary parts of the same scheme for disposing
of surplus population. The total number of Poor Law migrants
to the northern manufacturing districts was slightly under 5,000;
in a roughly equivalent period the number of Poor Law emigrants overseas was about 6,400.[1] In each case the majority of
the persons affected came from the East Anglian counties of
Norfolk and Suffolk; and in general both movements were concerned with the removal of people from those south-eastern
counties whose natural outlet for movement was in the direction

[1] *P.L.C., 2nd Ann. Rept.*, App. D, No. 13, pp. 571–3; *3rd Ann. Rept.*, App.
C, No. 6; cf. Mackay, p. 228. See Table III.

of London. The attraction of London helps to explain a common characteristic of the two movements. No Poor Law migrants were taken from either Surrey or Hertford, no Poor Law emigrants were taken from Hertfordshire between 1835 and 1837, and only twelve were sent out from Surrey.

TABLE III

POOR LAW EMIGRATION JUNE 1835 TO JULY 1837.

County						1835–6	1836–7	Totals
Bedford	.	.	.	.	.	18	29	47
Bucks .	.	.	.	.	.	25	—	25
Berks .	.	.	.	.	.	30	15	45
Cambs	.	.	.	.	.	39	29	68
Hants .	.	.	.	.	.	182	—	182
Hunts .	.	.	.	.	.	27	13	40
Kent .	.	.	.	.	.	320	156	476
Lincoln	.	.	.	.	.	17	—	17
Middlesex	.	.	.	.	.	88	22	110
Northants	.	.	.	.	.	23	11	34
Norfolk	.	.	.	.	.	3,068	286	3,354
Oxford	.	.	.	.	.	11	46	57
Somerset	.	.	.	.	.	11	40	51
Sussex .	.	.	.	.	.	248	156	404
Suffolk.	.	.	.	.	.	787	296	1,083
Wilts .	.	.	.	.	.	347	25	372
Devon .	.	.	.	.	.	—	7	7
Essex .	.	.	.	.	.	—	13	13
Gloucester	.	.	.	.	.	—	6	6
Surrey	.	.	.	.	.	—	12	12
Totals		.	.	.		5,241	1,162	6,403

The selection of migrants and emigrants according to place of birth followed the line of least resistance; apart from the East Anglian counties, home migration was carried on most strongly from counties north of the Thames, whereas emigration was especially prominent in Kent, Sussex, and Wiltshire. Some slight lack of co-ordination between the two schemes is apparent from the transfer of a score or so of Suffolk people to Somerset, while twice that number of Somerset people were being assisted to emigrate overseas. The home migrants sent to Somerset were placed with Messrs. Sascon and Brothers, of Bruton, probably a silk-throwing firm. In spite of this accession,

I

Bruton declined in population between 1831 and 1841, the decrease being attributed to the stoppage of two silk factories.[1]

On the whole the Poor Law emigration scheme stood a better chance of success than the contemporary scheme for home migration. The Commissioners themselves preferred the home migration scheme, as being a less expensive method; the parishes, on the other hand, favoured emigration, because this made it more difficult for the paupers to return or to be brought back to their place of settlement. Accordingly, Poor Law emigration continued after the untimely death of the home migration scheme in 1837, though the numbers of emigrants dwindled markedly after the first two years of the scheme. The annual average of Poor Law emigration between 1835 and 1846 only amounted to 1,400 persons, while the total *recorded* emigration from the United Kingdom during the same period averaged 84,700 persons yearly;[2] so that Poor Law emigration was almost insignificant as a factor in the more general problem of movement overseas.

Nor was the parallel movement of home migration so important numerically as might be thought from the heated controversy which it aroused. As already seen, the total number of migrants sent to Lancashire was less than two thousand during the two years for which the scheme was in operation. Dr. J. P. Kay had estimated statistically that during the preceding decade (1821–1831) there had been an immigration into Lancashire of nearly seventeen thousand persons annually, taking one year with another; and there had been a progressive increase in the annual influx since the census records began.[3] On this estimate, the home migration scheme cannot have been more than a small disturbance on the broad stream of independent movement towards the manufacturing districts.

Despite its numerical insignificance, however, the Poor Law migration aroused heated controversy, even after it had long been abandoned. In that age social confidence had ebbed so low that any official interference with the flow of labour was

---

[1] *1851 Census*, Pt. I, Vol. I, Divn. V, pp. 72–3.
[2] *1851 Census*, Pt. I, Vol. I, App. to Rept., p. cxxxii, Table 47; cf. Hansard, *3rd Series*, XCIII, p. 104.
[3] P.L.C., *1st Ann. Rept.*, App. B, No. 11, pp. 183–5.

bitterly resented. Parish apprenticeship had been popularly imagined to be a kind of transportation in the eighteenth century; and the same name was given (with perhaps greater justification) to all the attempts at the official organization of 'poor' emigration during the early nineteenth century. It was, therefore, almost inevitable that Oastler and other opponents of the New Poor Law should regard the Commissioners' home migration scheme as 'transportation into slavery'. This judgment was echoed in the protest of one poor woman who, when offered assistance in migrating to the manufacturing districts, replied that she had done nothing wrong, and did not wish to be transported; she would rather stay in her own country.[1]

In general, Oastler and his friends regarded the Poor Law migration as part of a diabolical design framed by the 'three despots of Somerset House' and 'penny-a-line' Chadwick— 'that monster in human shape'—to drive the agricultural labourers into factory slavery; the centralized regulation of migration was akin to the centralized control of poor relief under the 1834 Act, and the centralized organization of factory inspection under the 1833 Act. Especially bitter were the attacks on Dr. J. P. Kay. As a private medical practitioner, Dr. Kay had ruthlessly exposed the wretchedness and squalor of the factory towns, but as Assistant Poor Law Commissioner he was foremost in urging the agricultural poor to migrate thither.[2]

Putting aside personal vituperation and rhetorical denunciations, however, there were undoubtedly serious grounds for distrusting the Commissioners' interference with the normal course of migration. The policy of home migration rested on the alleged coincidence of an acute labour scarcity in the manufacturing districts with a serious glut of labour in the agricultural districts. But the accounts of labour scarcity in Lancashire were (to some minds) hard to reconcile with the evidence of widespread unemployment among handworkers there.

In the borough of Bolton, to which some of the agricultural paupers had

---

[1] *24th Rept. P.L.A.A.*, 1838, p. 21.
[2] Baxter, *Book of Bastiles*, 1841, pp. 356, 366, 412; an attack on Dr. Kay was also made by W. B. Ferrand in the House of Commons.

already been sent, there were not less than twenty-four thousand individuals entirely dependent upon handloom weaving for their support,
and who were represented to be in a state of considerable distress. . . .
It was evident that the low rate of wages which prevails amongst thousands
of workmen whose service could be made available in the staple manufactures of Lancashire and Yorkshire afforded the strongest presumption
that there was a redundancy of labour in those counties. Under these
circumstances the transportation of agricultural labourers into the manufacturing districts would aggravate the privations of the handloom weavers
and engender very serious discontent, without improving the condition
of the agricultural labourers.[1]

As for the alleged glut of labour in the agricultural counties,
it was a favourite doctrine of the Poor Law Commissioners that
no such labour surplus actually existed, apart from the vicious
operation of the Old Poor Law; and the evidence collected by
their Assistant Commissioners during the period of the home
migration scheme seemed to corroborate this opinion. From
Kent, where 'those who had left their parishes were so small
in number as hardly to deserve mention', it was reported that
'the enormous mass of apparently surplus population that was
before the curse of this county has been almost entirely absorbed'. In Sussex, also, the 'facility of absorption of the pre-
tended surplusage by the demand for labour in the county
itself' was considered to be fully proved. Some of the most
progressive landlords maintained that 'instead of having too
many labourers, we now have not enough; . . . and what is more
extraordinary, we know few, if any, labourers have left the
neighbourhood, but are all employed in it'.[2] If this was so,
where was the necessity for any elaborate organization for the
encouragement of home migration?

The Poor Law Commissioners could, of course, reply that the
initiative had not been with them. They had, in the first instance, merely acted as intermediaries between manufacturers
asking for labourers and labourers asking for employment; and
it was only after the scandalous treatment of some of the earlier

[1] Hansard, *3rd Series*, XXVII, p. 358: Charles Hindley, supporting an
unsuccessful motion by John Fielden for the production of the correspondence relating to the early experiments in home migration.

[2] *P.L.C., 2nd Ann. Rept.*, App. B, No. 2, pp. 191, 196; No. 3, p. 210; and
No. 6, p. 275.

migrants had become notorious that the Commissioners had acceded to the many requests for a centralized control and supervision of the movement.

The motives of the manufacturing employers who received the migrants, and of the parish authorities who sent them, were more open to question. Some mill-owners went out of their way to be affable, at any rate to the earlier migrants. Letters of migrants give pictures of the great Thomas Ashton, of Hyde, talking amiably with his new workpeople; and Moses Cheetham, of Heywood, gave his protégés their first week's meals 'at his table and in his parlour'. At Mellor, 'Mr. Clayton gave all the families a load of coals each on their arrival, and charged them nothing at all for the first nine days' rent. He also offered to lend them money to enable them to buy furniture.'[1] There was, however, another side to the picture. The mill-owners' unusual affability suggests that the native workpeople were, if not openly hostile, at any rate suspicious of the movement. Moreover, the elaborate precautions taken to bring the migrants into the mills without ostentation show that the masters had reason to fear the activities of the trades unions, and especially the turbulence of the Irish.[2]

The whole movement is to be studied in relation to the outbreak of trades unionism which culminated in the Grand National Consolidated Trades Union of 1834. That part of the employers' anxiety for labourers arose from hostility to the labour unions seems clear enough from their early letters suggesting the migration. In July 1834 Edmund Ashworth, of Turton, wrote: 'I am most anxious that every facility be given to the removal of labourers from one county to another, according to the demand for labour; this would have a tendency to equalize wages, as well as prevent in some degree some of the turn-outs which have been of late so prevalent.' R. H. Greg, writing three months later, had more personal cause to oppose the union: 'My parlours are without doors, having been sent

[1] *P.L.C., 1st Ann. Rept.*, App. B, No. 11, p. 197; *2nd Ann. Rept.*, App. B, No. 20, pp. 420–21.
[2] *Ibid.*, pp. 411, 429–30.

some time since to be altered, and their progress having been stopped by a meeting of the joiners.'[1]

Of all the mill-owners Thomas Ashton, of Hyde, had most cause for wishing to break the power of the unions. On January 3rd, 1831, his son, Thomas Ashton the younger, had been shot dead in cold blood at the Woodley Mills. The crime was, perhaps, never proved to be the work of the unions; but it occurred during a strike of the local spinners. Moreover, the murderers, when brought to trial in 1834, declared that the crime was instigated, planned, and paid for by the Spinners' Union.[2] In the circumstances, it may easily be imagined that the employers were anxious to stop this violent tendency; from the employers' point of view it was, as Thomas Ashton bluntly put it, 'impossible for too many hands to be sent; they are wanted, and must be had, and if the agricultural districts will not send them, the Irish will'.[3]

The mill-owners emphasized the fact that the encouragement of migration from the south was not against the interests of the native mill-workers. 'In order to find employment for them, we have not found it needful to dismiss any one from our service. . . . The rates of wages of such hands have not been lowered. . . . Their neighbours or fellow-workpeople have not treated them as unwelcome or intrusive.'[4] It was said that the migration actually increased the employment available for some classes of the native workers, by supplying piecers and other inferior grades of workers, for whom there was an urgent need. The migrants especially desired were, of course, children and young persons between the ages of thirteen and eighteen.

Serious friction between the native workers and the newcomers did not at once arise, partly because in 1835-6 the cotton trade was exceptionally prosperous and there was work enough for all. Nevertheless, it is clear that the official stimulation of migration must have contained some elements of danger

[1] *P.L.C., 1st Ann Rept.*, App. C, No. 5, p. 213.
[2] *Ann. Reg.*, 1834, App., pp. 290–6; and *Manchester Guardian*, August 9th, 1834.
[3] *P.L.C., 1st Ann. Rept.*, App. C, No. 5, p. 221.
[4] *P.L.C., 1st Ann. Rept.*, App. C, No. 5, p. 219.

to the established standard of living in the manufacturing districts. In at least one case the arrival of the Poor Law migrants caused open conflict. This was in August 1836, at the mill of Messrs. C. Ainsworth and Company, Little Bolton. Eighty cardroom hands left work without notice through the introduction of several families from Suffolk at wages much below the current rates. Six or seven of the old hands had been discharged, therefore the rest determined not to instruct the new-comers, and 'turned out', causing 435 persons altogether to be thrown out of work.[1]

The movement inevitably tended to lower the wages of the native cotton workers. The wages of the new-comers were necessarily below the rates then current in the manufacturing districts; for the migrants were mostly unused to machinery, and required to be taught the trade before they were worth even the 'apprenticeship' wages for which the employers contracted. One witness estimated that the migrants' wages were never more than two-thirds of the wages earned by the other millworkers.[2] Moreover, the importation of child labour, if continued on any large scale, must have tended to increase the parasitic action of the manufacturers in using up labour quickly, and then rejecting it (through the poor removal system) in favour of a fresh supply of human raw material. This seems to have occurred to some extent in the years following the collapse of the home migration scheme. In 1835–7 seventeen southeastern counties had sent nearly five thousand persons to the north-western textile districts; in the wholesale poor removals of 1841–3 those seventeen counties received back only 328 persons from the manufacturing towns whose poor removals have been analysed, though nearly forty times that number of poor persons had been removed from the various towns.

By the local authorities in the agricultural counties migration

---

[1] *Bolton Chronicle*, August 13th, 1836, p. 3; the reference was kindly pointed out to me by Miss C. V. Bradley.

[2] *24th Rept. P.L.A.A.*, 1838, pp. 22, 24; *25th Rept., ibid.*, pp. 4, 6, 7; with the details of migrants' wages given in *A. & P.*, *loc. cit.*, compare lists of industrial wages round Manchester in 1832–3 in *P.L.C., 1st Ann. Rept.*, App. B, No. 11, pp. 202–4.

to the manufacturing districts was too often regarded merely
as an outlet for the disposal of their most troublesome paupers.
R. M. Muggeridge, the migration agent, complained of 'a disposition on the part of the boards to make a very improper
selection of families and individuals for migration';[1] and it was
declared that in many cases the scheme was used as a bogey to
scare off applicants for relief. How far this was true it is impossible to say; but Muggeridge himself claimed that the scheme
had been useful as a test for malingerers. A hostile critic put
a different emphasis on the matter by declaring that 'if all the
persons must have gone to the factories that they offered the
factory work to, they would have had to build a great many
more factories in Lancashire than there are now, many as there
are'.[2]

The worst features of Poor Law migration showed themselves
after the collapse of trade in 1837. Muggeridge, in writing his
final report in July 1837, claimed that the new migrants were
doing better than might have been expected. The majority of
them were still in work, although many of the native workpeople were unemployed. This, of course, was early in the depression. As the gloom deepened, the new-comers, unused to
mill-work and town life, seem to have fared worse than the
established workers. With the bad times came smallpox and
fever; the migrants got their full share of the diseases, and many
died. Some families returned home to claim the relief for which
they were ineligible in Lancashire; others were compulsorily
sent home under poor removal orders. In the West Riding
many were among those relieved from funds subscribed by the
public.[3]

It is a point in favour of the migration scheme that the
families engaged through the official agencies do not seem to
have suffered so keenly as some of the independent migrants.
The Poor Law migrants were, theoretically at least, protected

[1] *P.L.C., 2nd Ann. Rept.*, App. B, No. 20, pp. 409, 413.
[2] *25th Rept. P.L.A.A.*, 1838, p. 4.
[3] *P.L.C., 3rd Ann. Rpt.*, App. B, No. 4, p. 92; No. 7, pp. 96–7; *37–39th
Repts. P.L.A.A.*, 1838, pp. 44–5; *21st Rept., ibid.*, pp. 6–7; cf. Hansard, *3rd
Series*, LXVI, p. 1026.

from sudden unemployment by their three years' contracts. As the depression deepened, therefore, the factory masters were hard put to it to find a way out of their obligations. Some of the manufacturers began to complain of the bad character and improvident disposition of the southern migrants. Others adopted more direct methods in evading the contracts. Some of the parishes received complaints that the migrants had been put on short time, and were only being paid for the time worked, the original contract being used as a scale of wages for a full week's work.[1]

Thus obscurely and ignominiously ended what was, after all, a remarkable experiment in social economics. Its failure discouraged any further attempt at direct interference with the course of migration; and enemies of the New Poor Law found it an effective taunt, in depicting the distress of the agricultural labouring classes, to inquire: 'Do you intend to have another migration scheme, by which you may transport them from Buckinghamshire to Lancashire?'[2]

[1] *1st Rept. P.L.A.A.*, 1837, p. 56; *17th Rept.*, *ibid.*, 1838, p. 2; *6th Rept. Set. P.R.*, 1847, p. 2; *P.L.C.*, *3rd Ann. Rept.*, App. B, No. 5, p. 95.
[2] Hansard, *3rd Series*, LVIII, p. 1534.

CHAPTER VII

'THE HUNGRY 'FORTIES'

IN the years following 1836 there could be no question of using
the manufacturing districts as an outlet for the surplus labour
of the southern agricultural counties; for industries in general,
and the northern textile industries in particular, were then ex-
periencing a trade depression of unusual severity and persistence. The first signs of the coming storm were already detected
during the summer of 1836, amidst the apparent prosperity of
manufactures and commerce. The prices of raw materials were
advancing ominously, and manufacturers found themselves unable to make anything like corresponding increases in the prices
of their finished products. Orders for English manufactured
goods were being countermanded, and a strong demand from
America for gold instead of goods was springing up.[1]

American conditions already exerted an important influence
upon the course of trade in England; and financial changes of
the greatest commercial significance were taking place in
America during the 'thirties. The overwhelming victory of
Andrew Jackson in the presidential election of 1832 had led to
the withdrawal of the charter of the United States Bank. This
opened the way for a great expansion of the credit currency
issued by the various State Banks in America. Many of the
States had borrowed extensively to meet expenditure on internal
improvements; and at the same time speculation in the purchase
of western lands was becoming feverish. To finance these operations the various State Banks found it necessary to expand their
credit currency; this in turn led to a general wave of speculative
enthusiasm, which was reflected in the exceptional prosperity
of English trade during the years 1833–6.

The speculative 'boom' in America culminated in the sum-

[1] *3rd Rept. on Agric. Distress*, 1836, pp. 342, 401.

mer of 1836. In July of that year the United States Government ordered its land agents to take payment only in specie, or in the notes of specie-paying banks; this checked land speculation and crippled the western banks. The shock to credit quickly spread, and before the end of 1836 several important business houses in England had collapsed under the strain. The alteration of the official ratio of gold to silver in America added to the difficulties of business in England by inducing a drain of gold to America. This led the Bank of England to restrict its issue of credit and to raise the bank rate. In 1837 the full force of the economic collapse was felt both in America and in England, and the next six years were a time of almost unrelieved commercial depression on both sides of the Atlantic. In May 1837, the New York banks suspended cash payments, and within two months two hundred and fifty bankruptcies took place; the value of American real estate was said to have depreciated by more than forty million dollars in half a year. The American banknote circulation was rapidly contracted from 149,000,000 dollars in 1837 to 58,000,000 dollars in 1843, and the sales of public lands diminished steadily from twenty million acres in 1836 to one million acres in 1841.

In Great Britain, meanwhile, grievous reports of distress were being received in 1837 from all the manufacturing districts. At Paisley fourteen thousand men, generally employed in the weaving of fancy goods, had been unemployed for the whole of the summer, and the relief funds were exhausted. In the lace and hosiery districts of Nottinghamshire and Leicestershire, business failures were alarmingly frequent, and many thousands of workers were in desperate distress. Riots were taking place against the harshness of the New Poor Law, the operation of which was now for the first time being actively felt in the manufacturing districts. The effects of distressed trade were especially severe in the Lancashire cotton district, the fortunes of which were already closely bound up with the trade conditions of the United States. At Manchester, during the summer of 1837, fifty thousand workers were said to be out of employment, and most of the large establishments were working only half-time. At

Wigan there were four thousand weavers entirely out of work; and the same situation was found elsewhere throughout the county. The entire trade of the district was brought to a standstill, and well-informed observers feared that unless trade improved rapidly half a million workers, at least, would be idle in the manufacturing districts, in the very worst time of the year.[1]

There had, of course, been trade depressions in almost regular sequence during the previous generation; but the most terrible feature of the depression beginning in 1836–7 was its long continuance. The troublous times of the later 'thirties were succeeded by years of still severer distress in the early 'forties. In 1841–2 trade was reported to be going from bad to worse in all the manufacturing districts, and especially in the Lancashire cotton area. At Stockport it was reported in 1841 that between six and seven thousand 'hands' had been displaced from employment; and in 1843, when trade was believed to be recovering, horse-power adequate for the employment of over five thousand operatives was still standing idle. In that neighbourhood the wages for cotton-spinning had been reduced from 2s. 11d. per thousand hanks in 1839 to 2s. 6d. in 1841, and 2s. 1d. in 1842, for precisely the same work; and this 30 per cent. reduction was said to be 'about the general rate for spinning'.[2] In the Manchester area the number of bankruptcies was still abnormal in 1842, and many factories were being closed down; some of the mills had been closed ever since 1836–7, and mill fires seem to have been curiously frequent.[3]

A trade depression of such persistence inevitably caused important displacements of the manufacturing population, and checked for a time the current of townward migration. The 1841 census returns reveal a thinning of the population in many of the manufacturing townships through the stoppage of factories and the removal of factory workers in search of employment; while some other industrial towns were only saved

[1] *Ann. Reg.*, 1837, pp. 27, 55–6, 126–7; cf. Muggeridge, in *P.L.C., 3rd Ann. Rept.*, App. B, No. 4, p. 90.
[2] *Rept. M. & B.U.*, 1841, p. 6; S. C. Johnson, p. 58; Wood, p. 67.
[3] *F.I. Repts.*, Dec. 1842, in *Repts. from Commssnrs.*, 1843, XVI, No. 429, pp. 25–7.

from a decrease of population through the employment afforded by railway construction. Cobden asserted that in Stockport one house out of every five was empty through the dispersal of the unemployed industrial workers.[1] At Oldham, it was reported, no less than 1,800 houses were standing empty, and in many cases several families were living together in the same house; a similar report concerning the elasticity of demand for house accommodation was received also from the neighbouring townships of Rochdale and Saddleworth, as well as from Sheffield.[2]

At a time when all the manufacturing areas were suffering simultaneously from extreme depression, wandering in search of employment was a desperate and demoralizing ordeal. Many hitherto respectable workers were reduced to begging from door to door for bread; others, more ingenious, picked up a precarious living in all sorts of curious ways. 'Some have acted as porters and carriers; some have begun to sell hardwares; some have hawked salt for sale; some sand; some have gone about the country with vegetables . . . some go about hawking the various cheap publications of London.' Other textile workers, hitherto unused to heavy manual labour, became accustomed to spade work, and found employment 'working on the road, or quarrying in the stone quarry, or assisting builders'. Detailed analysis of the reabsorption of one thousand labourers, displaced through the closing of a cotton-spinning mill near Bolton, showed that dispersion had taken place over the area of a circle forty miles in diameter.[3]

Such readjustments of labour within and around the same industrial area may suffice to tide over minor fluctuations of trade, but were quite inadequate in so prolonged a depression. Luckily, the period of the depression was marked by great activity in the construction of new railways, which provided a

[1] See also T. E. Ashworth, *An Account of the Todmorden Poor Law Riots . . . and the Plug Plot*, privately published, Todmorden, 1901, p. 19, for the distress in Stockport.
[2] Thorold Rogers, *Cobden and Political Opinion*, 1873, p. 20; *1st Rept. Children's Employment Commission*, 1842, App., Pt. II, p. 839; *1841 Census*, pp. 147, 382, 395.
[3] *Rept. on Truck*, 1842, pp. 98–9; *Rept. M. & B.U.*, 1841, pp. 6, 7, 23.

welcome outlet for much unemployed labour in both industrial and agricultural districts. In 1836, before the effects of the depression had shown themselves, Muggeridge (the migration agent) anticipated that railway construction would absorb all the surplus able-bodied labour of the country. He had in mind the Leeds and Manchester Railway, which (he said) 'passes through a line of country where at the present moment there is not an able-bodied man out of employ who is willing to work'. Apart from this, there was, in the north of England, a demand for labour on the North Midland, Midland Counties, Selby and Hull lines. In the south of England the Commissioners had already encouraged labourers to find work on the line of the London and Birmingham Railway (requiring nearly eight thousand hands), and Muggeridge recommended that similar encouragement should be given with respect to the Great Western line to Bristol, which was then under construction.[1]

Some labourers were actually sent to railway work under the Poor Law migration scheme, and such work seems to have been better liked than factory work, since it yielded higher wages and did not entail such a long migration. The Birmingham line drew labourers from most of the counties along its length, its effect being apparently strongest in Hertford. The Great Western caused temporary increases of population in Berkshire and Wiltshire. In Kent, the South Eastern Railway was finding employment for local labourers; in Sussex many were working on the Southampton line or the London and Brighton. In Essex, the Eastern Counties Railway was causing local increases of population.[2]

The activity of railway construction in the later 'thirties helped to mitigate the distress of industrial depression on the cotton districts round Manchester. In Cheshire, labourers were employed on the Manchester and Birmingham line, the Chester and Crewe line, the Manchester and Sheffield Railway, with

---

[1] *P.L.C., 2nd Ann. Rept.*, App. B, No. 20, pp. 417–18, 432.
[2] *P.L.C., 2nd Ann. Rept.*, App. B, No. 2, p. 201; No. 3, p. 222; No. 4, p. 242; No. 6, p. 275; No. 15, pp. 385, 387; *3rd Ann. Rept.*, App. B, No. 3, p. 95; *2nd Rept. on Agric. Distress*, 1836, qq. 8194–7, 8511, etc.; *Lords' Rept. on Agric. Distress*, 1837, qq. 507–10; *1841 Census*, pp. 9, 134 ff., 89–92, etc.

its branch line to Glossop. The Manchester and Sheffield line also helped to employ the distressed cotton workers of Ashton-under-Lyne and Openshaw. In the centre of Lancashire the situation was being relieved by the construction of the Bolton and Preston line. Fleetwood, also, had grown in five years from an uninhabited rabbitwarren to a town and seaport, through the formation of a railway to Preston. Altogether, it was estimated that railway construction provided employment for about fifty thousand men during the great depression.[1]

Another promising outlet for unemployed labour was by emigration; all the principal trades fed the movement overseas. Many iron-founders, engineers, millwrights, and machine-makers left the country, some for the Continent, others for America; some of the bricksetters, also, were emigrating to America, while others were going to Australia.[2] This emigration of artificers in the engineering and building trades was particularly helpful to those foreign countries which were becoming serious industrial rivals of England. It was said that foreign manufacturers were draining the great English manufacturing firms of their best mechanics. From Germany it was reported in 1840 that the factories were rapidly increasing by the importation of British machinery, and by the influx of British engineers and machine-makers; cotton-spinning was being carried on 'as well in Austria proper as in Austrian Italy, worked principally by machinery imported from England . . . and in many places by English workmen, who are much encouraged'.[3]

Nevertheless, movement overseas did not appeal to industrial workers so strongly as to agricultural labourers. Factory industry abroad was still in too rudimentary a state to absorb many immigrants accustomed to the standard of living of the English skilled artisan, low as that was according to modern ideas. In 1842 'many skilled factory operatives, who had emigrated from this country in the vain hope of finding lucrative

---

[1] *Ibid.*, pp. 28-31, 51, 140-6; *Census of Ireland*, 1841, Rpt., p. x.
[2] Henry Ashworth, 'Statistics of the present depression of trade at Bolton', in *S.J.*, V, pp. 75-6.
[3] *Ann. Reg.*, 1839, p. (34); *Repts. Hd. Lm. Wvrs., Foreign Countries*, 1840, pp. 509-10, 514.

employment in factories abroad', were returning home disappointed; and an emigration office which was opened at Stockport in 1843 sold only ten passages for Canada in the first season, and forty-seven for Australia.[1] The weakness of industrial emigration, as compared with emigration from the agricultural counties, may be demonstrated from statistics collected in 1841. Industrial emigration was at that time, probably stronger than at any previous period of the century, owing to the trade depression. When the 1841 census was taken, the parishes were instructed to state the numbers who had emigrated in the previous six months (January to June). The comparative results may be briefly stated for four representative counties as follows:

County	Total Population	Emigrants, Jan. to June 1841	Proportion per 1,000
Lancashire . . .	1,667,054	1,362	0·8
Yorkshire (W. Riding). .	1,163,580	944	0·8
Cornwall	342,159	795	2·3
Sussex	300,075	758	2·5

It is therefore evident that while more people were, at that time, emigrating from the manufacturing districts than at any previous time, yet the proportion of industrial emigrants was even then much smaller than the proportion of agricultural emigrants, when compared with the total populations of the respective counties.

Voluntary dispersion from the manufacturing districts being insufficient to prevent social distress and unrest, the local authorities in many instances fell back on the drastic method of poor removal for the purpose of reducing the pressure of pauperism upon the local rates. The blackest years of the depression were marked by an extraordinary number of poor removals from the north-western textile districts. In the three years from 1841 to 1843 no fewer than 15,365 persons were removed from various manufacturing towns in Lancashire, Cheshire, and Yorkshire to their places of settlement. A return

[1] *F.I. Repts.*, loc. cit., pp. 29–30.

ordered by the House of Commons in 1846[1] gives full information concerning the removals, the number of families and persons removed, their occupations prior to removal, the length of their residence in the manufacturing districts, and the parishes to which they were removed. In many cases the information given is vague or ambiguous; but even an approximate analysis produces interesting results.[2] Out of 12,628 cases of poor removal from nineteen towns in Lancashire, Cheshire, and the West Riding, it has been possible to trace the destination of 12,359 persons, and so to determine the main features of the movement. In general, the analysis tends to confirm conclusions already reached concerning the characteristics of townward migration during the preceding period. The majority of the poor removals were to places in the same three counties of Lancashire, Cheshire, and Yorkshire, or in the neighbouring counties of Staffordshire and Derbyshire. Beyond this area of short-distance movement, the places of settlement to which poor persons were removed lay fairly uniformly round the centres of dispersion; the only important stream of long-distance movement was to Ireland.

By 1843 trade was showing some signs of recovery from its long stagnation; in Lancashire, cotton factories which had been stopped for years were being started again, and new mills were being built.[3] This promise of 1843 was fulfilled during the next two years. By the summer of 1845 the trade revival was complete, and industrial activity was even becoming feverish; while a succession of good harvests helped to mitigate social distress and prevent the necessity for a drastic use of the powers of poor removal. But even amid the apparent prosperity of 1845, Peel detected signs of renewed trouble. 'I should shudder at the recurrence of such a winter and spring as those of 1841–2,' he wrote, at the end of August.[4] A damp summer was then developing

[1] *A. & P.*, 1846, XII, No. 209.
[2] See Tables IV and V on p. 127.
[3] Léon Faucher, *Manchester in 1844*, pp. 141–3; *F.I. Repts.*, June 1843, in *Repts. from Commssnrs.*, 1843, XVI, No. 503, p. 13.
[4] C. S. Parker, *Sir Robert Peel*, 1899, III, p. 194, quoted J. F. Rees, *Fiscal and Financial History*, 1921, p. 102.

into a soaking autumn and while the corn was rotting in the ear news came from Ireland that a blight had fallen on the potatoes. The failure of the Irish potato crop led to a famine the horrors of which were unprecedented even in that most distressful country.

The direct reaction of this terrible Irish famine upon English social conditions, through the locust-like swarm of destitute and disease-stricken peasants which descended on this country, may best be studied along with the wider question of Irish migration to England. Here must be noticed its indirect effect upon the settlement question in England. The Irish famine made inevitable the repeal of the corn laws; and the repeal of the corn laws, in turn, provided another incentive for relaxing the settlement regulations, so far as these were considered to impede the circulation of labour. For some years previously the questions of poor-law settlement and corn-law repeal had been closely connected. The manufacturing interests, when accused of adopting an inhuman policy of poor removal, could reply that their policy was made necessary by the effect of the corn laws in producing distress and pauperism throughout the manufacturing districts. Repeal of the corn laws, therefore, opened the way for a reform of the settlement regulations. Sir Robert Peel, in introducing his Corn Law Bill, promised that the Government would, in this way, partially compensate the landlords for the loss of the corn monopoly. 'We propose not only to relieve the land, but to do an act of justice to the labouring man.'[1]

This was attempted by the Poor Removal (Amendment) Act of 1846 (9 and 10 Vict., c. 66), which made non-removable all persons who had been resident in a parish for five years without receiving relief from the local authorities. In practice this Act worked very unjustly against the town parishes. As already seen, the necessity for poor removal had quite commonly been avoided by the payment of non-resident relief by parishes to their 'settled' poor living elsewhere. The Act had attempted to secure that such 'assisted' residence should not be used to transfer the liability of settlement; but, through error or oversight, it was

[1] Mackay, pp. 313, 319, 341-2.

TABLE IV

SUMMARY OF POOR REMOVALS FROM NINETEEN TOWNS IN LANCASHIRE,
CHESHIRE, AND YORKSHIRE, 1841–3

Towns	No. Removed	Towns	No. Removed
Congleton	109	Preston	791
Macclesfield	197	Wigan	128
Ashton-u.-Lyne	807	Bradford (township)	764
Bolton	561	Halifax	46
Burnley	184	Rotherham	47
Chorley	150	Sheffield	227
Clitheroe	23	Stockport	1,997
Lancaster	31	Huddersfield (Union)	272
Manchester–Salford*	4,426	Leeds (township)	1,440
Oldham	428		
		Total	12,628

* 1841 Return for Manchester–Salford incomplete.

TABLE V

APPROXIMATE DISPERSION, ACCORDING TO COUNTIES, OF PERSONS
REMOVED FROM NINETEEN TOWNS IN LANCASHIRE,
CHESHIRE, AND YORKSHIRE, 1841–3

Counties	No. Received	Counties	No. Received
Bedford	6	Stafford	361
Berks	1	Suffolk	51
Bucks	24	Surrey	40
Cambs	1	Warwick	63
Cheshire	991	Westmorland	102
Cumberland	163	Wilts	28
Derby	461	Worcester	41
Devon	15	Yorkshire {East	143
Dorset	22	Yorkshire {North	223
Durham	32	Yorkshire, W. Riding	2,238
Gloucester	22	Anglesey	12
Hants	8	Caernarvon	27
Hereford	3	Carmarthen	2
Herts	2	Cardigan	2
Kent	17	Denbigh	99
Lancashire	3,686	Flint	171
Leicester	84	Glamorgan	6
Lincoln	36	Merioneth	9
Middlesex	74	Montgomery	22
Norfolk	37	Ireland	2,647
Northants	18	Isle of Man	3
Northumberland	13	Scotland	151
Notts	93	Not Placed	269
Oxford	5		
Salop	97		
Somerset	7	Total	12,628

not made clear whether this provision was to be retrospective or not. The law officers advised the Poor Law Board that the provision was not retrospective; the courts held the contrary view. The bearing of the new law being thus doubtful, many parishes which had been paying non-resident relief stopped their allowances; the effect of this was a sudden increase in the burden of pauperism in many towns. Moreover, many poor persons in the towns, who had previously been deterred from applying for relief by the fear of removal, now became chargeable. The Act also stimulated the efforts of country landlords to clear their estates of poor persons by such devices as the destruction or non-repair of cottages. Hitherto the towns had been able to counter such forced clearances by using their power of poor removal; henceforth this weapon was much weaker.

In the great manufacturing centres of the north and west the increased burden of pauperism after 1846 was, no doubt, chiefly a consequence of the Irish potato famine. Such towns as Norwich, however, were off the main track of the Irish influx; even in 1851 Norwich contained only 316 natives of Ireland.[1] Yet the burden of pauperism in Norwich during the years following the Act of 1846 amounted to nearly one-sixth of the total population. This was, of course, largely due to the general decline of manufactures in the city; but it seems clear that the local burden of pauperism had been greatly increased by the influx of poor persons from the surrounding agricultural parishes. This local influx was due mainly to the 'clearing' system adopted by large landowners in the neighbourhood.[2] The demolition of cottages as a device for clearing poor persons off the land was, of course, no new thing. In the years following 1846, however, local decreases of population from this cause became common in almost all the counties of southern and eastern England, from Cornwall in the west to Norfolk in the east. The 1851 census gives instances from at least twenty-three English counties. It is probable, nevertheless, that the resultant shifting

---

[1] *1851 Census*, Pt. II, Vol. I, Divn. IV, p. 321.
[2] *Repts. Set. P.R.*, 1850, pp. 25–7.

of population was of mainly local importance; for in most unions 'open' and 'close' parishes were fairly evenly balanced. This forcible shifting of labourers to and fro, from town to country and from country to town, attracted much attention at the time, and roused much public indignation; the economic and social effects of the great depression of trade, however, struck much deeper than this. The unrest and distress of the period inevitably quickened the process of economic transition, and precipitated many changes in industrial organization. Many old-established manufacturing centres which had, in the earlier 'thirties, still hoped for a revival of prosperity, now found themselves unable to battle any longer against the stronger forces of factory industry and power-driven machinery. It is, perhaps, not too much to say that the 'hungry 'forties' marked the end of a distinct epoch in the transition to modern industrial conditions.

Up to the 'thirties, the localization of the cotton industry was still far from complete. During the 'forties, however, local decreases of population, through the abandonment of cotton mills, were taking place, in such widely-spread counties as Stafford, Nottingham, Derby, Cheshire, Yorkshire, Cumberland, Kirkcudbright, Renfrew, Dumbarton, Stirling, and Fife; henceforth, Lancashire was the undisputed centre of the English cotton industry.[1] The great depression also played a decisive part in the battle between the West Riding and the older clothing districts of East Anglia and the West Country. As already shown, the crisis of 1836–7 may be said to have marked the end of the industrial greatness of Norwich.[2] Similarly, almost all the clothing towns of the West Country declined in population during the 'forties, and in most cases this was specifically stated to be due to the decay and abandonment of the woollen manufacture.

It was at this time, moreover, that the power-loom finally

[1] A. J. Taylor, 'Concentration and specialization in the Lancashire cotton industry, 1825–1850', *Economic History Review*, I, Nos. 1 and 2, 1949, pp. 114–116.
[2] M. F. Lloyd Prichard, 'The decline of Norwich', *Economic History Review*, III, No. 3, 1951, pp. 371–7.

overcame the desperate resistance of the handloom weavers in the cotton and woollen trades, and became definitely recognized as of superior commercial efficiency. The position of the handloom weavers had, indeed, been growing more precarious ever since the beginning of the century; but until the 'thirties it remained doubtful to many practical manufacturers, even in the cotton trade, whether the productive advantages of the powerloom outweighed its commercial disadvantages.[1] The rates of wages for handloom weaving fell on the whole throughout the period, but revived at each breath of brisker trade. After 1836, however, the rate never again revived, even in 'boom' periods; it remained practically at a dead level until 1861, by which time the handloom weavers were quite inconsiderable as a factor in production.[2]

There is some evidence that the persistent distress of the handloom weavers after 1836 was accompanied by, and perhaps dependent on, a change in the racial composition of the class. After 1836 a great many English and Scottish handloom weavers gave up the trade in despair of earning a decent livelihood; but the number of handloom weavers did not immediately dwindle, because the places of the native weavers were taken by Irish weavers used to a lower standard of living. By 1840 it was estimated that in most centres a majority of the handloom weavers in distress were Irish. In Manchester there were said to be comparatively few English handloom weavers after 1835. The strength of the Irish weavers in Lancashire is shown by the manifestoes of the local weavers' committees in 1839. The Manchester, Bolton, and Wigan returns were signed by Irishmen; more than one-half of the families in the Salford return bore Irish names, and about one-third of the families in the Wigan return. Most of the cases of pauperism at Manchester, whether settled or casual, were Irish weavers, and seventy per cent. of the juvenile offenders were the children of Irish parents.

---

[1] Kennedy, 'The Rise and Progress of the Cotton Trade', in *Proceedings of the Manchester Literary and Philosophical Society*; quoted Chapman, *V.C.H. Lancs.*, II, p. 384.

[2] Wood, p. 112.

The same report as to juvenile crime was also made from Macclesfield. At Leeds two-thirds of the woollen stuff weavers were Irish.[1] The situation was much the same in the Scottish textile districts. The Irish weavers came in as the Scots were gradually withdrawing from the trade. Out of the 3,072 persons given work by the Glasgow Relief Committee in 1837 no fewer than 2,884 were weavers; and of these 1,103 were Irish weavers, nearly all married.[2]

When this change in racial character is appreciated, the appalling social distress in the manufacturing districts during the later 'thirties and earlier 'forties acquires a new significance. The Irish leadership and turbulent character of the Chartist movement no longer requires special explanation. The flood of Irish pauperism which swept over England during the great potato famine no longer appears as an isolated disaster, but is seen in its true character as the culminating wave of a rising tide of Irish immigration which had been steadily creeping further over England for many years previously. This persistent exodus from Ireland was by far the most significant feature of British migration during the nineteenth century, and merits very full investigation. The general characteristics of the movement are discussed in the next chapter.

[1] *Repts. Hd. Lm. Wvrs.: Gen. Rept.*, 1840, p. 49; *Lancs. Rept.*, 1839, pp. 579–580; *West Riding Rept.*, p. 572; *Rept. I.P.*, 1835, G, p. 66; *Rept. M. & B.U.*, 1841, pp. 34, 47–8; *Rpts. Hd. Lm. Wvrs.:* W. E. Hickson, 'Notes . . . made during a Tour through the Weaving Districts', P.P. no. 639, 1840, p. 55.

[2] *Rept. I.P.*, 1835, G, pp. 109, 149, etc.: C. R. Baird, 'Observations upon the Poorest Class of Operatives in Glasgow in 1837', *S.J.*, I, pp. 167–72.

CHAPTER VIII

THE IRISH INFLUX (1)

CELTIC IMMIGRATION IN THE EIGHTEENTH CENTURY

AMONG the various currents of migration in Great Britain during the earlier nineteenth century by far the most striking was the influx from Ireland. This in its turn was part of a general Celtic movement which caused also a considerable exodus from Scotland and Wales. Irish, Scottish, and Welsh immigrants were, of course, already to be found in England before this period, though they did not form any considerable proportion of the population.

Some Irish vagrancy has been traceable in England since the Middle Ages. The statute of 1413 (1 Hen. V, c. 8), ordering 'that all Irishmen and Irish clerks beggars, called chamberdekyns, be voided out of the realm', was followed by a long series of laws, ordinances, and proclamations on the subject during the following centuries. At each recurrent scarcity of food in Ireland the inflowing stream of Irish vagrancy increased, calling forth complaints from the local authorities and repressive measures from the Crown. In the 'dearth of cattle and corn' between 1628 and 1633, for instance, there were bitter complaints from places so far apart as Pembroke, Bristol, Somerset, Dorset, Essex, and London. There was apparently a regular traffic of emigrant ships from Ireland to England, and the nuisance led to the organization of an elaborate system of poor removal through the seven specified ports of Bristol, Minehead, Barnstaple, Chester, Liverpool, Milford, and Workington.[1]

In the 'new' manufacturing districts, such as Lancashire,

---

[1] C. J. Ribton-Turner, *History of Vagrants and Vagrancy*, 1887, pp. 148–50; J. B. Bryan, *A Practical View of Ireland*, 1831, p. 125; G. Roberts, *Social History of the People of the Southern Counties of England*, 1856, pp. 187–8.

Irish immigration was not particularly important until the eighteenth century. The Manchester Constables' Accounts for the middle of the eighteenth century show frequent payments to Irish, Scottish, and, more rarely, Welsh vagrants; but they also record payments to vagrants and 'poor passengers' from such unlikely places as Constantinople and Bengal! In the smaller manufacturing centres of Lancashire contemporary vagrancy was fainter, and apparently included a greater proportion of Welsh beggars. Before 1790 the influx of Irish vagrants was alarming only in such south-western shires of Scotland as Wigtown, Ayr, and Kirkcudbright. There the Irish beggars were reinforced by an increasing class of 'troggers', or pedlars, who brought linen cloth from Ireland to be bartered for the Scottish woollen cloth.[1] Meanwhile the seasonal migration of Irish, Scottish, and Welsh harvesters was already noticeable in England. In Herefordshire (1794) the crops were harvested by Welshmen from Cardiganshire. In Norfolk (1774) much of the harvest was got in by itinerant Scotsmen; in Hertfordshire most of the reaping was done by Irishmen; while in Huntingdon, Bedford, and Cambridge the open-field farmers depended for harvesting labour either on the wandering Irish or on industrial workers from such counties as Leicestershire.[2]

As yet comparatively few Irish had made a definite settlement in England. In London, it is true, there had been serious anti-Irish riots in 1736; these were said to be due to the Irish 'not only working at hay and corn harvest as has been usual, but letting themselves out to all sort of labour considerably cheaper than the English labourers have; and numbers of them being employed by the weavers upon the like terms'. In 1768 the Irish coal-heavers round Wapping were in a state of riot, and one of their leaders, James Murphy, was executed for murder. The strength of the Irish colony in London by the

[1] *Manchester Constables' Accounts* (ed. 1892), III (1743–76), *passim*; *Lancs. Parish Register Soc.*, XXXVII, pp. 50, 287, 296, etc.; Sinclair, III, p. 139; cf. *ibid.*, II, pp. 68n.–69n.

[2] Clark, *Herefordshire*, 1794, p. 29; Arthur Young, *Political Arithmetic*, 1774, pp. 103–4; Ernle, p. 300; Hasbach, *History of the English Agricultural Labourer*, 1908 ed., p. 82.

end of the century may be guessed from the fact that in 1796 the united parishes of St. Giles and St. George, Bloomsbury, paid £2,000 in relief of casual poor, 'which arose from the support of about 1,200 poor natives of Ireland'.[1]

Sir James Steuart, writing in the middle of the eighteenth century, accepted the regular immigration of Irish and Scottish settlers into England as a normal movement, and discussed seriously the contention of a contemporary writer that England would diminish in numbers if it were not constantly recruited from Scotland and Ireland. Most accounts agree, however, that Irish settlement on a large scale did not begin until nearly the end of the eighteenth century; some authorities refer its beginning directly to the distress following the rebellion of 1798. The first symptom of increased migration may, perhaps, be detected after the end of the American War of Independence. In 1782 and the following years, both Ireland and Scotland suffered severe famine, which strengthened the existing movement from the two countries.[2] The manufacturing towns and villages of Lancashire were then (1780–90) developing very rapidly, and by 1787 instances of Irish and Scottish settlement became more frequent. At that date Manchester was said to have an Irish population of more than five thousand, and the number of Irish in the neighbourhood increased rapidly until the French war began to restrict movement. By the end of the eighteenth century the Irish element was apparent not only in Manchester but in some of the smaller Lancashire villages, and Celtic names began to appear in the parish registers as names of residents as well as of vagrants. There were already strong and well-established colonies of Irish and Welsh in Liverpool, and during the last decade of the century these were notably strengthened.[3]

---

[1] Coxe's *Walpole*, 1798, III, p. 349; *C.H.O.P.*, 1766–9, pp. 343, 348–9, Nos. 903, 920, 925; Ribton-Turner, *op. cit.*, p. 214.

[2] Sir James Steuart's *Works*, 1805 ed., I, Chap. XV, pp. 125 ff.; *Rept. I.P.*, 1835, G, pp. iv, v; *1851 Census of Ireland*, Pt. V, Vol. I, pp. 150–1; for Scotland see Sinclair, III, p. 507; IV, p. 473, etc.

[3] *Rept. I.P.*, 1835, G, p. 69; *A. & P.*, 1846, XII, No. 209, p. 4; J. Holt, *Lancashire*, 1794, p. 213; T. Henry, 'Observations on the Bills of Mortality

The Irish movement into England in the nineteenth century was more important numerically than that of the Scots or Welsh, and was more fully observable by contemporaries, since the migration from Ireland involved a sea voyage. It is important to remember, however, that Scottish and Welsh migration was going on alongside the Irish influx throughout the period. In the closing decades of the eighteenth century there was considerable migration into England from Scotland. From Roxburghshire people were moving into Northumberland, and from Dumfriesshire into Cumberland. It was said that every year about ten thousand craftsmen (including wrights, carpenters, bakers, gardeners, and tailors) went from Scotland to London. Scots migratory labourers were becoming important also in East Anglia. As already seen, Scottish 'itinerants' were responsible for much of the harvesting work in Norfolk. In 1775 the Norwich 'Scots Society' was established for the purpose of relieving any poor Scotsmen who might come to the town. The scope of the Society was afterwards widened to include poor persons of other nations; but when an account of the Society's work was published in 1784, it was found that the Scottish poor were still increasing, and formed the greatest proportion of the persons relieved.[1]

In the same period Scotsmen were migrating also to Liverpool and the growing cotton towns of Lancashire. Many of the great trading houses of Liverpool were founded by Scotsmen; such a one was John Gladstone, who came to Liverpool in 1787. The leaders of the Lancashire cotton industry in the later eighteenth century included a surprising proportion of Scotsmen. Many of them came from a country district of Kirkcudbright in the early 'eighties of the century, following the machine-maker Cannan, who had come from the same district. This little group included the M'Connels, the Kennedys, and the Murrays, who were all prominent Manchester cotton

for Manchester', in *Memoirs of the Manchester Lit. and Phil. Soc.*, 1786, pp. 159–63; Mantoux, p. 359; *Lancs. Par. Reg. Soc.*, XXXVII, pp. 171, 290, etc.; E. Baines, *History of the County of Lancaster*, I, p. 165; Muir, pp. 304–5.
[1] Sinclair, I, pp. 7–8; II, p. 25; III, p. 218; IV, p. 106; Eden, II, p. 524.

spinners of the time.[1] The process by which Scotsmen thus gravitated to Lancashire in the later eighteenth century may be illustrated from the history of the 'Cheeryble' Grants, of Bury. The father of the family was a small farmer in the valley of the Spey in 'Morayshire'. In 1768 he lost his property through a flood; for the next fifteen years he earned a precarious living as a cattle dealer and drover, making several journeys into England. Then came the lean years following the famine of 1782. He and his eldest son took the drovers' road into England and came to Manchester by way of Yorkshire, bringing with them a letter of introduction to Richard Arkwright. They failed to get work in Manchester, and went on to Bury, where a brother Scot, Mr. Dinwiddie, of Hampson Mill, found employment for them in his printworks.[2] The same process may be traced in the history of the Bannerman family of Manchester. Henry Bannerman was a farmer in Perthshire. In the first decade of the nineteenth century he sent his eldest son to Manchester, to see what prospects the cotton trade held. 'He took a small warehouse in Marsden Square, and prospered so well as to induce his father to throw up the farm and bring the whole family south. . . . The new firm was styled Henry Bannerman and Sons, four out of the five sons having joined.'[3]

In many cases these successful Scots employers must have brought families from Scotland to work for them. The records of Messrs. M'Connel and Kennedy show at least one such case, the firm advancing money for the transport of a workman's family from Scotland. The same firm in the early years of the nineteenth century had among its workers and tenants many people with distinctly Scots names, as well as others with names as distinctly Irish and Welsh. There is, however, little evidence by which to judge the comparative importance of the Scots settlement in England until the middle of the nineteenth

---

[1] Daniels, p. 127, quoting Kennedy, *Early Recollections*, 1849, pp. 9–10. See also W. H. Chaloner, 'John Galloway (1804–1894), engineer, of Manchester . . .', *Trans. Lancs. & Ches. Antiq. Soc.*, LXIV, 1954, pp. 93–5.

[2] *Manchester City News*, N.Q., VI, p. 139; B. T. Barton, *History of Bury*, 1874, pp. 140–5; and information from Miss F. Collier.

[3] W. A. Shaw, *Manchester Old and New*, 1894, II, p. 3.

century. There are, it is true, vague references to the 'vast numbers of Scotch artisans . . . to be found in every factory in England'; and it is piquant to note that the only local complaint against Cobden as an employer at Chorley was that he employed too many Scots. Scots framework knitters were also employed along with Irish in the Midland hosiery districts. Such incidental references, however, are not particularly helpful.[1]

The main reason why so little is known about the Scots migrants is, perhaps, that they less frequently required poor relief than the Irish. This was noticed both at Manchester and at Liverpool, though in each town there was a considerable Scots colony. In London, also, there were very few Scottish beggars compared with the number of Irish, few Scottish families in distress, and few Scottish paupers brought before the City magistrates.[2] The paucity of information concerning the migration of Scots necessarily confines attention mainly to the more strongly marked Irish influx. The very inadequate account given may, however, help to place the Irish movement in its true aspect as part of a general Celtic movement which affected not only Ireland, Scotland, and Wales, but also such smaller centres as Cornwall, Brittany,[3] and the Isle of Man.

VAGRANCY

Both Irish and Scottish vagrancy in England is to be studied in relation to the existing practice of mendicancy in the countries of origin. In Ireland the Roman Catholic encouragement of alms-giving, and the absence of poor laws, made mendicancy

[1] M'Connel and Kennedy MSS., Manchester University, MS. Ledger, June 1806, folio 20; *ibid.*, MS. Rent Ledger, c. 1810–25; in a list of names, chosen at random, occur those of McMurdo, Glendinning, Kilgour, Baird, Murray, Inglescent, and Owen; J. B. Bryan, *op. cit.*, pp. 123–4; cf. *P.L.C.*, *1st Ann. Rept.*, App. B, No. 11, p. 185; *Rept. on Truck*, 1842, p. 80; *Rept. on Framework Knitters*, 1845, Pt. II, App., p. 52.

[2] *Lords' Rept. P.L.*, 1818, pp. 155, 168–9; *6th Rept. Sel. P.R.*, 1847, pp. 55, 76; *1st Rept. on Mendicity in the Metropolis*, 1815, pp. 7, 10, 13, 15; *2nd Rept.*, 1816, p. 15.

[3] On the seasonal migration of potato-diggers into Jersey, from Brittany, see G. F. B. de Gruchy, in *E.H.R.*, II, p. 736.

inevitable; and a report of 1819 laid stress on the effect of the numerous mendicant poor in spreading the contagious fevers from which Ireland was seldom free.[1] In Scotland, also, the system of poor relief did not provide adequately for casual pauperism, and was said to encourage begging. The more liberal administration of the poor laws in England up to 1834, therefore, gave an added inducement to migration from both Ireland and Scotland.

At the end of the Napoleonic wars the danger of an increased movement of beggars and vagrants into England was immediately felt. In the summer and autumn of 1815 droves of Irish cattle poured into England through Liverpool, Bristol, and the Welsh ports, covering the roads for miles—and blazing the trail for the droves of human beings who followed. Inquiries showed that the Irish already formed an alarmingly large proportion of the London vagrants. Of two thousand beggars examined in London, fully one-third were Irish. In the trade depression of 1816–17 attention was drawn to the serious and increasing problem of Irish pauperism in such manufacturing towns as Manchester, and to the unfair burden laid on seaports and border parishes by their duty of passing the unfortunate vagrants back to their country of origin.[2] Of the border counties, Cumberland complained most bitterly of the hardship experienced from the influx of Scottish and Irish poor, since the less liberal poor laws and settlement regulations of Scotland encouraged a persistent movement of destitute persons across the border. The poor rates of some English parishes near the border were in 1819 nearly five times as high as those of neighbouring parishes in Scotland. Another grievance was that in Scotland settlement was only gained by a three years' residence, while in England the Scots and Irish were said to be gaining settlements by a residence of only six weeks.[3]

In 1819 an Act was passed which facilitated the passing of

---

[1] *1st Rept. on Labouring Poor of Ireland*, 1819, p. 5.
[2] *1st Rept. on Mendicity in the Metropolis*, 1815, pp. 5–9, 40, and App., pp. 90–4; Brougham, in Hansard, XXXIII, p. 1097; *Lords' Rept. P.L.*, 1818, pp. 154–5, and App., pp. 41–2, 48.
[3] *Commons' Rept. P.L.*, 1817, pp. 84–5; *J.H.C.*, LXXIV, p. 152.

Irish and Scottish vagrants, and this was declared to have relieved many parishes. East Ham, for instance, had previously been troubled by an influx of Irish paupers every winter, after the harvesting, hop-picking, and other summer work failed, but it was found that the number of applicants decreased after 1819. The Act however, had the defect of being popular with the vagrants. Many Scottish and Irish poor applied to the London Mendicity Society to be passed, and Irish labourers (probably belated harvesters) petitioned Parliament from the parish of St. Giles in the Fields to be sent home 'to cultivate the bogs of Ireland'. Meanwhile, the number of Irish poor in England increased very rapidly, and the burden of passing lay heavily on such places as Bristol, Liverpool, and Cumberland.[1]

At that time (1821–3) the Irish influx was taking on a new and more formidable aspect. The failure of the Irish potato crop in 1821 was followed by a grievous famine and epidemic in 1822. The resultant increase of migration was so great that a recent writer has taken this date to mark the beginning of the main Irish movement into England.[2] It is, therefore, important to estimate the extent of Irish vagrancy at this time in England, and its relationship to the contemporary Scottish vagrancy. This can be done roughly by means of the accounts for sums paid by the various counties of England and Wales for the apprehension and removal of vagrants during the period in question. The result is interesting as showing the general distribution of the country between Irish and Scottish vagrants.[3] There were at that time apparently two main streams of Irish vagrancy in England, one starting from Bristol, Milford Haven, Newport, and other ports of South Wales, the other starting from Liverpool and Holyhead. Both streams converged on London and the surrounding counties, thus driving a broad

[1] 59 Geo. III, c. 12: Rept. on Vagrants, 1821, passim; J.H.C., LXXVII, App. 12, pp. 1342–3; Rept. D.S. Agric., 1821, p. 62; J.H.C., LXXV, p. 82.
[2] G. O'Brien, Economic History of Ireland from the Union to the Famine, 1921, p. 209; 1851 Census of Ireland, Pt. V, Vol. I, pp. 188–97, gives an extensive collection of references to the famine of 1822.
[3] A. & P., 1824, XIX, No. 250; see also ibid., No. 357, and J.H.C., LXXVIII, App. 12, pp. 1024–5; and Map F in Appendix.

wedge across the country. Wales was as yet little affected by
the movement, except along the north and south coasts.

The Scottish vagrants, instead of being confined to the northern counties, as might have been expected, held sway also down
through eastern England, as far as the fen country round the
Wash. The boundary-line between Irish and Scots in these
eastern counties is most clearly seen in the little county of
Rutland, whence it was reported that nineteen out of every
twenty vagrants passed through the western half of the county
went to Ireland; and the same proportion of those passed
through the northern half went to Scotland. The Scots were,
moreover, apparently holding their own against the Irish in
such southern counties as Surrey, Hampshire, Dorset, and
Devon. The strength of Scottish vagrancy in eastern England
may have been due largely to the movements of Scottish drovers,
taking cattle to the London market; the drovers followed the
Great North Road as far as Yorkshire, there diverging from it
to avoid turnpikes. With this southward movement of Scottish
drovers may be compared the eastward movement of Welsh
drovers across England. Welsh drovers are mentioned by both
Cobbett and Borrow: near Tregaron, Borrow talked with a
Welsh drover who was up in London every month, until the
'domm'd railroad' came into fashion.[1] The large proportion
of Scottish vagrants in many of the southern counties is not so
easily explained; it may have consisted partly of Irish or
English vagrants who wished to travel in a northerly direction.
It is, however, significant that the high proportion of Scots, in
both the eastern and the southern counties, is confirmed by the
census records of migration in the later nineteenth century.

The ten years following 1823 saw a great increase in the immigration from Ireland, including not only beggars and seasonal
labourers, but also a large number of poor people who settled
permanently in the growing towns. A further alteration in the
laws governing the passing of Irish and Scottish vagrants was
effected in 1829 (9 Geo. IV, c. 12, ss. 33–4), but had such poor
success that its suspension or repeal was strongly demanded.

[1] *Wild Wales*, Everyman edn., 1906, p. 515.

Between 1828 and 1833 there was a very great increase in the numbers of Irish passed home through Bristol and Liverpool, and the problem was felt to be so alarming as to 'require the particular attention of the legislature'.[1]

The general lines of Irish movement remained much the same as in 1823. South Wales, Herefordshire, and Monmouthshire were sorely troubled by a swarm of Irish people travelling up from Milford Haven, Bristol, and Newport in the direction of London. The West Country clothing districts reported that the tramps there were mainly Irish, mixed with a few Scots and a very small proportion of foreigners. Derbyshire, also, reported a preponderance of Irish; whilst in Northumberland the Irish were now beginning to challenge the former supremacy of the Scots. There was, about the same time, a noticeable increase in the number of Irish vagrants making their way towards Birmingham and the other large towns of Staffordshire and Warwickshire; in this the neighbouring county of Shropshire also shared. By this time, indeed, there were few counties in England to which the Irish wanderers did not penetrate. They were even remarked upon in Sussex, 'a county most distant from Ireland'.[2]

SEASONAL MIGRATION

Contemporary observers of the Celtic influx did not, in its earlier stages, distinguish clearly between ordinary vagrancy and seasonal migration. The seasonal migration of harvesters is, however, sufficiently interesting to warrant separate treatment, especially as similar movements were going on elsewhere in Europe.

The migration of Irish and Scottish harvesters into England was an extension of a similar practice of seasonal migration in the two countries of origin. In Ireland there was a seasonal movement, at the times of harvest and potato-digging, from the

[1] *Rept. on Irish Vagrants*, 1833, qq. 508–12, 637–41, 659; *P.L.C. Rept.*, 1834, App. A, Pt. I, No. 20, p. 802.
[2] *Ibid.*, No. 18, p. 671; No. 15, pp. 456–7; No. 13, pp. 386, 392–3; No. 5, pp. 126–8; *Rept. on Irish Vagrants*, 1833, qq. 607–18, 621–4, 632–6; Hansard, *N.S.*, XVIII, p. 959.

L

mountainous parts of Galway and Kerry into the lowlands of Limerick. Towards the end of the eighteenth century high-landers were employed as reapers in most parts of Scotland, coming from such shires as Argyll, Perth, and Ross and Crom-arty.[1] As already seen, both Irish and Scottish harvesters were to be found in England during the same period; but during the French wars between 1793 and 1815 this harvesting migra-tion into England appears to have been checked by the rapid progress of Irish and Scottish agriculture. There was, it is true, a wave of immigration from Ireland following on the famine and social unrest of 1811;[2] but this was allayed by good har-vests in the succeeding years.

After the famine of 1822 the influx into England of Irish harvesters increased so rapidly as to require some further explanation. Part of the explanation is found in the post-war agricultural depression, and the consequent changes in agri-cultural methods and tenure. Wartime prosperity in both Ireland and Scotland had led to an excessively minute sub-division of holdings.[3] As the profits of agriculture diminished after the end of the war, the smallholdings became inadequate to support the families occupying them, even on a very low scale of living. The smallholder, even when he retained his land, tended to seek day-labour for the employment of his unoccupied time; but there was no extensive outlet for such labour in Ireland. 'A man cannot obtain his living as a day-labourer. He must get possession of a plot of land . . . or starve.' Less than one-third of the labourers were employed all the year round; the rest got work only at harvest and the time of potato-digging. Even the possibility of getting harvest work in Ireland was very uncertain; and, in any case, the wages paid for harvesting work in England were much higher than any paid in Ireland or Scotland.[4]

[1] *Rept. S.P. Ireland*, 1830, pp. 505–6; *Rept. Employ. Ireland*, 1823, p. 25; Sinclair, I, p. 234; III, p. 515; *etc.*
[2] Smart, I, p. 258.
[3] *Rept. Employ. Ireland*, 1823, Rept. p. 7, Evid. pp. 53, 132; *Rept. Emig.*, 1826, qq. 741, 628–36, 1220–9; *Repts. S.P. Ireland*, 1830, *passim.*
[4] G. Nicholls, *1st Rept. P.L. Ireland*, 1838, p. 8; G. C. Lewis, *Local Disturb-ances in Ireland*, 1836, pp. 311–12.

Moreover, after the war, pasture land in many cases became more profitable than arable, and land which had been tilled during the war was now again laid down to pasture. This tendency was already threatening Irish agriculture by 1821, and was strengthened by the miseries of 1822. It was now to the interest of the landlord to convert small farms into large, and this soon became the general practice. The result was a further diminution of the amount of agricultural labour required, and the ejectment of many tenants. Some of the ejected persons took to the hills, and settled there; others flocked to the towns, and became dependent on charity.[1]

The general result of these agrarian vicissitudes was to swell the streams of emigration from Ireland, whether to Great Britain or to more distant countries. The strengthening of the seasonal migration from Ireland may also, perhaps, be attributed partly to the changing relations between town and country, and between manufactures and agriculture, in England. These changes diminished the amount of industrial labour available for harvesting purposes in England, and increased the field of employment for the Irish harvesters. How the Irish fitted into the scheme of English harvesting is admirably depicted in Cobbett's account of the bands of reapers making their way northwards from London through Middlesex and Hertfordshire in June 1822.

> We saw, all the way down, squads of labourers of different departments migrating from tract to tract . . . the mowers, with their scythes on their shoulders, were in front, going on towards the standing crops, while the haymakers were coming on behind towards the grass already cut or cutting. . . . It is curious to observe how the different labourers are divided as to the nations. The mowers are all English; the haymakers all Irish.[2]

Cobbett goes on to declare sarcastically that no Scotsman (when out of Scotland) ever follows such a laborious occupation as hay-making. In this he was not well-informed. Scottish harvesters continued to come to such northern counties as

---

[1] *Rept. D.S. Agric.*, 1821, pp. 308, 311, 328; *Rept. Employ. Ireland*, 1823, pp. 119, 122–3, 134, 154; *Repts. S.P. Ireland*, 1830, Rept. p. 4, qq. 869–70, 3109, 4386–8, 5025–7, 5236–41, 6919–20.

[2] Cobbett, June 19th, 1822.

Northumberland, and Welsh harvesters to the western Mid-lands;[1] but in each case they had to meet strong Irish com-petition, and the movement became more purely Irish as the half-century went on. In Scotland the highland harvesters were for some time able to maintain their position alongside the in-truders from Ireland. As many as five hundred persons left a single Perthshire parish in February and March 1821, to seek summer service in the Lowlands, and similar movements were reported from other parishes in the shire. In years when the fishing failed the highlanders were joined by the young men from the coast parishes; while in some parts of the Lowlands they worked alongside harvesters from the great towns. In Haddingtonshire, for instance, it was asserted in 1836 that the harvest could not be got in without the assistance of strangers from Ireland, the Highlands, Edinburgh, and Glasgow. Perth, also, sent out many persons to field labour during the summer.[2]

The Irish harvesters came in the main from the western and southern (less prosperous) parts of Ireland. Very few agri-cultural labourers emigrated to England from the more 'civil-ized' counties of Leinster. In the earlier years of the nineteenth century the movement was apparently confined to the mountain tenants of Connaught; and this province remained the principal source of harvest labour throughout the period.[3] As the move-ment developed, however, three main bodies of migrants may be traced, distinguishable by place of origin and by destination, as follows:

> (a) from Munster to Bristol;
> (b) from Connaught to Liverpool;
> (c) from Ulster to Scotland.

This grouping holds primarily for harvest labour, but is also true in some degree for the other classes of migrants.

---

[1] *Lords' Rept. P.L.*, 1831, pp. 135–6, 158.

[2] *1821 Census*, p. 528; *1831 Census*, II, pp. 988, 1017; *3rd Rept. on Agric. Distress*, 1836, qq. 9937–41, p. 31.

[3] *Rept. S.P. Ireland*, 1830, pp. 418–19; J. B. Bryan, *op. cit.*, p. 125.

(*a*) From the south and south-west of Ireland came harvest workers from the mountainous parts of Kerry and the barren tracts of Cork, who had previously harvested in the lowlands of Limerick. This diversion of harvesting labour from Limerick to England was commented upon in 1830, and was said to be caused partly by the hostility of the native Limerick labourers. 'They do not go so numerously as they used over Ireland; they come here in preference . . . they run no risks, and besides that they get better pay in England.'[1] These Munster migrants took ship mainly from Cork to Bristol and the southern ports of Wales. In 1835–6 it was observed that many more Irish labourers embarked at the port of Bristol than had ever disembarked there. This was accounted for by the fact that 'considerable numbers of the lower classes of Irish come over to the small ports on the Welsh coast, such as Swansea, Neath, Cardiff, etc., in the colliers which return from Ireland in ballast'.[2] The labourers arriving so cheaply in Great Britain generally managed to save a few pounds during the summer, and were therefore able to pay for a regular passage home in the autumn, if they were not lucky enough to get a free passage as paupers; in either case they returned through Bristol, and so produced a 'debit balance' of migration through that port.

The harvesters landing at Bristol or in South Wales made their way through all the counties between Gloucester and Middlesex, or, branching northwards, competed with Welsh harvesters in the western Midlands. In 1828, for instance, Irish harvesters were found to be displacing Welsh harvesters in Shropshire. In Hertfordshire and Middlesex, where they have already been noticed at work in 1822, the Irish harvesters continued to compete for the rest of the half-century. In Gloucestershire and Wiltshire they were particularly strong in the parishes near the great road from Bristol to London; while in Berkshire and some parts of Wiltshire it was said that the harvest could not have been got in without them. In Buckinghamshire they were employed at both haytime and harvest, and

---

[1] *Rept. S.P. Ireland*, pp. 108–9.
[2] *P.L.C., 2nd Ann. Rept.*, App. B, No. 20, p. 419.

in Bedfordshire also they were increasingly employed, especially after 1834.[1]

To the south of London the Irish had a great share in the hop-picking. In 1826 hop-pickers were reported to be scarce in East Sussex, and Irishmen were being taken on by the score, though Englishmen would have been preferred. Later in the century it was ascertained that out of nearly a thousand 'hands' employed by one hop-grower down in Kent about six hundred were Irish.[2]

(b) The harvesters entering England by Liverpool and North Wales came mainly from the province of Connaught. There the subdivision of holdings had become extreme, through the larger tenants' splitting up their land among their grown-up children. The regions chiefly affected were the counties of Mayo and Roscommon, the southern part of Sligo, and the northern part of Galway.[3] The migrants walked across Ireland in parties to the eastern ports, taking ship principally at Dublin, from which port there was regular steamboat communication with Liverpool and Holyhead. During the summer of 1841, 57,651 deck passengers crossed from Ireland to England. Of these 25,118 came from Connaught, embarked either at Drogheda or Dublin, and landed at Liverpool. Over 10,400 came from the county of Mayo alone.[4]

The harvesters landing at Liverpool seem to have spread across the country from Lancashire to Lincolnshire, through Yorkshire and Nottinghamshire, and even penetrated as far south as Northamptonshire. Their employment in Lancashire calls for no explanation: in the middle of the century they were regarded as indispensable there through the scarcity of English agricultural labour, and they continued to be extensively employed until quite recent years. In the West Riding of

---

[1] Hansard, N.S., XIX, pp. 1513–14; *1841 Census*, pp. 120, 177; *Lords' Rept. P.L.*, 1831, p. 295; *Rept. S.P. Ireland*, 1830, p. 66; *1st Rept. on Agric. Distress*, 1836, qq. 487–91, p. 32; P.L.C., *2nd Ann. Rept.*, App. B, No. 6, p. 275.

[2] *Ibid.*, App. B, No. 3, p. 223; *Rept. P.R.*, 1854, p. 467.

[3] G. Nicholls, *2nd Rept. P.L., Ireland*, 1838, App. 12, p. 70.

[4] *1841 Census of Ireland*, Rept., p. xxvi.

Yorkshire Irish competition was, by 1840, capturing the harvesting work from the local handloom weavers, even in that time of industrial distress. Lincolnshire had, in the early part of the century, been the haunt mainly of Scottish vagrants; but by 1831 the Irish had made their appearance there in considerable numbers, and were beating down the wages. Their intrusion was greatly resented by the local labourers, and agricultural riots broke out in consequence. Nevertheless, the Irish found harvesting work on the level of Ancholme, in the north of the county; and in the Lincolnshire Wolds it was said (1837) that their help in harvest-time was indispensable.[1]

(c) The northern group of migrants, coming from the counties of Donegal, Londonderry, and Tyrone, embarked chiefly at Londonderry and Belfast, and went to Scotland. Comparatively few migrants from the northern counties of Ireland went to Liverpool. The movements of the harvesters going to Scotland are not so well known as those of the other main groups. That they made their way across the whole of southern Scotland is clear from their appearance alongside native harvesters in Haddingtonshire; and they were repeatedly mentioned as competing with Scottish harvesters in Northumberland during the 'thirties of the century.[2]

The period of the year at which the Irish harvesters entered and left England was determined jointly by the time of the harvest in the midland counties and by the needs of the Irish potato crop. The potato plots were planted by the labourers before they left home; and they returned in time for the potato-digging. Thus they were in England usually during the months of May, June, July, and August. 'They mostly resort year by year to the same districts, where they become known; and the

---

[1] *Rept. P.R.*, 1854, *loc. cit.*; W. H. R. Curtler, in *V.C.H. Lancs.*, II, pp. 430, 436: cf. Hasbach, *op. cit.*, App. VI, p. 410; *Repts. Hd. Lm. Wvrs.* (*Yorkshire*), 1840, p. 536; *Lords' Rept. P.L.*, 1831, pp. 202–3; Cobbett: *Register*, August 20th, 1831; *2nd Rept. on Agric. Distress*, 1836, qq. 5882–5, p. 74; *2nd Rept. P.L.A.A.*, 1838, qq. 339–43.

[2] *6th Rept. Sel. P.R.*, 1847, p. 58; *3rd Rept. on Agric. Distress*, 1836, qq. 9937–41, p. 31; *Lords' Rept. P.L.*, 1831, pp. 135–6; *P.L.C. Rept.*, 1834, App. A, Pt. I, No. 5, pp. 126–8; *Lords' Rept. on Agric. Distress*, 1837, qq. 4696–7, p. 289.

English farmer not infrequently engages during the current harvest the labourers who are to come ... to assist him in getting in his crops in the next.' They worked as they travelled, each gang under its recognized head, who sometimes paid all their expenses and received their earnings.[1]

The extremely frugal manner of life of the Irish reapers was well described by a Nottinghamshire correspondent whose recollection of them covered the whole of the first half of the nineteenth century. 'They always bargain for money, milk, and some beer (taken with them into the field). At times I have known them live entirely on milk and bread—the latter of which they purchased at a neighbouring town, and with the loan of an ass and a sack procured a supply for several days.'[2] Sometimes they begged the goodwife of the farm to give them her cabbage water; this they flavoured with a little pepper and salt, and used it as broth to 'get their bread down'. Living thus sparingly, the Irish strove throughout the summer to save a little money with which to pay the rent of their small patches of ground at home. Their wages were never so high as those of the English harvesters, or they would not have been employed. Perhaps half-a-crown a day would be too liberal an estimate of their earnings. Yet they managed to save quite large sums in a short time. 'I have heard of ten and twelve guineas being brought home; but that five, six, or seven guineas is not at all uncommon.'[3]

Many of the harvesters secured a free passage home by declaring themselves to be destitute and submitting to be removed. This occurred not only at Bristol and Liverpool, but also in London. In some of the metropolitan parishes a considerable proportion of the persons relieved were harvest labourers. During the earlier phases of the movement these frauds were committed brazenly; men applied for passes both at Liverpool and Bristol with money in their pockets, and some

---

[1] *Rept. I. & S. Vag.*, 1828, pp. 9–10; G. Nicholls, *op. cit.*, pp. 30–1.
[2] *Rept. P.R.*, 1854, p. 668: for a vivid account of living conditions among later Irish potato-diggers in Scotland see Patrick MacGill's *Children of the Dead End*, 1914.
[3] *Rept. S.P. Ireland*, 1830, p. 19.

were successful. After the loss at sea of certain Irish packet boats with paupers on board, money was in some cases found on searching the paupers' bodies. A subtler way of getting a pauper's passage was to make a deposit in England of the season's savings and take an order for payment in Ireland. The more general practice, however, was to appoint one man banker for the party; he paid his own fare home and took the money, while the rest of the party got home free as paupers.[1]

The harvesters from the north and south of Ireland were not far from their own counties after completing the return sea-voyage; but the men from Connaught had a long tramp across Ireland after disembarking at Dublin. They made the journey in 'vast crowds', keeping together until they had crossed the Shannon, which they did principally by the Lanesborough bridge.[2]

In many cases seasonal migration or vagrancy led eventually to permanent settlement in England; but the annual visits of the Irish harvesters have left very little impression on the English agricultural districts. When the harvesters or vagrants decided to stay in England they usually settled in the large towns. The Irish never secured a footing in the more highly skilled branches of agriculture; they were good reapers, but not fit for anything else. Even in Scotland, where their position in agriculture became strongest, there were few Irish ploughmen or dairywomen.[3]

---

[1] *Rept. on Irish Vagrants*, 1833, qq. 111, 164, 364; *Rept. I. & S. Vag.*, 1828, pp. 7, 8, 12, 14–17; *Rept. P.R.*, 1854, p. 163, qq. 2300–2; *ibid.*, pp. 133, 495–496; the 'banker' would, of course, usually be the 'contractor' for the party.

[2] *Rept. S.P. Ireland*, 1830, p. 150; G. Nicholls, *op. cit.*, App. 12, p. 70.

[3] *P.L.C. Rept.*, 1834, App. A, Pt. I, No. 5, p. 126; *Rept. P.R.*, 1854, pp. 240, 246, 262.

CHAPTER IX

THE IRISH INFLUX (2)

SETTLEMENT

MUCH of the work done by the Irish in Great Britain was of the same general manual nature as their harvesting and agricultural labour. Some of the work was even of a similar seasonable character, as, for instance, that of bricklayers' labourers. In many places the Irish almost monopolized the lower grades of work in the building trades. In these trades, as in agriculture, they rarely reached the higher-paid posts, because they did not come over till they were about twenty-five years of age, when they were too old to learn the trade. In London they formed the lowest class of builders' workmen, employed in 'carrying bricks, making mortar, taking down and erecting of scaffolds', and similar jobs. An immense number of Irish were employed as hodmen in Lancashire, and in similar work in the West Riding. By 1833 there were at least seven hundred Irish hod-carriers working in Liverpool, and two years later it was said that four-fifths of the bricklayers' labourers in Stockport were Irish.[1]

Another source of hard manual employment for the Irish immigrants arose from the great improvements in transport which were being made in the earlier nineteenth century. The class of Irishmen who found work as bricklayers' labourers was also being employed in roadmaking and canal-cutting, in harbour works, shipbuilding, and dock labour. Wherever an extensive drain, or canal, or road was to be cut, it was quite usual for nine-tenths of the labourers employed to be Irish. In

[1] *Lords' Rept. P.L.*, 1831, p. 81; *Rept. Mfs.*, 1833, pp. 106–7; *P.L.C., 1st Ann. Rept.*, App. B, No. 11, p. 186; *17th Rept. P.L.A.A.*, 1838, p. 3; *22nd Rept., ibid.*, p. 21; *Rept. I.P.*, 1835, G, pp. 28, 86.

London the loading and unloading of ships, and the principal hard work all down the river, was done by Irishmen.[1]

After 1830 the construction of railways began to take the place of canal-cutting. This might have been expected to suit the abilities of the Irish 'navigator' admirably; yet comparatively few Irish were employed in the work at first. Between 1831 and 1841 it was estimated that about fifty thousand labourers had been drawn to railway construction; but a leading engineer calculated that the Irish labourers employed did not at any time exceed five thousand, or one-tenth of the whole.[2] This is easy to understand for the years of depressed trade after 1836, since at that time it was possible to get English labour as cheaply as Irish. Moreover, attempts to introduce Irish railway labourers met with violent opposition from the English labourers, and led to serious disturbances.

In most manufactures, as in outdoor work, the Irish supplied the lower grades of labour. In the Lancashire cotton industry, for instance, there were thousands of Irish workers, but they were rarely employed in the most highly paid processes, such as spinning. They were mostly to be found in the blowing-rooms and the cardrooms. It was declared by prominent employers that there were not a hundred Irish spinners in all Lancashire.[3] This is partially confirmed by the records of poor removals from Lancashire towns in 1841–3. Out of many hundreds of Irish families then sent back to Ireland, there were only two spinners mentioned.[4]

In the Scottish cotton-spinning mills the case was entirely different. When cotton-spinning machinery was introduced there in the later years of the eighteenth century the native workers were extremely reluctant to enter the factories. Therefore the employers brought in Irish labour. In Glasgow and Paisley the highest branches of cotton-spinning were undertaken by the Irish, and the tradition persisted in the nineteenth

[1] *Ibid.*, pp. vii, 86, 131, 139, 141–2, 144, 151; *Rept. P.R.*, 1854, pp. 319, 433, and App. 17, p. 665; *3rd Rept. Emig.*, 1827, q. 1761, p. 187.
[2] *1841 Census of Ireland*, Rept., p. x.
[3] *P.L.C., 1st Ann. Rept.*, App. B, No. 11, pp. 185–6, 197.
[4] *A. & P.*, 1846, XII, No. 209, pp. 18, 20.

century. In 1833 the majority of the workers in the Glasgow mills were said to be still either Irish or of Irish descent. The majority even of the spinners still came from Irish families, but were not usually Irish born. In Paisley, also, many Irish were employed as cotton spinners.[1]

In both England and Scotland, however, the main Irish influx to the cotton and other textile trades was composed of handloom weavers. The immigration of Irish weavers had in both cases begun before the end of the eighteenth century, and the distress of the handloom weavers became increasingly an Irish problem as the nineteenth century advanced. Throughout the period there were many complaints of decay in most of the Irish textile industries; and this decay caused an efflux of industrial workers (mostly handloom weavers) both to Great Britain and to America.

The Irish cotton industry experienced particularly marked vicissitudes during the period, and by 1830 was in a moribund condition. The steam-power which killed the Irish cotton trade ruined also the Irish woollen industry. The commercial panic of 1825–6 had especially disastrous effects by causing the dumping of English cloth on the Dublin market. Most of the Dublin manufacturers stopped work, and the local woollen trade never recovered from the blow. Between 1821 and 1831 thirty of the most eminent woollen manufacturers of the city of Dublin were ruined.[2] The Dublin silk trade (the chief manufacture of the city) followed the fortunes of Spitalfields. During the Napoleonic wars it suffered from a silk famine in 1809, caused by the operation of the Berlin decrees; and its doom was sealed when the protecting duties were relaxed in 1824–6. After that date the Dublin silk manufacturers found themselves quite unable to compete with English centres like Manchester and Macclesfield; many of them left the trade, and the Dublin silk weavers were in great distress.[3] The Ulster linen industry was saved by a timely adoption of power-spinning

[1] *Rept. Mfs.*, 1833, pp. 311–13; *Rept. I.P.*, 1835, G, p. 132.
[2] R. M. Martin, *Ireland before and after the Union*, 3rd ed., 1848, pp. 70, 72, 73; J. J. Webb, *Industrial Dublin since 1698*, 1913, pp. 35–6; J. B. Bryan, *op. cit.*, p. 51.   [3] *Rept. Silk*, 1832, pp. 836–8, and App. E, p. 930.

and the power-loom; but this in itself displaced many domestic workers and aggravated the distress of the linen handloom weavers. Throughout the period the rates of wages for linen weaving in Ireland were below even the starvation rates paid in England.

The effect of this general decline of the Irish textile manufactures in the early nineteenth century was to send into Great Britain a swarm of handloom weavers, of whom the Lancashire and West Scotland cotton districts bore the chief burden. The Irish handloom weavers, as already seen, formed a considerable proportion of the burden of pauperism in Manchester by the end of the Napoleonic wars; and their numbers throughout the Lancashire cotton district increased very rapidly during the next thirty years. From Dublin there was a noticeable movement of silk weavers to Manchester and Macclesfield throughout the period: after 1826 the movement was stimulated by public subscriptions. The same financial encouragement of migration by public subscriptions occurred also at Cork and Limerick. From the north of Ireland there was a dispersion of linen weavers both to Scotland and to the textile districts of Lancashire and the West Riding.[1]

Compared with this influx of Irish into the textile trades their share in the other great industries was small. In the coal and iron trades they supplied a good deal of the rough labour required, especially in Scotland. In Ayrshire, for instance, most of the coal-miners were Irish, though the 'headsmen' were practically all Scottish; the Scots were said to have a dislike for coal-hewing, even at high wages. In Cumberland the connection of Irishmen with the iron trade went back to the early days of the eighteenth century, and Irish blood is still strong in most colliery districts of the north of England.[2] In South

[1] *Repts. Hd. Lm. Wvrs., Ireland,* 1840, p. 611; J. J. Webb, *op. cit.,* p. 156; *Rept. Silk,* 1832, pp. 792, 838; *Rept. I. & S. Vag.,* 1828, pp. 12–13; *Rept. S.P. Ireland,* 1830, pp. 419, 484; *Rept. I.P.,* 1835, G, p. vii; Baines, *History of the Cotton Manufacture,* pp. 495–6.
[2] *Rept. P.R.,* 1854, p. 290; *ibid.,* p. 244, qq. 3257–9; Fell, *Early Iron Industry in Furness,* pp. 223, 229, 362; cf. Dr. J. Beddoe, 'Modern Ethnological Migrations in the British Isles', in *British Association Handbook,* 1874, Trans. of Sections, p. 145.

Wales, also, the coal and iron trades employed an increasing number of Irishmen towards the middle of the nineteenth century.

A less attractive class of work in which the Irish were largely engaged consisted of jobs which Englishmen disliked because the work was dirty, disreputable, or otherwise undesirable. Much of this was petty trading and huckstering, keeping lodging-houses and beerhouses. In Manchester three-quarters of the stall-keepers in the market were Irish, as were also most of the old-clothes dealers; the less fortunate sold mats, firewood chips, and similar commodities. Many of the Liverpool Irish were employed in soap-boiling; while in Bermondsey the Irish were chiefly employed in fellmongers' and tanners' yards, or in glue factories. The Irish in Birkenhead specialized in cockles and mussels, or sold sand and rubbing-stones.[1] The same classes of work gave scope for the Irish in the towns of Scotland. Practically all the brokers in Kilmarnock were Irish, and in Glasgow many of the fish and fruit hawkers. In Edinburgh the Irish were keepers of (and lodgers in) the low-class lodging-houses of Cowgate, Grassmarket, Canongate, and Westport.

The general distribution of the Irish in Great Britain is clear from the nature of their occupations. The permanent settlers were concentrated mainly in a small number of large towns. It is not possible, however, to discover the exact location of the Irish settlers until towards the middle of the century. The earliest census returns distinguishing the numbers of Irish-born persons living in Great Britain are those of 1841. Earlier estimates are interesting mainly for comparison with the later enumerations: the wildest guesses were made, varying in character according to the temperament of the individual writer.

Throughout the period Lancashire contained a greater number of Irish settlers than any other county. The majority of the settlers in Lancashire were concentrated in Liverpool and Manchester. In 1835 Dr. J. P. Kay estimated the Irish

---

[1] *Rept. P.R.*, 1854, pp. 430, 454, 538; W. Tomlinson, *Byeways of Manchester Life*, 1887, p. 177.

and their immediate descendants in Manchester at about sixty thousand, and in Liverpool at about fifty thousand, the total in the county being assumed to be about 145,000. G. C. Lewis shortly afterwards reduced this estimate to 35,000 in Manchester (including 5,000 Protestants) and 24,156 (not including Protestants) in Liverpool, the total number in the county being taken to be less than 100,000. This was probably a fairly accurate estimate (except for Liverpool); the 1841 census gave the number of Irish in Lancashire as 105,916, of whom 34,300 were in Manchester and 49,639 in Liverpool.[1]

With the 1841 census returns it becomes possible to see more clearly the way in which the Irish element distributed itself throughout Great Britain. The three main areas of Irish settlement at that date centred respectively round Lancashire, Glasgow, and London. Lancashire contained about one-quarter of the total number of Irish in Great Britain, and more than one-third of the number in England. The nine counties forming the three main areas of Irish settlement included nearly three-quarters of the Irish population of the island.[2] In general, the Irish settlers clung closely to the great manufacturing areas. Except round London, Bristol, and the seaports, the Irish were not numerous in the southern counties of England. In Wales their numbers were unimportant, except in the coal and iron districts of Glamorgan and Monmouth.

In Scotland the towns of Glasgow, Greenock, Dundee, Edinburgh, and Paisley contained the largest proportion of the immigrants. Only in the south-western counties of Scotland had the Irish settled in considerable numbers over the country-side. There the influx of Irish settlers was already alarming before the end of the eighteenth century in the shires of Wigtown, Ayr, and Kirkcudbright, and in those parts of Lanark and

---

[1] *P.L.C., 1st Ann. Rept.*, App. B, No. 11, p. 185; *Rept. I.P.*, 1835, G, pp. vi, vii, 42 ff.; *1841 Census*, Preface, pp. 14–17.

[2] (a) Lancashire, Cheshire, and West Riding = 133,000
(b) Lanark, Renfrew, and Ayr   = 88,000
(c) Middlesex, Surrey, and Kent   = 82,000

                                              ———
                                            303,000
                                              ———

Renfrew round Glasgow. In the next half-century there were frequent notices of the strengthening of Irish settlement in the shires named, and its gradual extension in the smaller towns of Lanarkshire.[1] While this Irish settlement in the south-west of Scotland was important, the great bulk of the Irish settled population, in Scotland as in England, remained in the great towns.

Between the census enumerations of 1841 and 1851 occurred the great Irish potato famine, which carried off by death over 700,000 persons, and caused about a million more to leave the country. The Irish influx into Great Britain was suddenly and enormously increased; and petitions poured in from all parts of the kingdom, complaining of the distress caused by this terrible racial invasion.[2] Liverpool, Glasgow, and the South Welsh ports bore the worst of the attack. In 1846 over 280,000 immigrants arrived in Liverpool from Ireland, of whom not more than 123,000 eventually sailed to foreign countries. In 1847 over 300,000 persons landed at Liverpool from Ireland; of these about 130,000 emigrated to the United States, about 50,000 were passengers on business, and the remainder were paupers—half-naked, starving, and often diseased. At Glasgow the numbers entering were smaller, but still alarming; between June 15th and August 17th, 1847, the port received 26,335 persons from Ireland. In South Wales the towns most severely affected were Swansea, Cardiff, and Newport.[3]

From these main points of entry the horde of starving, vagrant Irish pushed on into the interior of the country, carrying with them the famine-fever, dysentery, and smallpox. Many of the Irish landing at Liverpool went on to Manchester, to the West Riding, or through Cheshire to Staffordshire and Derbyshire. From Bristol the Irish passed on through Bath,

---

[1] E.g. *1821 Census*, pp. 496–7, 518, 538; *1831 Census*, II, pp. 942–3, 998, 1020–1, 1038–9; cf. Hansard, XLI, pp. 891–2, 1399; *N.S.*, XVI, p. 229; *N.S.*, XVIII, p. 959.

[2] T. W. Grimshaw, *Facts and Figures about Ireland*, 1893, p. 6; Weber, p. 64; see also Hansard, *3rd Series*, LXXXIX, pp. 597–8, 612, 770, 1323; XCI, p. 810; etc.

[3] *6th Rept. Set. P.R.*, 1847, pp. 57, 59; *1851 Census of Ireland*, Pt. V, Vol. I, pp. 278, 305; *Rept. P.R.*, 1854, pp. 358–70, 478, 481, 503, etc.

and threatened to overrun such south-western counties as Dorset and Devon, which until then had been comparatively immune. The same intensification of the influx took place round London. In the years following the famine the Irish vagrants made their appearance in great numbers in places where they had never before been seen. Sussex and Hampshire, which had hitherto been almost free from Irish, were now overrun with Irish tramps from March to October, and the influx was still increasing.[1]

The fevers and other diseases which the Irish refugees brought with them into Great Britain spread like wildfire amongst the settled population through the increased overcrowding in the Irish quarters of many towns. In the summer of 1847, out of 1,150 patients in the fever hospital at Glasgow 750 were Irish. Similar reports were made from Edinburgh and other towns of Scotland. Liverpool complained bitterly of the 'thousands of hungry and naked Irish perishing in our streets', and of the pestilences which followed in the train of famine and misery. At Manchester the people living in cellar dwellings were mainly Irish, and the fever introduced in 1847 was still raging in 1854. South Wales was inundated with a flood of half-naked, half-starved, and very filthy Irish from the south-western counties, 'bringing pestilence on their backs, famine in their stomachs'.[2]

A significant feature of the post-famine influx was the increased proportion of women who came over from Ireland. Up to that time the Irish harvesters had not usually brought with them their wives and families; but after the famine there were many references to the employment of Irishwomen in English agriculture. At Richmond, for instance, the English-women complained that market-gardeners were now engaging Irishwomen. At York some of the famine-stricken Irish found work in the cultivation of chicory, for which the district was then noted; and long after that culture had declined Seebohm

---

[1] *6th Rept. Set. P.R.*, 1847, pp. 57, 180; *Repts. Set. P.R.*, 1850, pp. 86, 88–9, 97; *Rept. P.R.*, 1854, pp. 443–5.
[2] *Ibid.*, pp. 358, 474–93; *1851 Census of Ireland*, Pt. V, Vol. I, p. 305.

M

Rowntree observed that some of the Irishwomen remaining in the city got their living by field labour, often tramping out for miles in the early morning to their work. This increased use of women's labour in agriculture was noticed also in Ireland itself after the famine.[1]

The year 1851 marked the climax of the post-famine influx, and the distribution of the Irish in Great Britain at that time is therefore particularly interesting (see Map G in Appendix). Between 1841 and 1851 the total number of Irish in Great Britain had increased from 419,256 persons to 727,326 persons. Allowing for wastage by death and secondary emigration, it is evident that at least half-a-million Irish people entered Great Britain during the ten years. This great influx did not, however, alter appreciably the general distribution of the Irish in Great Britain; it merely strengthened the existing tendency to concentration in the great towns, especially round the main points of entry on the west coast.

The problem of migration directly attributable to the famine filled the years 1847–54. In a broader sense, also, the middle of the century was the turning point of the Irish migration to this country. The population of Ireland, which was increasing rapidly during the first half of the nineteenth century, declined steadily in the second half. This was largely due to increased emigration. Before the famine there was some reluctance in Ireland towards emigration; after the famine a great wave of overseas movement set in, affecting a wide range of social classes. Among those eager to emigrate were domestic servants, mechanics, town artisans, country labourers, and 'even strong farmers'. With increased mobility came a change of direction away from Great Britain and towards the United States. Not only the seasonal immigration of harvesters, but also the influx of permanent settlers into England, began to shrink from about this time; and as the nineteenth century advanced the percentage of Irish-born persons living in Great Britain decreased steadily.

---

[1] *A. & P.*, 1847–8, XV, No. 987, II: *Report on Vagrancy*, by W. D. Boase, p. 18; *6th Rept. Set. P.R.*, 1847, pp. 284–5; B. S. Rowntree: *Poverty*, pp. 9–10; *Rept. P.R.*, 1854, p. 91.

SOCIAL EFFECTS

The main social significance of the Irish influx lay in its tendency to lower the wages and standard of living of the English wage-earning classes. This clash of social standards had been clearly foreseen by the Committee on Emigration in 1827. 'Two different rates of wages and two different conditions of the labouring classes cannot permanently co-exist. One of two results appears to be inevitable: the Irish population must be raised towards the standard of the English or the English depressed towards that of the Irish. The question appears to your Committee to resolve itself into the simple point whether the wheat-fed population of Great Britain shall or shall not be supplanted by the potato-fed population of Ireland.' Cobbett put the same point of view more picturesquely in 1834. There were, he said, three countries under the Government's control. 'One of them had meat and bread and knives and forks, the other had oatmeal and brose and horn spoons, and the third had only potatoes and paws.' Was England also to become a country of 'potatoes and paws'?[1]

To contemporary observers the question might well seem to be answered in the great rush of famine-stricken and diseased Irish peasants to Great Britain in the years following 1846. The disastrous social effect of the Irish influx was, however, already apparent in the 'thirties. Much of the evil arose from the lower standard of living general in Ireland, which was transplanted by the immigrants into their new environment. The Irish in Great Britain always lived in the cheapest houses; families were often to be found sharing house with several other families, and they retained their native practice of keeping pigs in the house. With this lower standard of living went a lower efficiency as workmen, and a worse moral tone. The Irish were less provident, and more given to drunkenness; they were slovenly, careless, and stupid. On this account they were not usually put in charge of power-driven machinery, and were necessarily given the lower-paid work. They formed a submerged

[1] *3rd Rept. Emig.*, 1827, p. 7; Hansard, *3rd Series*, XXIV, p. 429.

class, always tending to drag down their neighbours to a lower level of living. 'Where they are a majority they banish providence, temperance, and quiet from the neighbourhood in which they reside.'[1]

Their effect in dragging down wages was most painfully seen in the case of handloom weaving, but was also a subject of complaint in agriculture. In the south-west of Scotland there were complete colonies of Irish weavers, and it was said that whenever an employer wished to reduce wages 'it is ten to one but the Irish are the first to accept his terms'. In agriculture there were complaints that the Irish were beating down wages in the southern Midlands, from Gloucestershire right across England to Lincolnshire.[2] This result of the influx is, indeed, hardly to be wondered at when the wages current in Ireland are compared with those in England. The ordinary labourer in Ireland got from sixpence to a shilling a day; more than a shilling was rare. In Great Britain he might earn as much as twelve shillings a week. In Manchester the bricklayers' labourers, a class very largely recruited from the Irish immigrants, were in 1835 earning sixteen to eighteen shillings a week. The Irishman was thus able to accept much less than the wages current in England, and yet be considerably better paid than he had been at home in Ireland.

One of the most important effects of the Irish influx was its influence on the development of an organized wage-earning class in England. Any such intrusion of a foreign (and lower) social standard necessarily tends to break up the solidarity of the labouring classes and retard the growth of a stable labour organization. This tendency was strengthened by the fact that many of the Irish regarded their stay in England simply as a means of earning sufficient money to take them to America.

A young unmarried man can earn two or three fold the amount necessary for his own maintenance according to the usage of his class in this country [Ireland]. Half a year's saving of this surplus may enable him to go well

---

[1] *Rept. I.P.*, 1835, G, pp. x, xi, xiv, 67; *Repts. Hd. Lm. Wvrs., Yorks.*, 1840, p. 572.
[2] *Ibid., South Scotland*, 1839, p. 19; *Lords' Rept. P.L.*, 1831, pp. 203, 295.

clad to England; there he may in a few months realize a sufficient sum to enable him to seek his fortune in America.[1]

From the employers' point of view the convenience of using Irish labour was very clearly stated by Alexander Carlisle (a Paisley cotton manufacturer) in 1835:

Ireland is our market for labour, the supplies of which are regulated on the same principles which regulate the supplies of articles of consumption and commerce.

This had been particularly so (he said) since the introduction of steam navigation between Ireland and England, which

affords peculiar facilities for readily answering every call made by us for additional hands, and also for carrying back whatever may be redundant in the supplies afforded. The boundless coalfields beneath us, and the boundless mines of labour, so to speak, existing for us in Ireland, form together one of the great secrets of the almost unparalleled prosperity of this part of Scotland.

How the system actually worked was described by James Taylor, a silk manufacturer, of Newton Heath, near Manchester. At that time (1835) Taylor employed 190 young Irish persons, aged seven to twenty years, as silk winders.

Eleven out of twelve of the Irish in my employ are Irish born in Ireland. The moment I have a turn-out and am fast for hands I send to Ireland for ten, fifteen, or twenty families. . . . The whole family comes—father, mother, and children. I provide them with no money. . . . The communications are generally made through the friends of parties in my employ. I have no agent in Ireland. I should think that more than four hundred hands have come over to me from Ireland, many of whom left me after they had learned their trade.[2]

The Irish were frequently used as strike-breakers. In a famous cotton strike at Preston in 1854, for instance, the employers 'imported persons from a distance to take the place of the strikers, and a number of the Irish who are now [1912] in the town are the children of parents who came to Preston in 1854'. Not all the Irish 'blacklegs' were so fortunate on this occasion; some

[1] *A. & P.*, 1838, XLVI, No. 270: plans for the relief of helpless poor, etc.; No. 3, by William Trench, p. 8. There were numerous references to this practice of temporary emigration to England, throughout the period.
[2] *Rept. I.P.*, 1835, pp. xxxvi–vii, 68.

of the children, imported for the emergency from a Belfast manufactory, were discharged as soon as the strike was over and shipped back to Dublin as paupers.[1] There was, of course, nothing in all this repugnant to the general opinion of the educated Englishman of the time.

> In the present state of the labour market [said the Rev. A. Campbell, of Liverpool] English labour would be almost unpurchasable if it were not for the competition of Irish labour. The English labourers have unfortunately been taught their rights till they have almost forgotten their duties . . . and in that case we are very frequently able to put on the screw of the Irish competition.

It was, indeed, generally assumed that Irish labour was indispensable to the prosperity of both the manufactures and the agriculture of Great Britain; and the Irish undoubtedly proved useful to the employers in keeping down the level of wages.[2]

Yet it may be questioned whether the employers did not, after all, overreach themselves in their use of Irish labour. The Irish immigrants were very active in many of the social disturbances and labour revolts of the period. A distinction is, perhaps, to be drawn in this respect between the Irish employed in agriculture and those working in the great industrial centres. In agriculture, and rural work generally, the Irish labourers earned a good character as 'being sober, well conducted, and inoffensive . . . living hard and labouring hard'. Even in agriculture, however, their employment frequently led to social disturbances. In 1830–1, for instance, there were destructive fires among the Kent farmsteads, and riots in Cambridgeshire and Lincolnshire, which were attributed in part to popular resentment at the introduction of Irish labour; and later in the decade, there were pitched fights between English and Irish haymakers.[3]

Mention has already been made of the intense hostility

---

[1] H. W. Clemesha, *History of Preston*, 1912, p. 226. *Rept. P.R.*, 1854, pp. 132–3.

[2] *Ibid.*, p. 370. For manufacturers' evidence see *Rept. I.P.*, 1835, G, p. xxxvi; for agricultural evidence see *Lords' Rept. P.L.*, 1831, pp. 158, 168; G. Nicholls, *2nd Rept. P.L., Ireland*, 1838, p. 31; *Repts. Set. P.R.*, 1850, p. 133.

[3] Cobbett, *Political Register, loc. cit.*; *Ann. Reg.*, 1838, Chronicle, p. 961.

between English and Irish labourers working on the construction of new railways during the period. On more than one
occasion this racial hostility broke out in open conflict. In 1838
a regular battle took place near Preston between English weavers
and Irish 'navvies' working on the North Union Railway.
Some hundreds of persons were involved, swords and guns were
used, and many casualties occurred. A still fiercer fight took
place in the following year, on the line of the Chester and
Birkenhead Railway. Three hundred Irish labourers engaged
two hundred and fifty English labourers in a three days' war-
fare which ended only when the Irish were besieged in Childer
Thornton by troops called up from Liverpool and Chester. In
many parts of the country English railway 'navvies' would not
allow Irishmen to work with them, and it was necessary to keep
the two races separate in order to avoid fighting. The intrusion
of Irish workers caused much friction also in industrial centres.
At Manchester it was well known that the Irish weavers did
not get on well with their English fellows, and had to be kept
separate at work; and most of the riots at Manchester in the
early nineteenth century were with the Irish.[1]

Besides being of different race, the Irish were mostly Roman
Catholics in a Protestant country. The revival of Roman
Catholicism through the Irish influx was regarded as alarming,
particularly in the Scottish Lowlands. Glasgow in 1835 was
said to contain more Roman Catholics than all Scotland did
in 1679; and Dundee, where in the later eighteenth century
the Roman Catholics amounted to no more than fifty, contained
in 1835 about five thousand, who were strongly reinforced
before the end of the half-century. At Stockport the hostility
between English and Irish developed into a religious feud. In
June 1852, this broke out in a serious fight, which lasted three
days and was accompanied by some loss of life; the immediate
occasion of the fight was the annual Sunday School procession
of the Catholics through the town.[2]

---

[1] *Ann. Reg.*, 1838, p. 78; *ibid.*, 1839, pp. 200–2; *Rept. S.C.F.*, 1816, p. 313;
many other references in *Rept. on Railway Labourers*, 1846.
[2] *Ann. Reg.*, 1836, Chronicle, p. 71; *ibid.*, 1852, Chronicle, pp. 90–3.

In spite of racial and religious hostility, however, the Irish were very prominent in labour and political organizations in Great Britain. The Irish weavers from Newton Heath took part in the 'Peterloo' demonstration of 1819. In consequence of injuries received on that day Thomas Redford, of Middleton, sued Colonel Hugh Birley for 'unlawful cutting and wounding'; of Redford's two leading witnesses at the trial in 1822, one (Alexander Anderson) was an Irishman who came to Manchester in 1800, and the other (William Mickleroy) defined a bludgeon as 'something like a shilelah'.[1] Mention has already been made of the large proportion of Irish among the Manchester weavers, and their prominence as secretaries and members of the weavers' committees; in Glasgow, also, the Irish weavers (though not particularly active in the work of organization) were the more daring spirits in actual disturbances, and 'more prone to use violence without regard to consequences'. Considering the large proportion of Irish among the Glasgow cotton spinners, it was natural that the spinners' union there in the early 'thirties should have received its chief support from the 'daring character of the Irish'; but it is, perhaps, a little surprising that in the Manchester area, where so few of the cotton spinners were Irish, the leading spirit in the burst of labour combination after 1829 was John Doherty, a cotton spinner from Donegal.[2]

If the Irish were thus prominent in the labour struggles of the early 'thirties, they were still more active in the Chartist disturbances later in the decade. The movement in the north of England was largely recruited from the distressed handloom weavers, of whom a majority were said to be Irish. Their leader, Feargus O'Connor, was 'as much an Irish Nationalist as he was a Chartist';[3] and among the other Chartist delegates, agitators with Celtic names such as O'Brien, O'Neill, M'Grath, and Murphy were plentiful.

[1] Samuel Bamford, *Passages in the Life of a Radical*, 1893 ed., II, p. 153; *Ann. Reg.*, 1822, App., pp. 353-6.
[2] *Rept. I.P.*, 1835, G, pp. 28, 108-9.
[3] Hovell, *The Chartist Movement*, p. 283; D. Read and E. L. H. Glasgow, *Feargus O'Connor, Irishman and Chartist* (1961).

CHAPTER X

EMIGRATION

IRISH AND SCOTTISH EMIGRATION

Aᴺ adequate account of overseas emigration is beyond the scope of this book; but some treatment of the subject is necessary as a background to the study of internal migration. Emigration and internal migration are complementary aspects of the same general movement of population, having different characteristics in some respects, but springing from the same causes, and reacting continually upon each other.

All the various currents of migration within the United Kingdom, which have been described in the preceding chapers, were ebbing and flowing in close relationship to similar streams of British emigration to countries beyond the seas. The unemployed agricultural labourers of the southern counties, and the destitute weavers of East Anglia and the West Country, were not only seeking work in London, or Birmingham, or South Wales, but also in America, Australia, or South Africa. Starving cotters from the Highlands of Scotland were not only crowding into Glasgow, but building up a new Scotland in Canada. Poverty-stricken peasants from Ireland were creating grave social problems, not only in England, but also in the United States. Unless the connection between migration and emigration is constantly borne in mind, the full significance of the movements may easily be missed.

The Irish influx, for instance, had a very serious effect upon the question of emigration from England. There was apparently a great surplus of agricultural labour in some parts of England for which the natural outlet was considered to be emigration to the colonies; but this seemed useless in view of the distressed masses of population in Ireland, ready to flock into England to fill the vacant places of the emigrants. This point of view was

clearly expressed by the Committee on the State of the Poorer
Classes in Ireland in 1830: 'Emigration as a remedial measure
is more applicable to Ireland than to any other part of the
Empire. . . . Emigration from Great Britain, if effectual as a
remedy, must tend to raise the rate of wages in the latter
country, and thus to increase the temptation of the immigration
of the Irish labourer.' It was, therefore, essential that any
schemes for assisted emigration should apply primarily to
Ireland.[1]

The reasons in favour of this policy were strengthened by the
fact that, even in the eighteenth century, both the Irish and the
Scots had shown a much greater disposition to emigrate than
had the English peasantry. In the period before the American
War of Independence the emigration from north Ireland was
considerable, arising partly from the depression of the linen
manufacture, and partly as an aftermath of rebellion at home.
Altogether 43,720 persons are said to have emigrated from the
five ports of Belfast, Newry, Derry, Larne, and Portrush between
1769 and 1774.[2] In the same period emigration was also taking
place from many parts of the Scottish Highlands, especially
from the Hebrides and from the shires of Sutherland, Inverness,
and Argyll. This emigration of 'tacksmen', husbandmen and
farmers from the north and west of Scotland was said by the
Edinburgh Magazine of the time to be numerically unimportant;
but it caused much discussion, and was a source of grave anxiety
to the Government.[3]

The danger of excessive emigration from Scotland was
brought to the notice of the Government as the result of a trial
of Paisley weavers for unlawful combination, in 1773. 'As some
thousands of weavers were concerned, and threatened to go off

[1] *2nd Rept. Emig.*, 1827, Evid., qq. 559–60, p. 46; *Ann. Reg.*, 1827, App.,
pp. 385–6; *Rept. S.P. Ireland*, 1830, p. 49.
[2] Arthur Young, *Tour in Ireland*, Pt. I, pp. 108, 112, 125; Pt. II, pp. 30–1;
C.H.O.P., 1770–2, pp. 478–9, 571; *ibid.*, 1773–5, p. 67; *Gentleman's Magazine*, XLIV, p. 332.
[3] Sinclair, I, p. 448; III, pp. 246–7, 582; IV, pp. 132–3, 140 ff.; J. Murray
Gibbon, *Scots in Canada*, 1911, pp. 63–5; Arthur Young, *Political Arithmetic*,
1774, pp. 319–21. Cf. also M. I. Adam, 'The Highland Emigration of
1770', in *Scot. Hist. R.*, XVI, pp. 280–3.

in a body to America, the trial became very delicate.' Lord Justice Clerk Miller was terrified by this threat of wholesale emigration. 'I pray God, for the sake of this country, that such ideas of migration to America may not become epidemical. . . . In this part of the kingdom transportation to America begins to lose every characteristic of punishment.' About the same time, at an Ayr county meeting, Sir Adam Ferguson produced a printed paper which had been circulated throughout Ireland and the south-west of Scotland to induce people to emigrate to North America. Very attractive terms were offered to intending settlers, and the attempt met with considerable success in the north-west Highlands and in Ireland. The movement was also spreading to the Lowlands, and affecting not only the husband-men but also some of the better sort of farmers and mechanics. Joint-stock associations were formed for buying land in the colonies, and the Lord Justice Clerk thought that the movement might in time 'as effectually depopulate this country as the mines of Peru and Mexico have depopulated Spain'.[1]

The emigration from both Scotland and Ireland revived unabated at the end of the American War. In the year following the peace of 1783 eleven thousand persons are said to have emigrated from the port of Dublin alone, the emigrants still coming mainly from the north of Ireland. In Scotland, also, the emigration continued as before to be mainly from the Highlands of the north-west. Even in the first fifteen years of the nineteenth century, in spite of the war with France, several schemes for colonization from the north-west Highlands were projected or carried out. Telford, in making his 'Survey of the Coasts and Central Highlands of Scotland', found that in the previous year (1801) about three thousand persons had left the north-western Highlands, and three times that number were preparing to go. In 1803 a further emigration from Glengarry received the official support of the Government, and a settlement was made in Canada near the earlier emigrants from the same district. In the same year Lord Selkirk organized a successful movement from the Highlands to Prince Edward Island; he promoted a

[1] *C.H.O.P.*, 1773–5, pp. 92, 95, 98, 204–6, 218–19, 384, 398–400.

168 LABOUR MIGRATION IN ENGLAND

second scheme in 1811, though this was not carried out so happily. In 1813 Colonel Talbot, a member of the Lieutenant-Governor's staff in Canada, began a regular system of organized emigration from Scotland, and by 1823 is said to have had twelve thousand people under his control at Port Talbot, on Lake Erie.[1]

After the end of the Napoleonic wars the Celtic emigration became still more pronounced. In 1815 there was a considerable emigration from Scotland to North America, and in the same year letters from Newfoundland reported that the arrivals from Ireland exceeded any previously recorded by the Customs authorities.[2] Emigration from Ireland had by this time become a movement to be encouraged rather than repressed. During the French wars the extension of tillage and of the cultivation of the potato had led to a reckless increase of population in Ireland ... 'a more rapid increase than has probably taken place in any other country of Europe'. In the depression of agriculture after 1813 it became clear that the population had been 'pushed much beyond the industry and present resources of the country'. For this over-abundant population in Ireland some outlet must be found, if only to prevent it from flooding England with its misery.[3]

The most pressing problem was to stimulate movement from the southern counties of Ireland, which were grievously over-populated. In 1821 Cork, a county mainly agricultural and containing many barren tracts, had an enumerated population of 730,444. The whole of London at that date contained only 1,378,947, or less than twice the population of Cork. Limerick, with 277,477, had a larger population than Warwickshire, which included such manufacturing towns as Birmingham and

---

[1] *J.H.C.*, LVIII, App. 42, p. 936; *Rept. of the Coasts and Central Highlands of Scotland*, 1803, p. 15; J. Murray Gibbon, *op. cit.*, p. 70; S. C. Johnson, p. 11; M. I. Adam, 'The Highland Emigrations of 1783–1803', in *Scot. Hist. R.*, XVII, pp. 73–87.

[2] *Ann. Reg.*, 1815, Chronicle, pp. 35, 41.

[3] On the alarming increase of population in Ireland during the late eighteenth and early nineteenth centuries see *Rept. Employ. Ireland*, 1823, Rept. p. 7, Evid. pp. 28, 121, 123, 154; Malthus, Bk. II, Chap. X; and K. H. Connell, *The Population of Ireland, 1750–1845*, 1950.

Coventry. In 1821–2 there was a famine in Ireland almost comparable with the famine of 1846–7; and a Parliamentary Committee of Enquiry in 1823 found that the distress was most urgent in the southern and western counties. The Government voted £15,000 to facilitate emigration from the south of Ireland to the Cape of Good Hope. Nevertheless, it was remarked in 1826, and again in 1830, that emigration from Cork was still not so active as from other parts of Ireland. The belief still lingered that government emigration schemes were only 'a genteel mode of transportation'.[1]

Shortly after 1830 emigration from Ireland became more general, taking place from the south and west as well as from the north. Between 1831 and 1841 the average annual emigration from Ireland to the colonies or foreign countries is said to have been about forty thousand persons; the average annual emigration from the whole of the United Kingdom during the same period was about 74,700 persons. If the figures are even approximately correct, the movement from Ireland outweighed the emigration from England, Wales, and Scotland combined. Of the Irish emigrants to the colonies or foreign countries the largest proportion (twenty per cent.) embarked at Belfast, but nearly the same numbers were now sailing from Cork; and emigrants were also leaving by way of Sligo, Dublin, and Londonderry.[2]

Despite this general emigration, the population of Ireland continued to grow with ominous rapidity, and to 'press upon the means of subsistence'. The census of 1841 showed that in the rural parts of Ireland 46 per cent. of the families occupied only a single room each (with the pig); in the towns 36 per cent. of the families occupied only a single room each, and two or three families sometimes shared the same room. To a population in such a state of congestion every scarcity of food was bound to bring the scourge of epidemic disease. Food scarcity

[1] *Rept. Employ. Ireland*, 1823, p. 4; *Rept. Emig.*, 1826, Evid., q. 2185, p. 200; *Repts. S.P. Ireland*, 1830, q. 3108; cf. Hansard, *N.S.*, XII, p. 1360.
[2] *1841 Census of Ireland*, Rept., pp. x, xxviii; *1851 Census of Ireland*, Pt. V, Vol. I, pp. 210–11, 243; *1851 Census of Great Britain*, Pt. I, Vol. I, App. to Rept., p. cxxxii, Table 47.

had occurred in Ireland at fairly frequent intervals since the Middle Ages, and had almost always been attended with typhus; conditions were now again pointing unmistakably to the danger of social catastrophe.[1]

The popular consciousness of impending disaster found expression in the sudden increase of emigration from Ireland in the years *preceding* the great famine. In 1842 the emigrants from Ireland were estimated to reach the abnormal figure of 89,686, out of a total for the United Kingdom of 126,509. At Dublin it was stated that more people had embarked for America than in any previous year, and a similar report was made from Limerick. At Athlone great shoals of people were reported to be passing through on their way to Dublin for America; and corroborative accounts in the same strain of astonishment were received from many other ports.[2]

From 1841 to the end of 1845 the emigration from Ireland averaged 61,242 yearly. The number rose to 105,955 in 1846, and to more than double this number in 1847. In the succeeding years the movement fluctuated in strength, reaching its highest point in 1851, when the emigrants amounted to 249,721; after this the number gradually decreased to 150,222 in 1854. In 1853, when the British emigration statistics first distinguished emigrants as coming from England, Scotland, or Ireland, the Irish emigration was *much more than double* that from the rest of the United Kingdom. Altogether nearly a million people left Ireland in six years, and the population shrank from 8,175,124 in 1841 to 6,552,385 in 1851.[3]

In many ways the great famine of 1846–7 was the beginning of modern Irish history; it was especially important as a turning point in the history of population. From that time there was a steady diminution of the population of Ireland throughout the rest of the century, caused mainly by emigration to America and

---

[1] Cf. O'Connell's motion on famine and disease in Ireland, in Hansard, *3rd Series*, LXXXIII, pp. 1052, 1064.

[2] *1851 Census of Ireland*, Pt. V, Vol. I, p. 230.

[3] *Ibid.*, p. 243; E. Levasseur, 'Emigration in the Nineteenth Century', trans. in *S.J.*, XLVIII, p. 70; G. B. Longstaff, 'Rural Depopulation', in *ibid.*, LVI, pp. 392–3.

accompanied by a rise in the standard of living. The total loss of population in the latter half of the century amounted to more than forty per cent., the greatest absolute and proportional decrease being in the province of Munster.

Emigration from Scotland between 1815 and 1850 had no such dramatic effects as the contemporary movement from Ireland; nevertheless, a considerable emigration went on from most of the highland shires and from many parts of the Lowlands. Up to the 'twenties the movement had no appreciable effect in checking the increase in population. From Cambuslang (Lanarkshire) it was reported that emigration had merely made room for more inhabitants; and similar reports were made by many highland parishes.[1] In the later 'twenties, however, emigration began to cause local decreases of population in many shires, both highland and lowland. Between 1831 and 1841 local depopulation through emigration became common in all the highland shires without exception, and the situation was almost as serious in the shires along the southern border. In the Lowlands the most persistent reports came from Roxburgh; yet the population of that shire increased quite steadily throughout the half-century, and did not reach its maximum until 1861. Many other shires were more unfortunate. Perth, Kinross, and Argyll reached their maximum populations in 1831, Inverness in 1841, Sutherland, Ross and Cromarty, Dumfries, Kirkcudbright, and Wigtown in 1851.[2]

ENGLISH EMIGRATION

Large-scale emigration began much later from England than from Ireland and Scotland, and up to the middle of the nineteenth century was of much less proportionate importance. During the first fifteen years of the century the war with France prevented any considerable emigration from England—directly through wartime restrictions on overseas travelling, and indirectly through the prosperity of agriculture. As soon

[1] *1821 Census*, pp. 514, 519; cf. pp. 528, 532.
[2] *1851 Census*, Pt. I, Vol. II, Scotland Divn., *passim*; G. B. Longstaff, *loc. cit.*, p. 389.

as the war was over, however, emigration became the panacea for all social ills. Malthus himself, while he recognized the inadequacy of emigration, as a general remedy for over-population, strongly recommended it as 'a partial and temporary expedient' to relieve the post-war burden of unemployment. Government assistance to emigration began immediately on the conclusion of hostilities; and transports sailing from the Clyde to bring back soldiers from Canada were advertised to take passengers out at low rates. The official explanation of this was that 'the object of the Government was merely to divert those who had been determined to emigrate, from the United States to Canada'.[1]

The emigrants' preference for the rebellious colonies, which had been clearly shown in the critical days of 1775, thus persisted now that American independence was recognized; this was a source of anxiety to the British Government throughout the earlier nineteenth century. In the years after 1815 the attraction of the United States remained 'unabated'. Portsmouth was crowded with intending emigrants; from Havre, also, every packet boat conveyed numerous passengers to America. As a counterblast to American attractions the Government decided to encourage emigration to the Cape of Good Hope, which had been ceded to England in 1814. A Parliamentary grant of £50,000 was made in July 1819, for a colonization scheme at Algoa Bay. The idea proved attractive, and by the beginning of November, in the same year, so many applications had been received that the Government closed the lists.[2]

A similar scheme was promoted in Nottinghamshire, where the distress among the framework knitters was acute. In this case two subscriptions of £5,000 each were raised—one for emigration, the other for relief works. The colonization scheme was, however, distrusted by the poorer classes who, with bitter memories of Luddite days, called it 'transportation'. Very few people could be got to emigrate from Nottinghamshire, and

[1] Malthus, Bk. III, Chap. IV; Smart, I, pp. 439–40; Hansard, XXX, pp. 52–3.
[2] *Ann. Reg.*, 1819, pp. 25–6, 91; Hansard, XI, pp. 1549 ff.

half of the subscriptions had to be returned. Eventually two vessels left Hull for Algoa Bay; but the great majority of the emigrants taking part in that settlement were from the London district. Some operatives who refused to go to South Africa went over to France, as offering more scope to manufacturing skill. About the same time there were other (independent) emigrations to America from Nottinghamshire and Yorkshire; but the total number of emigrants was small, and (like the contemporary Scottish emigrations) did not cause even local decreases of population.[1]

Between 1821 and 1827 the Government made four grants in aid of emigration, amounting to £68,760, £15,000, £30,000, and £20,480 respectively. In 1826 a Committee on Emigration was appointed and issued an important report, recommending colonization in the overseas possessions as the only means of mitigating the evils arising from a redundant population.[2] As the result, an elaborate scheme was set on foot for emigration to Nova Scotia, New Brunswick, and Prince Edward Island, but the project was eventually abandoned. The contemporary industrial depression made it doubtful whether the emigration of handloom weavers was not more urgently needed than that of agricultural labourers, and the danger of stimulating an already serious influx from Ireland helped to kill the scheme. Moreover, the probability that emigrants to Canada would cross into the United States[3] took away the Government's hopes of being repaid for the expense occasioned.

Nevertheless, it was in this decade (1821–31) that emigration first became an appreciable drain on the population of England. The census returns for 1831 reported local decreases of population through emigration from numerous districts in the south of England, from Cornwall and Wiltshire in the west to Kent and Lincoln in the east. In Nottinghamshire, also, the emigration was now leading to local decreases; there was a strong

---

[1] *Lords' Rept. P.L.*, 1831, pp. 238–41; *1821 Census*, pp. 249, 378, 417; E. A. Belcher, *Migration within the Empire*, 1924, p. 101.
[2] *Rept. Emig.*, 1826, p. 4.
[3] See J. B. McMaster's *History of the People of the United States*, VI, p. 79.

movement from the East Riding of Yorkshire (where the agricultural distress was serious) and from the lead-mining districts of the North Riding. Of the East Anglian counties, Suffolk was apparently losing most heavily;[1] but local decreases through emigration were also reported from counties so widely scattered as Norfolk, Northumberland, Sussex, Caernarvon, and Pembroke.

Between 1830 and 1833, there was a great increase in the volume of emigration, occasioned partly by the prevalent agrarian depression. Viscount Goderich reported that in 1831 the voluntary (i.e. independent?) emigration from England and Ireland was nearly double that of any previous year. In 1832 the recorded yearly emigration from the United Kingdom for the first time exceeded a hundred thousand, and in 1833 the Committee on Agriculture reported that 'emigration has taken place from all parts of the United Kingdom, and continues increasing from year to year'. The demand for labour in some parts of America was at that time very keen: railway and canal contractors on more than one occasion sent agents to Great Britain to recruit labourers.[2]

Emigration as an official method of relieving pauperism continued to be regarded with suspicion. Cobbett, in the 'twenties, had raged against 'the folly, the stupidity, the insanity, the presumption, the insufferable emptiness and insolence and barbarity, of those numerous wretches who have now the audacity to propose to *transport* the people of England, upon the principle of the monster Malthus'. In 1831 the National Union of the Working Classes, in its petition concerning the corn laws, annual parliaments, universal suffrage, and vote by ballot, included the plea 'that there might be no Transportation Laws, and no Starvation Laws'. The presenter of the petition (Hunt) interpreted 'Transportation Laws' as referring to the scheme of the Colonial Secretary for compulsory emigration, which the

---

[1] *1831 Census*, I, pp. 77, 260, 267, 269–71, 344, 482, 486; II, pp. 607–23, 695, 734–45, 770–85; see also *Lords' Rept. P.L.*, 1831, pp. 14, 156, 198–9; *2nd Rept. on Agric. Distress*, 1836, Evid., qq. 5430–49, pp. 53–4.

[2] Hansard, *3rd Series*, IX, p. 1147; *Ann. Reg.*, 1833, App., p. 350; McMaster, *op. cit.*, p. 81.

petition characterized as 'an unjust, wicked, and unconstitutional measure'.[1]

From the standpoint of the central and local authorities, however, assisted emigration was an effective and cheap method of disposing of the surplus population. Many parishes, especially in the southern counties, were financing emigration as a relief to the poor rates. In Wiltshire, for instance, the parish of Corsley organized an emigration to America in 1830; and in the following years parties went out to Canada, the United States, Australia, and South Africa from several other places in the West Country clothing district. Parishes in Kent and Sussex, also, were adopting the same remedy. The accounts received of emigrants' progress overseas at this period were very mixed. Some were doing well, but it is evident from both British and American sources that the labour market in America was becoming temporarily glutted, and that the emigration fever among the English labourers was cooling.[2]

By 1841 emigration had caused local decreases of population over a great part of southern and eastern England. Of the counties on the east coast, only the mining county of Durham had failed to report such decreases, and on the south coast only Dorset and Hampshire, where the growth of Southampton had produced a counterbalancing influx. The attractive force of London had checked emigration from the counties of Hertford, Bedford, and Huntingdon to the north, and from Surrey and Berkshire on the south-east. In general it may be said that by 1841 emigration was causing an appreciable (but not alarming) drain of population from most parts of southern and eastern England, except round the rapidly growing towns and ports. The north-western and north-midland parts of the country were as yet not suffering even local decreases of population through emigration, though it is known that considerable numbers of agricultural workers had emigrated from such counties as Derby, and an uncertain number of artisans and operatives from all the manufacturing counties.

[1] Hansard, *3rd Series*, V, pp. 927–8.
[2] *P.L.C. Rept.*, 1834, App. A, Pt. I, Nos. 8, 12, and 15, *passim*.

In the next decade (1841–51) the fever of emigration spread yet further over the country, though persisting most strongly in the south-eastern counties. Hertford, Surrey, and Hampshire still remained comparatively unaffected; but Bedford and Huntingdon were now feeling the drain. In the south-west, emigration was general even in Dorset, which had previously been outside the main current of the movement. In the midlands and north, the drain of emigration had spread from Northampton to Leicester, Rutland, Derby, and the agricultural parts of the West Riding. In Wales, every county except Anglesey had by 1851 reported some local depopulation through emigration.

Artisans' Emigration

The emigration of artisans attracted a good deal of attention throughout the early nineteenth century, especially in relation to the growth of foreign industrial competition. In the eighteenth century a comprehensive body of legislation had grown up forbidding the emigration of artificers in the chief trades of the kingdom. This policy was especially strong in the decade 1780–90, when the former American colonies became foreign territory, and when English manufacturing industry was adopting many technical inventions.[1]

The number of these restrictive Acts implies that serious efforts were being made by foreign agents to attract skilled English workmen out of the country, and this is supported also by other evidence. The Home Office papers of the time contain much correspondence concerning schemes for the emigration of iron-workers to Continental countries, especially to Sweden and Russia; and attention has already been drawn to the threats of wholesale emigration from the textile districts of Scotland. In the closing years of the century public meetings were held in Manchester to raise funds for the prosecution of persons attempting to export machinery and seduce artisans;

[1] See *22 Geo. III, c.* 60; *25 Geo. III, c.* 67; *39 Geo. III, c.* 56, etc.

but this did not prevent the well-known manufacturer Liévin Bauwens from smuggling forty Englishmen and seventeen spinning mules, bearing 16,000 spindles, into the Netherlands in 1805.[1]

In 1811 the English and Scottish cotton centres, in petitioning against the obnoxious Orders in Council, declared that 'great numbers of Artists have been compelled, for want of employment . . . to emigrate to foreign countries'. In the post-war trade depression, however, some emigrants from the textile districts were as hardly hit as the workers who remained at home. British weavers returning from America in 1816 reported that they could not get a livelihood in America because the market there was flooded with cheap British goods. The American ports were said to be crowded with British emigrants wanting a passage home.[2] Nevertheless, the displaced workers in decaying textile trades continued to regard emigration as the most hopeful remedy for their troubles. In 1817 the Leeds wool-dressers and shearmen petitioned unsuccessfully for assistance in emigrating to North America. They declared that through the spread of gig-mills and shears during the previous ten years many of the wool-dressers had been reduced to poverty—yet the laws prevented them from emigrating. In the following year they presented a further petition asking for permission to emigrate to foreign countries; but this petition also was ordered 'to lie on the table'.[3]

By this time the demand for the freedom of artisans' emigration had become a favourite method of calling attention to distress in the manufacturing districts. The Carlisle weavers, for instance, were in May 1819, rioting against a reduction in the wage-rates for weaving gingham; they held a meeting on the sands, and resolved to petition the Prince Regent to send them all to America—in the same spirit as the London

---

[1] Timperley's *Manchester Historical Recorder*, 1845, p. 56; Scrap Book in Chetham's Library: 31366, p. 64; Chapman and Knoop: *V.C.H. Lancs.*, II, p. 354.
[2] *J.H.C.*, LXVI, pp. 311, 383; *Ann. Reg.*, 1816, Chronicle, p. 176.
[3] Hammond, *The Skilled Labourer*, p. 189, quoting H.O. papers; *J.H.C.*, LXXII, p. 49; *ibid.*, LXXIII, p. 263.

Irish were then petitioning to be sent home to cultivate the
bogs of Ireland. In the following year the Glasgow operatives
made similar petitions, asking that means might be granted to
enable them to emigrate to Quebec. Their prayer was not
answered; but the 1821 census return for Glasgow remarks on
the falling-off of population there since the post-war trade
depression, through emigration and kindred causes.[1]

In the programme of the Radical reformers restriction of the
emigration of artisans ranked with prohibition of workmen's
combinations as a flagrant offence against *laissez-faire* principles.
The principle of freedom was recognized by the Committee on
the Poor Laws in 1817, which recommended that the restrictive
legislation should be repealed and reasonable facilities granted
for the emigration of artisans to the colonies.[2] During the next
seven years the kindred questions of industrial combination and
emigration were vigorously advertised by a little knot of
politicians drawing their inspiration from Francis Place. The
Gorgon—the mouth-piece of the movement for the abolition
of the Combination Laws—also advocated emigration as a
means of relieving the labour market. Many persons who
could not support the repeal of the Combination Laws were in
favour of allowing artisans' emigration. When Joseph Hume
asked for a Committee on the two questions, 'Mr. Huskisson
shrunk back. He advised Mr. Hume to forego his intention of
moving for a Committee on the Combination Laws, and to
take in only the emigration of artisans and the exportation of
machinery.'[3] Eventually a Committee was formed, in 1824,
to discuss both questions. Very conflicting evidence was
received as to the numbers of artisans who had emigrated. One
witness said that as many as 16,000 had emigrated during 1822
and 1823. It was said that in several large factories in France
the majority of the workmen were obtained from Scotland or
England, while a more cautious estimate made out that there
were only between 1,300 and 1,400 English workmen in

[1] *Ann. Reg.*, 1819, Chronicle, p. 31; *J.H.C.*, LXXV, p. 403; *1821 Census*,
p. 520.
[2] *Ann. Reg.*, 1817, App., p. 288.
[3] Graham Wallas, *Life of Francis Place*, p. 209.

France altogether.[1] The Committee recommended 'that artisans may be at liberty to go abroad, and to return home, whenever they may be disposed, in the same manner as other classes of the community'; and the laws against artisans' emigration were eventually repealed at the same time as those forbidding workmen's combinations.[2]

In the trade 'slump' after 1825 the new freedom of emigration was eagerly used by workers in the textile and metal trades. In 1825–6 several vessels sailed from Liverpool with Yorkshire and Lancashire operatives for American print-works, and Parliament was again asked to help in sending out handloom weavers to the colonies from Glasgow and Lanarkshire, and from Carlisle. Between 1826 and 1828 Parliament received nearly a hundred similar petitions for assistance to artisans' emigration, mainly from the cotton districts of Scotland, but including one from the 'Manchester Emigration Society'; other petitions were from Balfron (Stirling), Glasgow, 'Natives of Ireland residing in Glasgow', and the 'Irish Friendly Emigrant Society' of Renfrew. In later years petitions to the same effect came from Manchester, from 'Members of the United Emigration Societies of Glasgow and neighbourhood', and from 'Hutcheson's Emigration Society'. The Glasgow Spinners' Union made a practice of paying emigration benefit in order to prevent the excess of labour from depressing wages. Henry Houldsworth, a Glasgow manufacturer, stated that between 1830 and 1833 not less than eighty or a hundred spinners were shipped off in this way from Glasgow, out of a total number of between 700 and 800; one-half of all the mechanics educated in Scotland were said to emigrate, some to England, others to America.[3]

The desire for emigration was nearly as strong in some of the English manufacturing towns. In 1830 an American ship's captain advertised in the *Manchester Times* that at a certain date he would be at a Deansgate inn to contract with passengers

[1] W. O. Henderson, *Britain and Industrial Europe, 1750–1870*, 1954, p. 141.
[2] Smart, II, pp. 229–30; *5 Geo. IV, cc.* 95–7.
[3] *J.H.C.*, LXXXV, p. 423; Hansard, *N.S.*, XVI, p. 229; *Rept. Mfs.*, 1833, pp. 311, 317; S. C. Johnson, p. 57; Smart, II, p. 334; *J.H.C.*, LXXXII, *passim; ibid.*, LXXXVII, p. 497.

for Baltimore. On the appointed day he found the inn sur-
rounded by a crowd of between 600 and 700 persons offering
their services as bondsmen in return for their passage to
America. Many weavers from Bolton emigrated to New York
or Philadelphia about that time; and from the midland iron
districts emigration had taken place to France, the emigrants
being generally skilled iron-workers.[1]

After a brief spell of prosperity between 1833 and 1836 the
industrial centres settled down to a prolonged period of bad
trade; the years from 1841 to 1843 were a time of especially
severe distress, and mention has already been made of the
increased emigration of artisans in those years from the northern
textile districts. The partial revival of trade in 1843 marked the
beginning of a new era in trade union policy; revolutionary
unionism was being abandoned, along with political Chartism,
and the labour leaders of the more 'respectable' trades were
accepting the current middle-class views of the orthodox
economists. So far as emigration was concerned, this did not
involve any break with the policy of the earlier labour organizations. Emigration and the threat of emigration had been a
recognized weapon of labour since the eighteenth century; and
many of the early unions had offered emigration benefits to their
members.[2]

This policy accorded well with the economic views of the new
trade union leaders, who had accepted the view that wages
must depend on the relation between demand and supply in
each class of labour. From this it seemed to follow that one of
the most effective means of permanently raising wages was by
reducing the supply of labour. For some fifteen years after 1843
many of the larger trade societies maintained emigration funds,
and in some cases organized emigration societies, much in the
same way as had been done in pre-Chartist times. In 1844, for
instance, the Operative Potters organized a 'Potters' Joint-
stock and Emigration Company' for the purchase of 12,000
acres of land in the Western States of America, to be re-sold

[1] McMaster, op. cit., p. 81; Rept. Mfs., 1833, pp. 707–8, 583.
[2] See Webbs' History of Trade Unionism, 1919 ed., Chap. IV.

to members at cost price on the instalment system. Later references show that many Staffordshire potters became members, and emigrated in due course. The *Potters' Examiner* was, in 1848, converted into the *Potters' Examiner and Emigrants' Advocate*, and henceforth was concerned chiefly with the promotion of emigration. Other unions pursuing the same policy included the Flint Glass Makers, the Compositors, the Bookbinders, the Iron Moulders, and the Engineers.[1] The emigration fund was particularly prominent in trade union affairs between 1850 and 1860, but in some societies it lingered on for the rest of the century. It was, of course, an expensive and futile policy, especially as many of the assisted emigrants eventually returned home.

[1] S. C. Johnson, pp. 80–1; Webbs, *op. cit.*, pp. 197, n. 1, 201.

CHAPTER XI

CONCLUSION:
THE PROCESS OF MIGRATION

I

BROADLY regarded, the study of migration in England during the earlier nineteenth century becomes an attempt to visualize the social aspect of the Industrial Revolution. It is by this time a commonplace to emphasize the evolutionary character of the transition, and to deny that the modern phase of economic and social life began with dramatic suddenness between 1760 and 1830. Ideally, the whole prospect of a nation or an industry may be altered in a day by the invention of a new machine or the discovery of some new source of motive energy; but such discoveries ordinarily take whole generations or centuries to become fully absorbed into the fabric of human society.

The tardy, lagging character of economic and social transition is reflected with especial clearness in the movements of population. The workers in a decaying branch of industry do not decide in a body that their occupation is gone; and that they must seek a livelihood elsewhere. They feel an ever-increasing difficulty in maintaining their customary standard of living, and a few of the more enterprising men may migrate to some rising centre of their own industry. The great majority, however, cling to their old homes; in slack seasons they seek the nearest work available, returning to their original occupations at every revival of trade. Even when the last breath of specialized trade has deserted an industrial town, most of the population may be retained inertly, offering through their low standard of living a temptation to the introduction of new industries dependent on low-grade labour. If this is true of an industrial population, it is even more strongly the case with an agricultural population,

182

which is usually of a slower mental habit and has a deeper attachment to its original home.

From such general considerations it seems probable that the population changes which accompanied the Industrial Revolution did not consist of a simple transference of population from the south and east of England to the north and west, as some writers have casually assumed. The most spectacular growth of population occurred, it is true, in the north-western manufacturing counties of which Lancashire is the type; but London, in the south-east, was by far the greatest single centre of attraction, and absorbed the bulk of the migrants from the south and east of England.

All the rising centres of industry and commerce were attracting workers by a process of short-distance migration from the surrounding country; where the attractive force of a large town was exerted over a wide area the inward movement took place usually by stages. The majority of the migrants to the town came from the immediately surrounding counties, their places in turn being taken by migrants from places further away. The characteristic features of this process, up to the middle of the century, are very clearly seen in the statistics of migration collected at the 1851 census.[1]

Of the people who had moved into the three Lancashire towns of Liverpool, Manchester, and Bolton the overwhelming majority had come either from Lancashire and Cheshire or from Ireland. Beyond the inner belt of intense migration was an outer belt showing less strong, but still considerable, movement; this outer belt was bounded on the south-east by Leicestershire, and in other directions lay fairly evenly round the centres of attraction, except for a prolongation through the densely populated counties of Warwick and Gloucester, a prolongation which would disappear if the migrants were expressed as a percentage of the population of their native counties. None of the south-eastern counties had sent many migrants to the Lancashire towns, though there was a large special migration from London.

[1] See Maps D and E in Appendix.

The bulk of the migrants to the West Riding towns of Leeds, Sheffield, and Bradford had come from Yorkshire itself. The outer belt of counties showing considerable migration was in this case limited to Lancashire, Derbyshire, and Nottinghamshire; Lincolnshire, also, contributed moderately considering its relatively scanty population. Neither the migration from Ireland nor the special migration from London was anything like so large as in the case of the Lancashire towns: and the migration from North Wales, which was a considerable factor in the growth of the Lancashire towns, had apparently stopped short at the Pennine Range.

Migration into the midland iron towns of Birmingham, Dudley, and Wolverhampton had been stronger from the west than from the east. As before, the greatest proportion of the migrants came from the three 'native counties' of Staffordshire, Warwickshire, and Worcestershire: but there was also very considerable migration from Shropshire, Gloucestershire, and Leicestershire. The movement from the rest of the surrounding counties was weaker, though still appreciable.

Statistics of the migration into Glasgow confirm the substantial accuracy of the contemporary account quoted in Chapter IV above. Most of the migrants had come from the lowland shires between the Clyde and the Forth. To the north lay a band of shires (Argyll, Perth, and Forfar) which had experienced intense southward migration, and the movement tapered off quite uniformly in the shires still further north. Of the shires along the southern border of Scotland, Wigtown, and Dumfries contributed most strongly.

The migration into London had been affected in some measure by special migrations from all the great manufacturing and commercial centres; but the general characteristics of the movement remained the same as for the other great towns. A very great number of people had come from the extra-metropolitan parts of Middlesex and Surrey; there had also been strong migration from Kent, Essex, Hertford, and Berkshire. Beyond this inner belt there had been a considerable influx from all the southern and south-eastern counties, the north-western boundary of active movement running from Gloucestershire through Warwickshire to Leicestershire. The counties to the north-west of this line sent a relatively small proportion of people to London; but the attractive force of the capital city was felt in every part of the United Kingdom.

That there was a fairly uniform lessening in the intensity of migration as the distance from the absorbing centre increased may be demonstrated by tracing the proportion of migrants coming from the various counties along any given line of direction. Among every ten thousand people in Lancashire in 1851 there were (coming from the south-east) eighty-one who had been born in Derbyshire, ten who had been born in Leicestershire, six from Northamptonshire, and two from Bedfordshire. Coming from the south, there were four hundred and eight from Cheshire, forty-five from Shropshire, and three from Herefordshire. In every ten thousand inhabitants of Warwickshire at the same date there were (coming from the south-west) three hundred and seven from Gloucestershire, thirty-three from Somerset, twenty-six from Devonshire, and six from Cornwall. The migration into London, as already stated, was in some respects abnormal; but almost as uniform a lessening in the intensity of movement may be traced in several directions where the special disturbing forces were absent. Every ten thousand inhabitants of London included one hundred and three from Hertford, thirty-three from Bedfordshire, forty-five from Northampton, twenty-five from Leicestershire, and twenty from Derbyshire.

The movement out of any county was practically the reverse of the process already traced: the outward migration lessened in intensity as the distance from the home county increased, at any rate until some active centre of attraction was reached. Reversing the first instance taken above, for example, it is found that out of every ten thousand natives of Lancashire who were enumerated in England in 1851, twenty-nine were living in Derbyshire, three in Leicestershire, two in Northamptonshire, and one in Bedfordshire; out of every ten thousand natives of Bedfordshire, two hundred and fifty-seven were living in

Northamptonshire, twenty-seven in Leicestershire, fifteen in Derbyshire, and thirty-three in Lancashire. These two processes of migration, opposite in tendency but similar in form, may be traced in all parts of the kingdom. In each case the area affected was roughly circular; the process of absorption was centripetal, the process of dispersion centrifugal. The great majority of the migrants went only a short distance, and migration into any centre of attraction having a wide sphere of influence was not a simple transference of people from the circumference of a circle to its centre, but an exceedingly complex wave-like motion.

This short-distance movement was especially characteristic of agrarian migration. At first sight it seems probable that industrial migration would be more specialized in direction, and that industrial workers would tend to go where their technical skill and previous training could be utilized. The available evidence, however, seems to show that even industrial workers, when migrating in search of a livelihood, were influenced more by considerations of distance than of previous training. This weakness of special industrial migration is less surprising when it is realized that the main demand in the growing industrial towns of the early nineteenth century was for the labour of children and young persons. The father of a family would in most cases pursue a declining trade as long as he could, hoping for a turn of the tide; in the last resort he moved with his family to the nearest growing town. The unspecialized labour of the children was there readily absorbed; the father remained unemployed or under-employed, and became dependent in his declining years on the earnings of his children, in a manner which remained common until recently in all manufacturing districts.

If the dominant feature of migration was its short-distance character, how did the balance of population become shifted from the south-east of England to the north-west? A partial explanation lies in the fact, already noted, that migration was by stages, in a wave-like motion: the movement of population persisted over a wide area, even though most of the migrants did not make any long journey. Due emphasis must also be given to the importance of the Irish influx (which was mainly to the north-west) in disturbing the balance of population. It may be remarked that such phrases as 'balance of population' are vague, and may be misleading unless some numerical meaning is attached to them. In 1801 the collective population of the six northern counties of England (i.e. Cumberland, Northumberland, Westmorland, Durham, Lancashire, and Yorkshire) was slightly greater than that of the six south-eastern counties (i.e. Kent, Surrey, Middlesex, Sussex, Hampshire, and Essex); in 1851 there was still less than half-a-million difference between the respective populations of the two groups of counties. At that latter date the natives of Ireland in the six northern counties outnumbered their fellow-countrymen in the six south-eastern counties by 147,000; so that the Irish-born element alone, without reckoning the numerous children of the immigrants, would account for fully thirty per cent. of the errant 'balance of population.'

II

If the foregoing account of the main features of migration is admitted to be substantially true for the earlier nineteenth century, the interesting question arises whether the short-distance character of the movement was merely a reflection of the transport difficulties of the period, and was therefore to be greatly modified in the latter half of the century by the increasing influence of the railways in stimulating the mobility of labour and encouraging long-distance migration. In earlier chapters it has been assumed that the cheap and rapid steamship passage between Ireland and England, as contrasted with the slow, wearisome, and relatively expensive journey by waggon or canal boat from the south of England, was a partial explanation of the greater mobility of the Irish peasantry as compared with the English. If this was so, the popularization of the railway in England must surely have tapped a vast stagnant reservoir of labour in the English countryside and transformed the character of English migration.

Even in the first half of the century the railways were already beginning to exert an appreciable influence on the movements and distribution of the population. So early as 1830, many of the places on the Stockton and Darlington Railway found that the line was tending to increase their population and importance: Stockton, in particular, had benefited by its new connection with the coalfield.[1] During the next twenty years the main framework of the English railway system was brought into being, and the work of construction proved a most welcome source of employment in periods of severe trade depression. By the middle of the century local increases or decreases of population were occurring in country villages throughout England, according to the proximity or absence of the railroad. Villages which had a railway station were, almost without exception, increasing in population. Folkestone, a member of the old Cinque Port of Dover, received a larger life as a port of embarkation for the Continent after 1843, when the South-Eastern Railway was completed. West Ham, which had received its first impetus from the construction of the East- and West-India Docks, was before the middle of the century swelled by the large colony of railway workmen living there in 'Hudson's Town'. In Cheshire, the growth of Monks Coppenhall concealed the nascent greatness of Crewe, which was already becoming an important railway junction.[2]

By the middle of the century, too, the passing of the old transport system was depleting the population along the main mail-coach roads. No longer did the coaches roll over Bagshot Heath along the great west road. At Woodstock the Marlborough Arms (once a noted posting inn) had closed its doors, like many another of its kind. Inland and coastal navigation was suffering also from the changes in transport, and local decreases of population were being reported from many parts as due to the decay in canal traffic. One of the parishes in Cambridge was declining because the Eastern Counties Railway had absorbed the carrying trade of the Cam. Bewdley, once a considerable centre of

[1] *1831 Census*, I, pp. 166–8, 172–4.
[2] *Ibid.*, I, p. 180; *1851 Census*, Pt. I, Vol. I, Divn. II, p. 37; Divn. IV, p. 13; Vol. II, Divn. VIII, p. 21.

the Severn carrying trade, had been declining since 1831. Bowness, the port of Carlisle, was declining through the construction of railways from Carlisle to Maryport and Lancaster.[1] From the rapidity with which its effects were felt all over the country the transition to railway transport probably deserves the name of 'revolution' better than any other aspect of economic development in the eighteenth and nineteenth centuries.

The extent to which the railways modified the character of industrial migration in the later nineteenth century may be gauged from the history of Middlesbrough, which was practically created by the railway. Up to 1829 Middlesbrough was a small and inconsiderable hamlet. Shortly afterwards the Stockton and Darlington Railway was extended to Middlesbrough, and harbour works were constructed there. This, together with the construction of the Clarence Railway, made Middlesbrough a principal shipping place for the South Durham coal trade, and was sufficient to cause a small increase of population by 1831. From that time the population of the township grew at a tremendous rate, increasing from forty persons in 1821 to 7,631 in 1851. As yet, its growth had been the result of short-distance migration mainly; in 1861 nearly three-quarters of its population was still Yorkshire by birth. During the next ten years, however, the population of the town more than doubled itself, and miners and iron-workers flocked in from Durham, South Wales, Staffordshire, and other centres. In 1871 only one-half of the inhabitants were natives of Yorkshire; of the remaining half of the population 13·3 per cent. had come from Durham, 3·9 from Wales, and 2·6 from Staffordshire. Improved transport facilities had evidently strengthened industrial migration sufficiently to cause an appreciable (though slight) modification of the general trend of movement.[2]

The influence of railway transport on agricultural migration is more difficult to define, though it was undoubtedly important. In 1847–8 the London and North-Western Railway

---

[1] *Ibid.*, Pt. I, Vol. I, Divn. II, p. 17; Divn. III, pp. 35, 41, 43, 53, 61; Divn. V, p. 43; Divn. VI, p. 69; Divn. X, p. 51.

[2] E. G. Ravenstein, 'Laws of Migration', in *S.J.*, XLVIII, pp. 215–16.

was already providing special facilities (in the form of cattle trucks) for the carriage of Irish harvesters from Liverpool right across the country to such places as Rugby, Peterborough, and Watford.[1] If the Irish agricultural labourers could use the railways, so could the English. It is noteworthy that in a midland area traversed by the London and North-Western Railway the decrease of population first became noticeable in the districts touched by the main trunk line;[2] while the first English county to report a general decrease in population (Wiltshire, in 1851) was on the main line of the Great Western Railway.

While railway communication evidently strengthened the volume of migration from the country districts to the towns, it does not seem to have changed the main characteristics of the movement. The railway, it is true, induced many people to migrate for long distances who would otherwise not have moved far; but it also induced many more people to migrate for short distances who would otherwise not have moved at all. Statistical students of English migration in the later nineteenth century described the process in terms which might have been applied equally well to the movements taking place in the previous half-century. Ravenstein, writing in 1885, when railway travel was half-a-century old, found that the great bulk of all migration was for comparatively short distances, 'consequently there takes place a universal shifting or displacement of the population, which produces "currents of migration" setting in the direction of the great centres of commerce and industry'. It followed from this that the *process* of migration was by stages. 'The inhabitants of the country immediately surrounding a town of rapid growth flock into it; the gaps thus left in the rural population are filled up by migrants from more remote districts.'[3]

The preponderance of short-distance movement by stages thus appears to be a permanent feature of labour migration, and has been recognized as such by the greatest English econo-

---

[1] *A. & P.*, 1847–8, XV, No. 987, pp. 16–17.
[2] Ashby and King, 'Statistics of Some Midland Villages', II, in *E.J.*, III, pp. 195–7.
[3] Ravenstein, *loc. cit.*, pp. 182–3, 198–9; cf. Weber, pp. 255–7.

mist of the last generation.[1] 'Movements of population within a country are generally by small stages . . . it is seldom necessary to induce individual men, and still less whole families, to migrate over long distances. . . . Districts in which employment is offered on favourable terms draw labour from neighbouring districts; and they in turn replenish their supplies of labour from districts on the other sides of them. . . . Thus a level is maintained approximately over a wide area; though the greater part of the migration necessary to maintain it has been over only short distances, and has been set in movement by comparatively small forces.'

[1] Marshall, *Money, Credit, and Commerce*, 1923, pp. 7–8.

LIST OF MAPS AND SOURCES

MAP A: Migration between Counties in England.
1851 Census, Pt. II, Vol. I, p. clxxxii, Table 26.
This is defective in that Wales and Yorkshire are returned as single units. The requisite details for the several Welsh counties have been obtained from *ibid.*, p. cclxxxviii, Table 39. The parallel details for the separate ridings of Yorkshire are not obtainable from the census. It has, therefore, been assumed that the West Riding attracted a balance of immigration *at least* half as great as that of Cheshire, in proportion to their respective populations. This has involved a complementary correction of the balances of migration for the other two ridings, to bring the final result in conformity with the census tables. This estimate almost certainly errs on the side of moderation.

MAP B: Approximate Distribution of 4,680 Poor Law Migrants, 1835–7; and of 6,403 Poor Law Emigrants, 1835–7.
Accounts and Papers, 1843, Vol. XVI, No. 254.
P.L.C., 2nd Ann. Rept., App. D, No. 13. *P.L.C., 3rd Ann. Rept.*, App. C, No. 6.

MAP C: Approximate Dispersion of 12,600 Persons Removed from Nineteen Towns in Lancashire, Yorkshire, and Cheshire, 1841–3.
Accounts and Papers, 1846, Vol. XII, No. 209.
Not included in this edition. The information it contains has been given on p. 127, above.

MAP D: Migration into London and Glasgow.
1851 Census, Pt. II, Vol. I, Divn. I, p. 31; Vol II, Scotland Divn., p. 1041.
London and Glasgow are to be regarded separately, as two distinct maps.

MAP E: Migration into Liverpool, Manchester, and Bolton.
Ibid., Vol. II, Divn. VIII, p. 664.

MAP F: Irish and Scottish Vagrancy in England, *c.* 1823.
Accounts and Papers, 1824, Vol. XIX, No. 250.

MAP G: Distribution of Irish-born in Great Britain, 1851.
1851 Census, Pt. II, Vol. I, pp. cclxxxviii–ccc: Tables XXXIX to XLI.

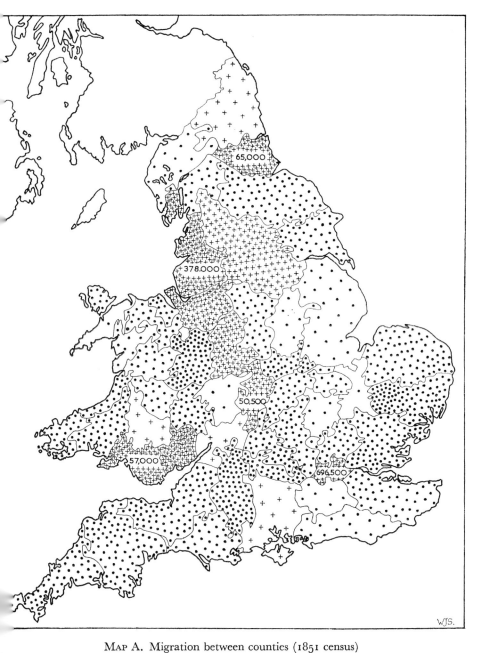

MAP A. Migration between counties (1851 census)
Crosses represent balance of inward migration and dots balance of outward migration.
ch dot and cross represents 500 migrants. Figures give actual balance of migration.

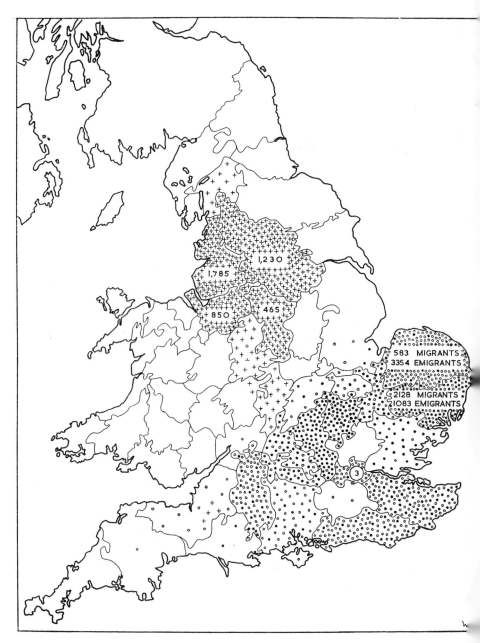

MAP B. Approximate distribution of 4,680 Poor Law migrants and
6,403 Poor Law emigrants (1835–7)

Each dot represents 5 outward migrants
Each cross represents 5 inward migrants
Each circle represents 5 overseas emigrants

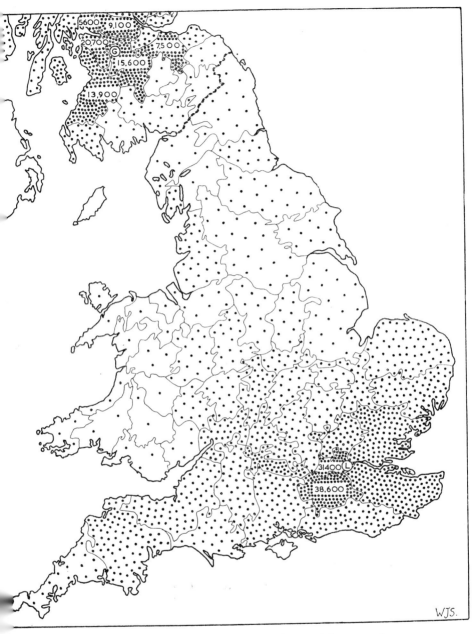

MAP D. Migration into London and Glasgow (1851 census)

London and Glasgow are to be regarded separately, as two distinct maps. In Scotland, each black dot represents 100 migrants to Glasgow; in England, each black dot represents 500 migrants to London. In addition, Glasgow received 59,801 Irish and 8,057 English; while London received 108,548 Irish and 30,401 Scottish.

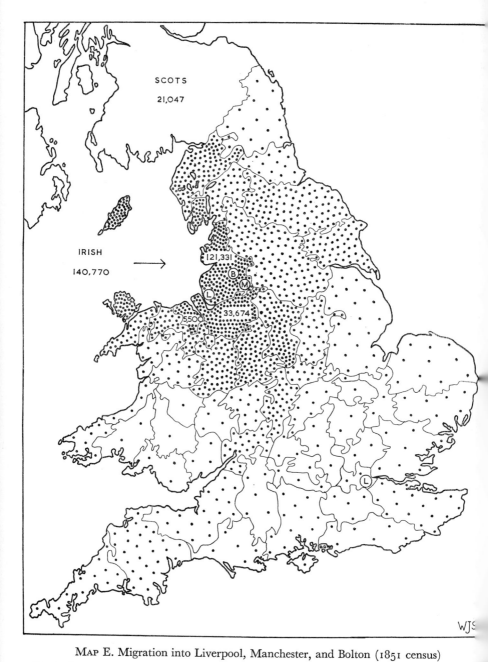

SCOTS
21,047

IRISH
140,770

121,331

B
M
L

5500
33,674

L

WJS

MAP E. Migration into Liverpool, Manchester, and Bolton (1851 census)
    Each dot represents 100 migrants to one of the three towns, lettered L, M, B. From Lond
there were 10,300 migrants.

MAP F. Irish and Scottish vagrancy, c. 1823

The numbers indicate the ratios between Irish and Scottish vagrants recorded. The broken
line indicates the approximate limit of Irish vagrancy, 1823.

o*

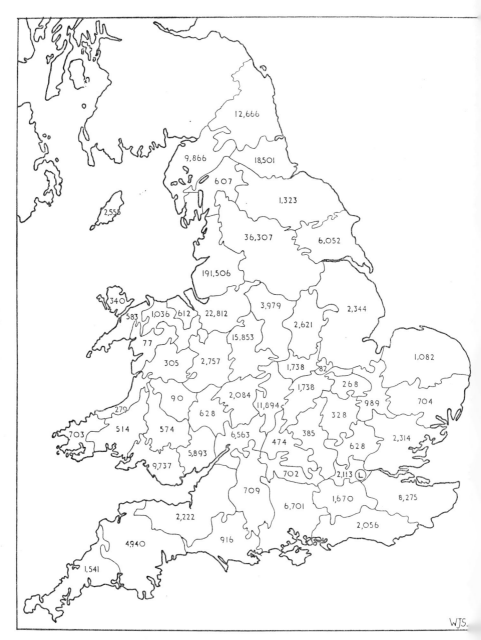

Maps G1 and G2 (opposite). Distribution of Irish-born residents in Great Britain (1851 census)

The figures give the actual numbers of immigrants to the various areas.

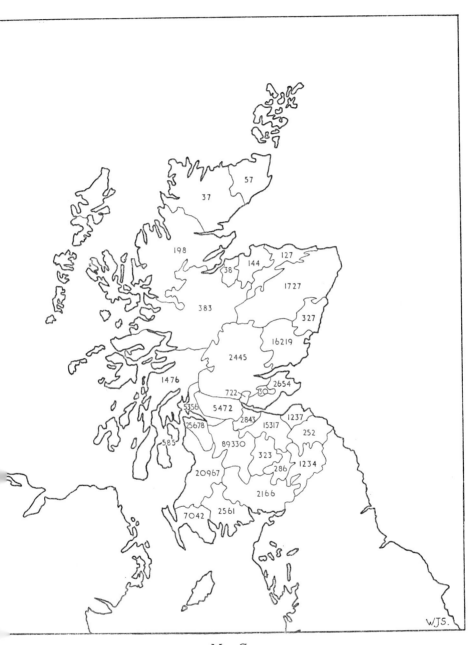

MAP G2

INDEX

Abbotshall, 51
Aberdare, 56
Aberdeenshire, 38, 76, 78
Abingdon, 90
Abruzzi, 5
Adam, M. I., 166n., 168n.
Addingham, 46
Agricultural depression, 73–6, 142–143, 168–9, 174, and Chaps. V–VI, *passim*
— — transition and migration, *see* Chaps. IV–V, *passim*
— — in Ireland and Scotland, 142–143, 168–9
Alcester, 48
Algoa Bay, 172–3
Alien immigrants, 3–4, 16–17, 141–2
Allotments, *see* Smallholdings movement
Alston Moor, 58, 73
America, *see* United States, South America, Uruquay, etc.
Ampthill, 103
Ancholme, 147
Anglesey, 64, 127, 176
Antrim, 39
Apprenticeship, 23, 30–3, 52, 58–9, 87, 115
—, parish, 32–3, 39, 52 and Chap. II, *passim*
Argyllshire, 78–9, 142, 166, 171, 184
Arkwright, Sir Richard, 20–1, 103, 136
Ashby, A. W., 65n.
Ashby, Joseph, 190n.
Ashford, Kent, 26
Ashreigney, 48
Ashton, Thomas, 105, 113–14
Ashton, T. S., 59n.
Ashton-under-Lyne, 41, 64, 123, 127
Ashworth, Edmund and Henry, 25, 63, 101–2, 105n., 113, 123n.
Asturias, 5
Athlone, 170
Australia, 123, 165, 175

Austria, 123
Auvergne, 7
Ayrshire, 56, 66, 133, 153, 155

Bacup, 64
Bagshot Heath, 188
Baines, E., 33n., 135n., 153n.
Baker, Robert, 105, 107
Baker, William, M.P., 89
Balfron (Stirling), 179
Balkan peninsula, 3
Baltimore, 180
Bamford, Samuel, 164n.
Bandon, Cork, 38
Banffshire, 78
Bannermans, of Manchester, 136
Barnsley, 51
Barnstaple, 132
Basques, 2–3, 5
Bath, 156
Bauwens, Liévin, 177
Bavaria, 88
Bayonne, 3
Beard, Rev. James, 103
Bedfordshire, 15, 71, 94, 103, 108–9, 127, 133, 146, 175, 185–6
Beggars and begging, *see* Vagrants and vagrancy
Belfast, 36, 37–8, 49–50, 99, 147, 162, 166, 169
Belgium, 5
Bere Forest, 73
Berkshire, 76, 90, 108–9, 122, 127, 145, 175, 185
Bermondsey, 48, 154
Berwickshire, 76
Bewdley, 188–9
Bexley Heath, 73
Bilston, 60
Birkenhead, 154, 163
Birmingham, 18, 27, 34, 59, 65, 95, 122, 141, 165, 168, 184
Bispham, 69
Black, 'Dr.' John, 100
Blackland, 66
Bledlow, 102

200

DATE

DE 14 '84	
GAYLORD	